THE ESSENCE OF
ENLIGHTENMENT

THE ESSENCE OF ENLIGHTENMENT

Vedanta, the Science of Consciousness

James Swartz

SENTIENT PUBLICATIONS

First Sentient Publications edition 2014
Copyright © 2014 by James Swartz

A paperback original

Cover design by Kim Johansen, Black Dog Design
Book design by Timm Bryson

Library of Congress Cataloging-in-Publication Data
Swartz, James Bender.
  The essence of enlightenment : Vedanta, the science of consciousness /
James Swartz. — First [edition].
    pages cm
  ISBN 978-1-59181-277-7
  1. Vedanta. I. Title.
  B132.V3S945 2014
  181'.48—dc23
                            2014022427

Printed in Canada

10 9 8 7 6 5 4 3 2 1

SENTIENT PUBLICATIONS

A Limited Liability Company
1113 Spruce Street
Boulder, CO 80302
www.sentientpublications.com

Contents

INTRODUCTION

In the last forty-five years, previously uninformed Western cultures have steadily become aware of the idea of enlightenment. While the quest for enlightenment is hardly a mainstream preoccupation, a vibrant subculture of seekers has developed since the invasion by swamis, lamas and roshis of America in the late sixties. From the point of view of an individual life, forty-five years is a long time, but from the point of view of a culture capable of serving the needs of seekers of freedom, it is very short indeed. Cultures dedicated to the knowledge of material objects evolve relatively quickly. The development of a sophisticated scientific, psychological or literary culture takes much longer—a few hundred years, perhaps. But a comprehensive body of knowledge of the nature of consciousness and the psyche, and how both relate to the material world and the human need for freedom, takes much longer. Though the West's long religious tradition has certain spiritual aspects—non-dual thinkers appeared from time to time—a spiritual culture centered around the idea of non-duality never evolved.

Material success came quickly after World War II and disgust with it followed soon after. It did not serve the needs of the soul. Because the culture offered no solutions, people had to look elsewhere. So Western young people in the tens of thousands—perhaps more—enthusiastically descended on Asia, particularly India, in search of fulfillment. Over the years they eagerly consumed exotic Hindu and Buddhist ideas and practices like a horde of hungry locusts. Though they only scratched the surface, they imagined they had mastered the enlightenment game and returned home laden with confidence that what they had acquired would transform their lives and save their country from materialism. Their attempt to integrate Eastern spirituality into the culture of their birth has created a vibrant subculture. But the culture of non-duality that is beginning to take shape here is still in its infancy, as is obvious to anyone who understands the history of enlightenment.

Consequently, the Western spiritual world is a strange hodgepodge of initially appealing, partially assimilated and conflicting, dual and non-dual notions and practices that quickly fade, leaving the heart hungry for more. Forty-five years ago my teacher, an Indian mahatma, told me that at the beginning of the twenty-first century the West would be ready for Vedanta, the granddaddy of all Asian spiritual cultures and a complete and perfected science of enlightenment teachings. I thought nothing of it at the time, but it seems he was prophetic. The reason is simple: Many seekers have worked diligently on themselves for years and have matured as human beings. Consequently, they are well prepared to understand the counterintuitive and radical message of Vedanta—to wit: appearances to the contrary notwithstanding, reality is non-dual consciousness. What this means and how it benefits human beings in their quest for freedom from limitation is the subject matter of this book.

In 2009 I wrote a book entitled *How to Attain Enlightenment*, which presented Vedanta to the Western world in clear, modern English. Vedanta never caught on in the West, either because people weren't ready for it or because the idea of non-duality was saddled with the trappings of Hinduism. The ochre clad swamis with glowing eyes and strange names spoke Hinglish—Hindi accented English—and laced their teachings with unpronounceable Sanskrit words. More often than not it was presented as a Hindu philosophy, although it has nothing to do with Hinduism and is not a philosophy at all. It is the knowledge of reality and as such is beyond time and place, religions and philosophies. In any case it apparently didn't appeal to many Westerners until my book came out in 2009. Since then my hitherto simple, contemplative life has become a flurry of activity as I jet around the world teaching Vedanta.

I will resist the temptation to say that this is a completely different book. The core teachings are eternal. They were revealed several thousand years before the Christian era. Vedanta as a means of enlightenment evolved slowly since then as great minds contributed dispassionately to the teaching tradition, which reached perfection in the eighth century. Just as nobody is trying to invent a new wheel, no one can improve Vedanta, because it does what it purports to do: set us free of our sense of limitation. So the basic logic of this book is the basic logic of the first book because Vedanta is the knowledge of reality and reality never changes. However, it is not the same book. It is written in a different, perhaps more accessible, style and develops certain teachings introduced in the first book. It adds a chapter on the topic of values and the enlightened person. It discusses *dharma* and the essence of enlightenment in considerable detail, thoroughly explaining the relationship between consciousness, the individual and the total.

Like its predecessor, this book sufficiently demystifies the topic of enlightenment. Although it is inspirational, it is not just another vague inspirational read. It is written in a simple style that I believe will make the science of self-inquiry accessible to seekers and finders everywhere.

—*James Swartz*

CHAPTER ONE

WHAT DO I WANT?

Motivations

Imagine yourself in the springtime in a mountain valley. Many beautiful flowers are blooming. Pick one of each, bring them home and lay them on a table. Each has its own beauty, but if you arrange them into a bouquet, the total becomes more than the sum of its parts. Vedanta takes all our experiences and arranges them in a way that gives us a perfect appreciation of our true nature and purpose.

Many things—wonderful skyscrapers and bridges, cell phones and the internet—are the result of humanity's collective knowledge. Similarly, our collective spiritual experience and knowledge has coalesced into a perfect bouquet of teachings that has the power to set us free. Nobody owns it because it belongs to everyone. This perfect bouquet, this most refined vehicle, is Vedanta,* the knowledge that ends the search for life's meaning.

The human heart will not rest until it understands who and what it is. Without the vision of non-duality, you will be forced to keep seeking. If you want to understand who you are and live free, you need to sign on to the logic as it

---

* *Veda* means knowledge in Sanskrit and *anta* means end. The compound word Vedanta has two meanings: 1) the knowledge that ends the search for knowledge and 2) the knowledge enshrined at the end of each of the four Vedas. The Vedas are the oldest extant texts on the topic of consciousness, the self.

unfolds in this book. If you can't accept the first teaching, you cannot benefit from the second. If you can't sign on to the second, the third will not make sense. Each teaching fits seamlessly into all the others because reality is one consciousness. Vedanta is its science. To get the most out of it you must be patient, because non-duality is challenging. Knowledge may come in a flash but it does not remain without constant exposure to the teachings. Incrementally, the vision of non-duality will coalesce in your mind. So read carefully. Never hurry. You will not be disappointed.

It is very important to see reality as it is, not as you think it is or want it to be. Everyone is proud of his spiritual knowledge, so you will have a tendency to evaluate Vedanta according to your own ideas, but this does not work. Once you have heard the teachings, you should evaluate what you know with reference to what you have heard, not the other way around. If you evaluate the teaching with reference to your beliefs and opinions, you will fail. A sense of incompleteness, separateness and limitation will remain.

The Unexamined Logic of Your Own Experience

Vedanta is an impersonal method of self-inquiry. The first stage is listening with an open mind, setting aside your personal views. Listening without judgment is difficult but not impossible. If you find yourself deciding whether or not you like what you hear, you are not listening. There is nothing to like or dislike, only something to know. If you listen without prejudice, the words will make complete sense, but if you are looking only for an explanation of reality that fits your views, Vedanta is not for you.

Once you have heard a teaching in full, as it is, you can let your beliefs and opinions interact with the truth, keeping those that make sense and discarding those that don't. This, the second stage of self-inquiry, is reflection or contemplation. If you surrender to this process, you will succeed.

You may understand a particular teaching well enough, but to succeed with self-inquiry you need to understand the truth that links all the teachings together in a beautiful necklace of meaning, like pearls on a string. The vision of non-duality is not gained by synthesizing teachings from different traditions. It is, however, easily gained if you consistently expose your mind to it.

I will introduce a few Sanskrit terms so that you understand that this is not my teaching. I have no teachings. I am simply a person who has been taught. I do not want you to believe me, to depend on me. I ask only that you listen with an open mind to this great knowledge. You will not be disappointed or cheated, because I follow the rules of the tradition. I have no agenda. Teachers outside the tradition, even the sincere ones, are usually unreliable guides to the truth because they know only that part of reality revealed by their own experience.

You will not get partial knowledge or be misled by an "enlightened" person if you listen to Vedanta, because it is a proven scriptural tradition. If you know the source of this great wisdom, you can check to see if I am teaching truth or merely what I think or believe. Teaching scripture protects me, too. If you have an argument with something you hear, the argument will be with the teaching, not with me. Hearing things you do not like is inevitable. Please don't blame me. I am a good person and I do not wish to upset you, but I sometimes have to deliver bad news.

I Want Security, Pleasure and Virtue

Vedanta's first inquiry is: what do I really want in life? It is clear that I do not want to be miserable. If misery comes—and it does—it is not because I want it. It is probably because I am incompetent or inefficient in my seeking owing to lack of understanding about myself and the world in which I live.

Everyone wants to be free and happy, to feel whole and complete. If you think there is another reason you are here on earth in this body, self-inquiry is not for you. When people want to be free and happy they chase things that they believe will make them free and happy.

The first thing we chase is security. It stands to reason, because life is insecure. You can't expect anything to last. There are many forms of security, the most obvious of which is financial security. Few feel they have enough money. It is a fact that everyone wants more money because desires are endless and money is required to get what you want. It is natural to believe that the more money you have, the more secure you will be, but it is not true.

Seeking is based on a sense of insecurity and insecurity has many faces. If you are financially secure, rest assured that you will feel insecure in other areas of life. You may be insecure socially or morally. When I ask if anyone has enough love, almost no hands go up. You always believe that you could love yourself more or receive more love. If you want attention, it means you are emotionally insecure. Before I go on enumerating the things we seek, you should know that not all necessarily apply to you. This is just a general list on the basis of which we are going to expose certain facts about the reality of worldly pursuits.

There is a famous book in the Vedic tradition on the topic of pleasure, the *Kama Sutra*. It is there because pleasure is something that people feel they need to know. Once you are financially secure, you want to enjoy life, so various forms of pleasure may become your goal. Western societies are financially successful and therefore we are obsessed with entertainment. Security is a necessity; pleasure is a luxury. Most westerners don't see people sleeping on the streets as do citizens of India, where luxuries are virtually nonexistent and people have no time to pursue pleasure. In our world luxuries have become necessities.

When you are emotionally insecure, you want to have a good time. See how much energy is put into entertainment: internet, sports, gambling, travel, music, sex, drugs—you name it. We don't really need these things, but they are available, so we want them. Sundari, my wife, calls them "weapons of mass distraction." I go through airports all the time and have to walk through a gauntlet of shops with all manner of tempting things: thousand-dollar handbags, mountains of chocolate and electronic toys too numerous to mention. A sane person does not need even one of these items. I bought a small digital scale on the plane yesterday to weigh my luggage so I would not get charged extra to carry my useless luxuries from one country to another. They printed a receipt from a tiny computer.

Pleasure is not a goal that is conducive to happiness, because moments of pleasure require three factors that are not always available: (1) *an object capable of giving pleasure*: sometimes I am out in beautiful nature surrounded by mosquitoes (2) *an appropriate, effective instrument for the enjoyment of said object*: sometimes beautiful music is playing but I have an earache; and (3) *the presence of the proper frame of mind for enjoyment*: sometimes I am feeling randy in the presence of a sexy, willing person but I am worried about losing my job. Because pleasure is dependent on these ever-changing factors, moments of pleasure are occasional and fleeting. This fact should—if I am a thinking person—lead me to conclude that there must be more fruitful pursuits.

Let's say you are secure financially and you are uninterested in pleasure because your life is good by the usual criteria. However, you don't feel that you are good enough as a person. You feel selfish, vain, arrogant and self-indulgent; perhaps you are cruel or none too honest. You know you have a moral problem and you feel guilty. Consequently, you would like to be more honest, pure, holy, sweet, generous and loving. What do you do? You pursue virtue.

In Christian cultures you learn that you are a sinner more or less as soon as you pop out of the womb. Yes, there is a grace period when Mom and Pop think you are God's gift to the human race and lavish affection on you, but before long they start to tell you that something is wrong with you. It's news to you, a rude awakening. Before you know it, you start to have a complex. You believe, without a shred of evidence, that you are not good enough. These days many people with low self-esteem work hard to become holy and good. This striving to be virtuous is very sad because nothing is actually wrong with you.

Some people feel weak and set out to seek power. They tend to make the lives of others miserable because they feel miserable inside. People want many other things, but the last one I will mention is fame or recognition. You feel small and unimportant because there is a small person inside—an inner child that never grew up, a small person that wants to be noticed and appreciated. So you become a needy pest, always seeking attention. You develop sophisticated strategies to get people to notice you.

There is no need to discuss all human pursuits; these are the basic ones. All are meant to make you feel adequate, whole, complete, happy and free. Let's see if they work.

We have now arrived at a very important point in our first inquiry. Some part of you is not going to like what comes next, but try to take this on board. Examine the logic carefully. Failure to understand the next teaching may disqualify you for enlightenment.

Does Happiness Exist?

Everybody has been happy for a minute or two, an hour, a week or a month. This proves happiness exists. But where does it come from?

Is It in Objects?

When you get what you want, you feel free, happy, complete and whole. Does this mean that the feeling of happiness-wholeness-completeness-freedom comes from the object? You do not chase things to make yourself unhappy. You pursue what you pursue because you believe the joy is somehow contained in the object.

But is it true? Is there happiness in objects? If it were true, the same object would give everyone happiness. A granny who knits socks and little wool caps for her grandchildren is not going to enjoy bungee jumping. Can you see granny standing on the edge of a bridge with bungee cords attached to her legs? And how happy is her teenage grandson who loves jumping off bridges going to be knitting socks?

If objects are the source of joy, it is reasonable to chase things in the world. Let's analyze the situation and see where the joy lies. You have a well-developed fantasy about the perfect person—your soul mate. You believe your loneliness will end and happiness will come when she appears. You go to a meeting. You see someone who fits your fantasy. Your eyes meet across the room. You feel an exciting buzz.

What happens to the fantasy when you actually connect? It disappears! Why? Because the object is present. A great feeling of love and happiness floods over you. You assume that the joy is coming from the object and immediately become attached to it. But your assumption is incorrect. *When the desire for the object disappears, the love that is the nature of the self immediately floods the mind.* The object is not the source of the feeling; it is just a catalyst that releases your inbuilt joy. The only reasonable conclusion I can draw leads me to ask: if happiness/love is my nature, why am I looking for it in objects?

If you cannot accept this fact right now, we can still teach you. Let's accept your contention that joy is in objects. Before we move on, let me ask you this question: what kind of happiness is it? You cannot claim that it is permanent happiness. When the experience ends, your sense of incompleteness returns and you try to reconnect with the same object or you seek a new object. You may argue that objective happiness works if you can stay connected to the things that seem to make you happy. But objects come and go. No object remains permanently in your life. The only constant is me, the subject! Vedanta contends that the nature of the subject is limitless bliss. It is a contention that we will prove in many ways. But if you are attached to your belief in the value of objects for happiness, please tentatively accept our view as a working hypothesis and listen to these teachings. You may change your mind.

Objects don't work as the source of happiness for a very simple reason: I seek completeness when I am already complete. I do this because I do not know who I am.

We should consider one more sad fact about objects: you do not get rid of the seeking when you get what you want, because the effort that went into obtaining the object is required to keep it. Everything is going south all the time. If you get a good job, your troubles have just begun; you must work hard to keep it. If you are lucky enough to have someone fall in love with you, you need to reciprocate more or less constantly or the love will go elsewhere.

Finally, not only are the objects inherently flawed in terms of their happiness content, the field in which the objects appear is set up in such a way that lasting happiness is impossible. The field of my experience, which is just my mind, is a duality. This means that because I do not know the non-dual nature of reality, I think in terms of opposites. For every upside there is a downside. Every gain entails a loss. For example, you fall in love and discover intimacy. But you also suffer attachment. To live in the house of your dreams makes you happy, but to do so you have to take a mortgage and pay through the nose for thirty years, which does not make you happy. Life is like that. There is no way to beat the system and get only the upside from life's experiences. As the poet says, life is "joy and sorrow woven fine." It is a zero-sum game.

Definition of an Object

An object is anything other than me, the subject. My body appears as an object in me. My feelings appear in me and are known to me. They, too, are objects, as are my thoughts, beliefs and opinions. Absolutely anything that I experience is an object, including the past, present and future. Experience itself is an object known to me. Please do not forget this definition because it is the essence of self-inquiry; you will need it right up to the end of your inquiry—and beyond. It is the basis of the practice that will set you free.

I Am Not an Object

If something is known to me, it cannot be me. Physical objects, thoughts and emotions and my experiences in the world are objects known to me.

Am I Separate from Objects?

Let's deepen our inquiry. Where do I end and the objects begin? Is there a separation? If there is, what kind of separation is it? If you analyze perception, you will see that the objects are not actually separate from the subject, me.

Light strikes objects and travels through the eyes, and the experience and knowledge of the object happens in the mind. The knowledge of the object is true to the object. If a dog is walking in front of you, you do not see a cat. What is the experience of the dog made of? It is made of your mind, the perceiving instrument. The mind is your consciousness taking the shape of various objects. It can know anything because it is formless and limitless. If you think about the experience of the dog, you can see that from an experiential point of view the dog is actually in your mind, not outside walking on the street. It looks as though it is outside, but if you try to experience it outside, you cannot. No matter how close you get to the dog, it is always an object. You cannot just jump out of your body-mind and experience objects, because objects are not located where they seem to be. They always seem to be away from us but they are not.

Here is one of Vedanta's counterintuitive assertions: objects are not real. When we say they are not real, we mean that they never stay the same from second to second and they are made up of parts. Which part of the dog is actually the dog? The hair, the teeth, the paws, the nose? And if the dog is the nose, what is the nose? It is an aggregation of particles changing according to various natural laws. So which particle is the nose particle? When you get very close to the dog, the dog is only a patch of hair.

When you investigate, all objects ultimately break down to the space in which the particles appear and the observer of the space. The observer is conscious of space and objects sitting in it, or they could not be known. And the consciousness of the observer is the consciousness that knows everything.

Definition of Real

Something is real if it never changes. Objects are not real because they change. If you think about it carefully, this fact will upset you because you would not pursue objects if you knew they were unreal.

In any case, we are trying to determine where objects are located and the relationship I have to them. Here is another exhaustive analysis of the relationship between the subject, me, and the objects that present themselves to me. This inquiry shows that the objects we identify and think we are experiencing through sensory perceptions are essentially nothing more than specific sensations created by the sense organs. The sensations we experience do not constitute the entirety of the object with which we associate them. For instance, the hardness we feel on our rear end when sitting on a wooden chair does not constitute the knowledge of the entire chair. The chair becomes a chair only because we make an inference based on an idea of what a chair is. What we experience is only certain distinct sensations in the body, which in turn are interpreted to mean something by the mind, which like the body, appears as an object in me, awareness. These sensations and the knowledge that arises with them do not equal either the experience of the chair or the knowledge of the chair. All we experience is hardness or softness (if the chair is upholstered) and an idea of *chair*. Greg Goode's book *The Direct Path* presents many concrete experiments that prove that objects seem to be out there but are not really located where they seem to be.

If you investigate further, you will see that the chair is nothing but the experience of the particular sense organ through which it is perceived. Furthermore, the independent existence of any sensation cannot be verified by an organ other than the organ that experiences it. For the chair to be objective and subject to common knowledge, it would have to be verified by some other organ of perception. But it is only when a given sensation appears in me that I experience what is called seeing, hearing, tasting, touching, or smelling.

Continuing to inquire, we discover that sense organs are essentially nothing other than me, the awareness that sees them. I do not experience them as instruments sitting around waiting to be used by me. I do not think "I want to smell the rose. I wonder where I left my nose? I had it yesterday but it seems to be lost. Let me call my wife, maybe she misplaced it." Analysis reveals that each organ is a unique function of awareness by virtue of which a particular type of perception occurs.

Finally, since awareness is required or the sense organ cannot sense, it is clear that the senses are dependent on awareness for their very existence—but awareness does not depend on them. You, awareness, exist whether or not you are sensing objects, as in deep sleep, for example. If they have no independent existence, the objects the senses seem to report—which is the basis of our knowledge of them—have no existence apart from me, the witnessing awareness, about which much will be said as we proceed. If the objects exist only as sensations and sensations exist only as me, the joy that is apparently caused by contact with objects is coming only from me. If we think one step further, it will become clear that I cannot separate the happiness I feel from me, the subject. Just as a wave is never separate from the ocean in which it "waves," the joy that waves up when I get what I want is just me, consciousness.

So we see that objects are not away from us in a world "out there." They are experienced and known "in" us. If we take our inquiry a bit further, we come up with the fact that is the basis of Vedanta, the knowledge that sets us free from dependence on objects: we discover that reality is non-dual and that we cannot depend on objects because they are us. If our analysis is true—and it is—then the objects we experience are not separate from the consciousness that makes the experience of them possible.*

The Objects Are Me

Let me ask a million dollar question. How far are you from your experiencing consciousness? And the answer is: you are not far at all. In fact, there is no difference between the real you, the non-experiencing witness consciousness, and your experiencing consciousness, the person you think you are. Although the person you think you are is an object known to you, like the physical objects are known to it, it is non-separate from you, the non-experiencing witness—the real you—just as a ring made of gold is not separate from the gold. If this is true, the objects are you! This is what we mean when we use the word *non-duality*. Duality, the distinction between the subject and the object, breaks down when you investigate the nature of perception.

But I Am Not an Object

The fly in the ointment of duality is this: the body cannot be you because it is an object known to you in the same way that any other object is known to you. Like the body, you are not your emotions or your thoughts or anything that happens in you, because all these objects are known by you. My hand is me, but I am not my hand. If my hand is removed, I am still the same. Of course, if I am the body, I am not the same. I am a body with one hand.

---

* The words *consciousness* and *awareness* are synonyms. Both refer to me, the subject. I have purposely avoided using the Sanskrit terms, Brahman and Atman, because we have no way to evaluate them outside the Sanskritic tradition. Both words refer to consciousness (*chaitanyam, chetena*) viewed from slightly different angles. And there is no difference between them. I tend to favor the word *awareness* because the Western mind tends to view consciousness as subjective objects appearing in consciousness, which creates a problem because the whole point of self-inquiry is to distinguish consciousness from objects.

This is an incredible fact to appreciate because it means that I am never in conflict with objects and I am free of them—particularly the unpleasant ones—at the same time.

Definition of Non-Duality

It is vitally important at the beginning of the teaching to understand the meaning of non-duality. It is easy to understand when you undertake the inquiry into perception, but it is very difficult to accept because it is contradicted by experience. We do not think deeply about the process of experience as we experience. We take the appearance of experience—that the subject and the object are separate—to be the reality and build our lives on it, when in fact nothing is separate from us at all.

It makes a huge difference to know that everything is actually you, not someone or something else. Conflict virtually disappears and the small conflicts that do develop are easily laid to rest. Furthermore, it makes an equally big difference to know that you are free of objects.

Finally, the icing on the cake of life is the fact that you are happiness itself. If happiness is not in the objects and there are only two categories in existence, the subject and the objects, then happiness can only be you. When you appreciate yourself as the subject, you will be blissful because you are always present.

If I am not happy, it is not due to the presence or absence of an object, it is due to a failure to distinguish myself from the objects that appear in me. Vedanta is a workable method for discovering both our oneness with everything and our freedom from everything.

Non-duality does not mean that you walk around in some kind of ecstatic, orgasmic spiritual daze unable to distinguish yourself from the objects and the experiencing consciousness —the "little" you. It doesn't mean that the person you have taken yourself to be for so long is not there. You hear spiritual people saying that a particular "enlightened being" is so "not there," as if there were virtue in being nonexistent.

For the record, that person—the one you are trying to change or rid yourself of—remains when you know who you are. It is just known to be an object non-separate from you, awareness, the non-experiencing witness. That person, the one that gives you so much trouble, is a problem only because you identify with it. When you understand clearly that you are not exclusively that person and identify with who you really are, he appears as a good friend, a toothless enemy, or at worst just an amusing bundle of irrational tendencies.

You may feel a little silly when you realize that you were tricked by duality and that you are actually awareness, the non-experiencing witness. Don't berate yourself for taking yourself to be the experiencing awareness for so long. Everyone is fooled by duality.

So far I have equated the understanding of the non-dual nature of reality with the word *happiness*. Maybe happiness is not a precise word to describe the result of the discrimination between the subject and the objects. The happiness we are talking about is not the result of a happening, getting what you want or avoiding what you don't. It is not "ha ha" happiness. Or "I won the lottery and fell in love" happiness. The kind of happiness that is the nature of the self is a subtle simple sense of wholeness and completeness, a quiet contentment born of an unquestionable sense of self-confidence: knowing that no matter what happens, good or bad, I am always okay because I am a partless whole. I am adequate. There are no divisions in me, no boundaries or borders separate me from anything.

So the self-inquiry process boils down to determining if I am whole and complete—and therefore free—or if I am incomplete, and therefore not free. If I am complete, then I needn't chase objects. If I am incomplete, I must keep chasing objects.

Self-inquiry is an existential, not a philosophical, intellectual, religious or mystical issue. The basic question is: what am I doing here on Earth in this meat tube? Who am I? What is life all about? If I could figure it out on my own, I would have done so by now. But the problem is too tricky. I need help. I need a means of self-knowledge. Vedanta is a means of self-knowledge. It reveals the hidden logic of our own experience and convinces us that if we are rational, it is to our advantage to abandon the pursuit of objects and to go for freedom directly.

We are almost at the end of the first teaching. If you want to move to the second teaching, you need to have signed on to the logic so far. If you can't accept it, the next teaching will make no sense, because you will still be expecting some kind of object—usually changed circumstances—to make you happy. If this logic is not enough—and it often isn't because of the ego's pig-headed insistence that objects are the source of happiness—please consider one last fact…

Life Is a Zero-Sum Game

As previously mentioned, the lid on the coffin of the object happiness idea is the sad fact that life is a zero-sum game. It is a zero-sum game because the world of objects is a duality. You cannot win every time. You lose as much as you win. I need money for security, but my desire to spend (what good is money if you can't spend it?) makes me insecure. The more pleasure I get, the more pleasure I want. Wanting is painful. I want power to be free of my sense of inadequacy and smallness, but power depends on circumstances not under my control, causing me to feel powerless. I want to be perfect, but the more perfect I become, the more hidden imperfections come to light. I want to enjoy the intimacy of a relationship, but to get it I need to be attached to the object, so I lose my freedom. If I want to be free, I have to sacrifice intimacy. The list goes on.

The Fourth Pursuit

We divided experience into three basic pursuits: security, pleasure and virtue. Objects can give us the first two, and the way we go about pursuing objects can give us the third. But actually, there is only one pursuit, the pursuit of freedom. Why? *Because I want an object for the freedom that comes when the desire for the object goes.* I don't want security. I want freedom from insecurity. I don't want pleasure, I want freedom from suffering. I don't want virtue, I want freedom from sin.

Nothing is wrong with objects, per se. But they are only an indirect means to temporary happiness. Since the real object of pursing objects is freedom, I need a direct path. On this path, I go directly for happiness. I understand clearly that objects will not help. You are not a mature, spiritually healthy person, one qualified for inquiry, unless you understand this teaching on objects.

This is the point where the rubber meets the road, spiritually. Everyone wants freedom, all right, but they want freedom *plus* the objects. They want to keep all their stuff and add the freedom object to their object pile. It doesn't work, but that does not stop them from thinking that it does. It doesn't work, because freedom is not an object that we can get as an experience. If we can, then it is not freedom at all, because all experiences come to an end one fine day.

Understanding that there is a direct path to freedom is perhaps the most important moment in life. To pursue anything properly, whether it is security, pleasure or virtue, you should commit yourself to it 100%. The more things you pursue, the less likely you are to get any one of them. You can get only so far with a particular desire before it conflicts with another desire. The next goal seems more attainable, so you drop the first. People hop from one thing to another, never finding success in one thing because they believe that something else will work better or faster.

If you are actually awareness and not the needy, wanting creature you think you are—and awareness is non-dual and always free of the objects known to it—pursuing anything else is not going to work. If you want to pursue security, pleasure, or virtue, or power, or fame, or whatever, then go for it. But there is no substance in those things. They give pleasure and pain intermittently, but not the self-confident happiness that comes from knowing that freedom is your nature.

CHAPTER TWO

KNOWLEDGE
AND EXPERIENCE

How Do I Get Free?

When you give up seeking in the world of objects you are ready for the spiritual option. When I was twenty-five and in the grip of a profound despair, I had an epiphany of epic proportions that turned my life around and set me on the path to enlightenment. However, the search needn't begin with a dramatic event. Perhaps a book like *The Power of Now* found its way into your hands and led you to other books until eventually you discovered the idea of non-duality. Or for health reasons you took up yoga and subsequently became interested in meditation, which led to the idea of enlightenment. Maybe you found a stone Buddha at a garage sale, stuck it in your garden and at the same time noticed that your mind was no longer preoccupied with the same worldly things. Perhaps somebody took you to see the famous hugging saint and something that you could not explain happened. When you are ready, you will discover innumerable paths purportedly leading out of the world.

If you thought the world was a gargantuan market of objects and activities, you soon discover that the spiritual world is also a big market of objects and activities. Like the pitchmen on TV, innumerable gurus, avatars, shamans, and yogis have just the deal for you! Freedom! Enlightenment! Kundalini! They say a hidden, snake-like energy sleeps at the bottom of your spine. To awaken her from her slumber, you're meant to eat like a bird, do exhausting breathing exercises, chant unpronounceable mantras, and deprive yourself of sleep. I ate spoonfuls of cayenne pepper and swallowed yards of cotton cloth strips which I retrieved from my innards laden with globs of mucus. Purification!

When she awakens, Kundalini slithers up your spine, passing through various energy centers. It is an exciting path, fraught with danger. She is not easy to control and can wiggle off into one of the minor nerve currents that wind around the central nervous system, hunker down there and cause all manner of mischief. But if everything goes right she continues on her upward spiral. Piercing the heart center, she releases unconditional love. When she penetrates the mind, wisdom flows like a rushing river. And finally—the grand finale!—she explodes through a mystic doorway in the top of the head and merges into consciousness, the limitless Self, setting off a mind-blowing spiritual orgasm that lasts forever and sets you free!

Or maybe you have an austere streak. You take up Vipassana, an ancient meditation technique, and find yourself sitting alone in a room watching your breath interminably. The connection between this activity and freedom is not always obvious but the teachers say that one fine day you will achieve a state of no suffering—*nirvana*. Maybe you stumble on a modern method and end up in a cult, wired to machines that monitor your brain waves, that are meant to "clear" you. They say there are ways to contact ascended masters who enlighten from extraterrestrial planes. Modern life is a veritable supermarket of other worldly paths.

Spirituality is an appealing, romantic, exotic, mysterious and promising world. But, sad to say, the basic psychology operating in it is no different from the psychology operating in the everyday world you just left: *do this and get that*. You have always worked hard for worldly things, so without much thought you assume that the pursuit of freedom is like the pursuit of any other object—it can be obtained by effort. So you get out your pick and shovel and toil in the spiritual salt mines.

Definition of Duality – Subject and Object

Eventually you find yourself at another crossroads. Lest you fall by the wayside, you need to sort out the issue of action before you can move on.

What is the basis of the idea that you can get freedom by doing something? For all intents and purposes it seems that action can free me because when I get what I want I do feel a sense of freedom. But can it?

The idea that *karma*—doing something—can set me free is based on the idea that reality is a duality. In its most fundamental formulation duality means this: "I am here. Objects are there. They are different from me. They have what I want." This is how reality presents itself to us and this is what we believe. From this premise my reasoning unconsciously proceeds: "Since I don't feel free and the experience of freedom is possible, it must be available elsewhere, so I need to do something to get 'there.'" In this case "there" means a different kind of experience, i.e., the enlightenment experience. Remember, experiences are objects too.

But from our analysis of the location of objects we know that reality is non-dual, *appearances to the contrary notwithstanding*. We said that objects are experienced in me by the experiencing instrument, the mind, and that the mind is an object that is also not separate from me. At the behest of some mysterious power the mind takes the shape of objects that seem to be different from me, the subject. It can do this because it does not have a structure of its own. It is formless.

Some teachings say the mind becomes the objects, but this is not true. If it became the objects, it could not modify to become a different object later and we would be stuck with a single experience forever. One second you can experience a tree and the next second you can experience a dog or a banana without any change in the nature of the mind. The mind keeps taking different forms without being affected by the form it takes. We say that the mind "appears" as objects. It is like a movie screen on which objects appear, causing no change to the screen. Objects are either relatively static or highly malleable structures in consciousness that have their own peculiar natures. Relatively static structures are the three bodies, about which more will be said later, and malleable structures are the predictable experiences that occur in the three bodies. The relatively static structures—the three bodies, three states, three qualities and the five elements—make the world reasonably workable so that it is possible for us to function. The nature of the mind, the Subtle Body, is to reveal objects. If objects were formless like the mind, purposeful work would not be possible. But the mind is formless consciousness-awareness.

Objects—structures—are formed out of awareness like a spider's web is formed out of the spider. And awareness, like the spider, is conscious, while the web, like the objects of experience, is not conscious. *Experience is awareness but awareness is not experience*; just as the web is the spider but the spider is not the web. If love or hate or anything else is the object of your experience, it is formed out of your own consciousness-awareness.

Physical objects look real because the senses, which are relatively permanent, organized functions in consciousness, structure consciousness in such a way that they seem to be solid. There is a power*—it is not in consciousness nor is it outside consciousness—that causes this to happen. It is a good thing because without this structuring nobody would get out of bed and go to work because nothing would follow its nature and life would be completely unpredictable. In other words, the senses make consciousness look like it is solid but it is not actually solid even though it is the permanent substrate of existence.

Because objects are not opaque but are actually the mind appearing as objects, the objects can be reduced to awareness. When you investigate material objects they resolve into atoms, protons, neutrons and electrons and then into quarks and mesons and even into other infinitely small bits of matter, right down to the Higgs boson. Once you get down to a certain level of matter, particles become waves and these waves appear in and disappear into "space." We can't even say what space actually is because it is not a sense object that we experience. And when you consider subtle objects—thoughts and feelings and memories, dreams, fantasies, etc—it is obvious that they are not substantial either. So there is nothing substantial for us to experience "out there," except ourselves as consciousness in the form of objects.

Furthermore, experience itself—the container of discrete experiences—is the only object that is permanent. Individuals come and go but experience remains. Discrete experiences are never permanent; what is called experience on the individual level is just the mind reflecting (and interpreting when the intellect is functioning) the objects appearing in it. And the mind is only consciousness, which is me. So I am already experiencing myself with or without gross and subtle objects. The only question remaining is: am I free or not?

Now that the nature of experience and objects is understood, let's return to the problem of action. Those who tout a path of action to enlightenment say that you can get freedom though spiritual practices: do this yoga, do that meditation,

---

* *Maya. It will be explained in detail later.*

chant a mantra or go to a guru and have enlightenment transmitted to you. It is amazing how much effort is invested in spiritual practice with the idea that it can deliver a permanent state of blissful enlightenment.

Every one of us takes the self to be a doer of actions, so if the teaching unfolded so far is true, we have come to a very difficult moment on the spiritual path. I lived in a mountain cabin once and it was necessary to kill pack rats if I wanted to stay. One by one I discovered their holes and blocked them, forcing them to run into my traps. Beware, Mr. Rat! The logic of Vedanta is now slowly closing your escape tunnels. The trap is about to slam shut. First you realized you cannot escape down the object hole. Now you are about to discover that you can't escape by running down the enlightenment tunnel. The hyperactive rat-like doer must die so we can get on with the inquiry.

What Is Freedom?

It is limitlessness. It means that boundaries don't hem you in, that nothing contains you, restricts you, defines you or modifies you. It is a worthwhile goal. In fact, it is the only goal.

As a limited being you act to get results that you wish to enjoy. With action you can get something, maintain something, change something, get rid of something, purify something or create something. But you cannot get what you already have by doing something.

The idea that enlightenment can be gained through action—the experiential notion of enlightenment—does not work, because it is contrary to the irrefutable non-dual nature of reality. It is based on the appearance of things, not on the reality of things. And appearances are not permanent, so an enlightenment that I may gain through action will not last.

There is only one limitless thing, which is not a thing. It is consciousness, your very self. In fact, there is only consciousness, appearances to the contrary notwithstanding. Reality is you, whole and complete non-dual consciousness.

This is the essence of Vedanta's teachings. So if you do not understand this—and don't feel bad if you don't, at least not until you have read this book—you will find yourself doing limited actions to get a limitless result, not knowing that the limitless result is you! One of the great sages in our tradition calls Vedanta the "*yoga* of no contact." *Yoga* means contact.

Paths Don't Work

Failure to appreciate this basic fact disqualifies nearly everyone seeking enlightenment. Because action does not work and seekers are committed to action, they are forced to rely on fantasies to set them free. Vedanta is not a spiritual path. It does not promise mystical experience. It does not try to connect you to anything because you are already connected. It does not try to change your experience, although your experience is transformed when you understand who you are. It does not try to fix you, because you are not broken. It does not try to heal you, because you are not sick. It is firmly based on reality. It is common sense existential knowledge.

Action is inevitable in the everyday world and it definitely has its place in the spiritual world, as we will see, but it is not a direct ticket to freedom. Some argue that Vedanta, self-inquiry, is an action, but it isn't; it is the nature of the self and that is why it is going on all the time in everyone. However, if you think it is we will not argue with you. But you should know that it has a different result from ordinary actions. It produces knowledge, not a particular experience.

To get what you already have, what can you do? You can only know that you have it and know what it means to have it. There is no other possibility. What conclusion can be drawn from this fact? Only one: if you want to be free you need to convert your desire for experience into a desire for self-knowledge.

I Want Self-Knowledge

The pursuit of self-knowledge is different from the pursuit of other kinds of knowledge because if you understand who you are, you will not need to understand anything else. Whereas, the knowledge of objects reveals only more ignorance. Vedanta says "What is it, knowing which, everything else becomes known?" If I understand who I am, my seeking stops.

What is self-knowledge? It is "I am consciousness-awareness." This knowledge sets me free because there is only me—all objects being only consciousness—and I am always present. If I am always free and always present all I need to do to become free is to realize who I am.

When am I not present as consciousness? If you possess an object and you believe the object is making you happy then you have a problem because no object will remain with you all the time. All objects—all states of mind, feelings, thoughts, ideas, circumstances, situations, loved ones and physical objects—come and go.

But I do not come and go. Objects arise and fall in me, but I stay the same. I am even beyond death. To say that I will not exist means that I would have to be present to observe my non-existence. But there is never a moment when I, consciousness, am not present. I am there to witness the death of my body and mind.

If you say that you or I (there is only one consciousness, so you and I are one) are not present in deep sleep, you will be wrong. Why do you prepare your bed and your bedroom with such care? When the kids next door come home drunk and crank up the stereo, are you happy to wake up? If you were not there, you would not be bothered by their noise. You are definitely present in deep sleep. Just because the person on your driver's license was not there does not mean that you were not there.

In sleep you enjoy yourself without objects. You are happy, complete and whole and everything is fine. When you wake up, you are taken away from the experience of bliss and happiness that is your nature and you are no longer happy.

If I am never not present and my nature is limitless bliss, then I do not have an action or an experience problem as far as freedom is concerned. I have a knowledge problem. If this is true, I need a means of knowledge because knowledge, including self-knowledge, does not happen on its own. It requires a means.

But before we take up the next teaching, the means of knowledge, it is important to put a few more nails in the coffin of experiential enlightenment. If you cannot accept these arguments, you will find that your path to enlightenment will be very rocky indeed. Most enlightenment teachings fall into the experiential category, so if you follow the logic you are going to be rather lonely once we finish our inquiry. Fortunately, Vedanta is the last man standing and it can set you free.

Debunking popular ideas does not make me popular but it is my duty to tell the truth. An open-minded person, however, is happy to hear the downside as well as the upside of things, including the enlightenment business. If some of the following ideas are associated with the names of people for whom you have devotion, do not think this is an attack on them. I am not trying to tear anyone down to build myself up. There is nothing personal in it. The logic speaks for itself.

Freedom from dependence on your experience of objects for happiness is liberation. Liberation is difficult because we are almost totally conditioned to the idea that what we experience defines and validates us. Thinking that it does is putting life's cart before the horse. It makes us victims of what happens, when in fact we are always beyond what happens. This profound truth will become more and more obvious as you listen to these teachings.

Enlightenment Myths

We are going to examine a number of popular enlightenment teachings from the non-dual perspective. If they come up short as means of enlightenment, it does not mean that they have no value. Indeed, some may be useful as practices to prepare the mind for self-knowledge. If you find yourself attached to one or more of these beliefs these inquiries will be challenging, no doubt. Ultimately, you will have to determine the nature of reality through your own investigation, but if your inquiry is disinterested and you follow the rules, you can only come to the conclusion: "I am and have always been ever-free, actionless, ordinary, non-dual, self-revealing awareness."

No Mind, Blank Mind, Empty Mind, Stopped Mind

As the self is always enlightened, the idea that "no mind" is enlightenment implies a duality between the awareness and thought. To say that the self is not experienceable when the mind is functioning means that the mind and the self enjoy the same order of reality, like a table and a chair. But experience shows that this is untrue. Do you cease to exist when you are thinking? Is there thought without awareness? In fact, thoughts come from you but you are much more than a thought. They depend on you, but you do not depend on them.

Does the mind hide the "I" and prevent you from experiencing the "I"? For you to know that the mind is empty or thinking you have to be aware. In both cases, with and without thought, I, awareness, am present. If I am aware at both times, I am not hidden by thought nor am I revealed by no thought. Whether thought is present or absent, I, the ever-free, ever-present self, am always directly experienced.

Awareness is always present. You can do nothing about it except know what it is and what it means to be awareness. It is ignorance of my nature as awareness that causes me to believe I can gain my self by stopping my mind or getting into a state of emptiness.

No Ego, Ego Death

This popular so-called teaching vies with the no-thought idea for top spot on the list of enlightenment myths.

Ego is the "I" notion, the idea we have about who we are. The list of identities that humans concoct in ignorance of their true identity is virtually limitless. Aside from the fact that there is no evidence that such an "I" exists, other than the thought that it exists, the absence of a limited identity does not equal enlightenment. If it did, plants and animals would be enlightened. And you would be enlightened in deep sleep because you have no identity there.

The teaching that the ego stands in the way of enlightenment is unworkable because the ego is the part of the self that wants to enjoy the results of its actions. If it killed itself it would not be there to enjoy the result i.e. enlightenment. So it will not kill itself. The ego is the self under the spell of ignorance; it thinks it is subject to birth and death, but it isn't. And if the ego is not conscious, it can only be a thought in consciousness, and no thought prevents the self from being and knowing itself. So there is no ego to kill, except the idea that the self lives or dies.

If you believe this myth you are a sucker for the spiritual version of the Hollywood ending: the ego kills itself and somehow gets the permanent enlightenment experience and enjoys endless experiential bliss. If you accept the fact that there is only one self and it is already enlightened and effortlessly and eternally enjoying itself, then understanding, not ego death is enlightenment.

Nirvana

This idea is another negative formulation of enlightenment. *Nirvana* is a desireless state of mind. This view is based on the idea that desire is suffering, which it is. To say that you want something means that you are not happy with what you have. This teaching is unworkable because a desireless mind is a contradiction in terms. When, except during sleep, do you not want something? Even at the end of life you want to continue living if life is still good, or you want to die if it is not.

On the surface the logic makes sense, but what is the cause of desire? Is it self-caused or is it the result of something else? If it is self-caused, then eliminating desire should eliminate suffering. But what if desire is an effect of self-ignorance? It is an effect of self-ignorance because there is only one self and it is a partless whole. It wants nothing. Will removing the effect remove the cause? Ignorance will not collapse when it is no longer supported by desire. It will just keep manufacturing more desires.

You may argue that ignorance sustains itself and it does, until it is known for what it is. It will collapse when it is exposed. If we continue to pursue our desires for objects, ignorance remains the hidden motivator for our actions and is, in fact, "reinforced" by the desires and the actions that flow from them. It remains hidden because our attention is turned away from the underlying cause of action.

It also remains to be seen whether desire is always suffering. Desire is just awareness functioning as the creator, sustainer and destroyer of the world. As long as my desires do not cause me to violate the physical and moral laws operating in the creation, why should I remove them? I am free to fulfill them. Enlightenment is the hard and fast knowledge that I am awareness and as such I am already free of desires so their presence or absence has nothing to do with me. Realize your nature and let desire be desire.

And finally, if I accept the contention that desire is suffering, how will I remove my desires without the desire to remove them? Once they are removed, who is going to remove the desirer?

The Now

Not to put too fine a point on it, the basic idea of the "now" teachings is: I am enlightened when I am present. Living in the past and the future means I am unenlightened. Aside from the fact that there is no time in a non-dual reality, let us inquire into this idea.

Does the word *now* refer to a period of time, which it certainly seems to, or is now a symbol for something else? If it refers to time, is there such a thing as objective time?

It is impossible to determine the nature of time because time is relative to the desires and fears of individuals and to the intervals between experiences. If my desires are being met and I am enjoying, time passes quickly. If I am suffering terribly, time passes slowly.

Are the past, present and future actual divisions in consciousness or only conceptual divisions? If time is objective, then everyone would be able to determine just when the past ends and the now begins. When I am in the now, how long does the now remain the now? Is it one second? Two? One minute? More?

Assuming I am in the now and want to remain enlightened, I should know when the now begins and ends. I need to avoid falling back into the past and travelling into the future. Perhaps I should hop up out of the time continuum just before the end of the now and jump back into it just before the past appears, keeping in mind how much time passes until I have to hop out again. Even if I am sitting still in the now I need to worry about the past and the future creeping into it.

Let's assume that there is only "now." Am I ever out of it? Experience takes place only in the present. How can you experience the past if it is not here? You can experience a memory but the experience of memory does not take you to the past. The memory appears in awareness and is experienced now. The experience takes as long as it takes and means whatever it is interpreted to mean. The same logic applies to the future. Nothing is ever experienced in the future. You may think about something that you imagine will take place at another time but if it happens, it happens only in the present, when it appears in awareness.

Direct experience shows that time is not linear. Objects, which are made out of thoughts, which are in turn made out of consciousness, appear in you—awareness-consciousness. They last as long as they last and are interpreted by your desires and fears, and then dissolve back into consciousness. When they appear in that part of awareness called the mind, they seem to change; but in reality it is only the mind that changes. Furthermore, if time were linear, everything would be evolving toward some kind of utopian state. The same experience would not happen again; but experiences keep repeating themselves over and over, ad infinitum.

If this is true, maybe *now* is a code word for the self, awareness. It is the humble opinion of the author that *now* is a misleading and inaccurate term for the self and should be banned from the spiritual debate because it is not helpful to refer to something that is eternal and out of time with a word that conveys a sense of time.

Experience of Oneness

To refute this idea let us revisit the location of objects teaching. Do you experience objects out there in the world or do you experience them in your mind? I experience them in my mind. How far is the object from your mind? Is it floating off the surface of the mind? No, it is not. Where is it then? It has merged into the mind and the mind has taken the shape of the object. The mind is formless, like water or air, and can take any form, just as gold can become a specific object, a ring, a bracelet or a necklace. How far are you from your mind? Is your mind floating above the surface of your awareness? Is there a gap between you and your mind? Do you need a bridge to travel over the gap?

I do not. Why? Because my mind is me. It is awareness. If this is true, then what you experience is not only in awareness but it actually *is* awareness. The objects in awareness and the subject—awareness—are one. If this is also true, then why do I need to experience oneness? I am already experiencing oneness with everything.

I want to experience oneness with everything when I am already experiencing oneness because I am in duality and have identified with the thought of separation, which causes suffering. Duality is not a fact. It is only a belief in the thought of separation. Instead of trying to remove the want by gaining the experience of a particular object, I should inquire into the thought of separation. Is it true? Am I really separate from my self? Or am I already the bliss that the object is meant to deliver?

Transcendental State, Fourth State

This myth asks us to experience enlightenment as a state beyond the mind. The mind is an interface through which awareness interacts with itself in the form of the physical objects. It is awareness in a form called *chitta*. The chitta makes it possible for awareness to apparently think, will, feel and remember. The mind is capable of a wide range of states, from the gross feelings associated with the physical body, including psychic experiences up to the most mystical and sublime *samadhis* of yoga. All states are in the mind and all change because they are in the dream of duality.

The self is non-dual and therefore it is out of time. It does not, nor can it, change. It is that because of which the mind's many states are known. It is conscious, but states of mind are not conscious. They are subtle energies that are only capable of reflecting consciousness. The subtler the mind, the more ethereal and luminous the states become. When you get to the interface between the self and the mind, the mind stuff is so refined and the self so close, that radiant "light" and intense bliss is experienced. It is very easy to mistake these higher states of mind for the self and think enlightenment is an amazing heavenly state or a state of endless experiential bliss. Experience belongs neither to the self nor to the mind. It occurs when awareness shines on the mind. Awareness and mind constitute the most fundamental duality.

Enlightenment is the nature of simple, unchanging awareness. It cannot be experienced as an object because it is subtler than the mind, the instrument of experience. A subtle object can illumine a gross object but a gross object cannot illumine a subtle object. So how is the ego-mind going to experience something that it is incapable of experiencing?

Enlightenment as Eternal Bliss

When someone accustomed to identifying with the ever-changing content of the mind wakes up to non-duality, the awakening is interpreted as a very positive event. But the feeling of bliss is not because it is experiencing awareness as a blissful object. The belief that it is, is caused by the absence of suffering, not because awareness "feels" good. If you have been suffering a toothache for days and the tooth is extracted, it is the absence of pain that feels good, not the bliss of the extraction. You have actually just gone back to normal, not attained an exceptional state. Enlightenment does not feel like anything. It is simply the hard and fast knowledge that I am limitless, partless, unchanging ordinary awareness. When this knowledge is firm, it has a very positive effect on the mind but it does not convert the mind into an endless bliss machine.

However, it infuses the mind with a sense of authenticity, wholeness and rock solid confidence. Henceforth the individual knows that it can weather any existential storm. When you know beyond a shadow of a doubt that you are awareness, you no longer desire to feel good, because you know you are the source of goodness.

Enlightenment Is Not a Special Status

Enlightenment is not a special status. It is the default, the nature of the self. You are not getting something you do not have; you simply realize that what you sought so frantically you had all along. If enlightenment is an experience, it should be cause for embarrassment, not jubilation. When an obscenely obese person goes back to normal, he is lauded by others as a courageous super-being for overcoming long odds, but the sloth that caused the obesity is conveniently forgotten. Was anything actually gained? Just as overcoming gluttony is not praiseworthy, enlightenment is not praiseworthy, because you are always enlightened; it is your nature.

Much of the striving for enlightenment is motivated by a desire to distinguish one's self, to excel and convince one's self that one is unique. You *are* unique, but not with reference to others. You are no more unique than I am because there is only one of us.

Here are other strange ideas of enlightenment: that enlightenment conveys amazing superpowers or is some rare "state" achieved by the chosen few; that it can be transmitted from one person to another in the form of some kind of special energy; that there are levels of enlightenment; that you will get everything you want when you are enlightened, etc. We need not address them now. As we proceed with the teachings of Vedanta, the fallacies behind all erroneous notions will be exposed.

CHAPTER THREE

THE MEANS OF SELF-KNOWLEDGE

Enlightenment is the hard and fast knowledge that I am ordinary awareness and not the experiencing entity I think I am. It is only knowledge for one simple reason: I am already free. As we have just concluded, any attempt to experience the self or experience enlightenment or attain a permanent state of consciousness is a waste of time. What I should be seeking is self-knowledge. But knowledge does not just land on one's window sill like a little bird and tweet itself. Knowledge, which is the content of everything, requires a means.

With our God-given means of knowledge—perception and inference—we can know things through experience and draw certain conclusions. These means require objects. The senses require objects. The heart needs feelings to feel. For its enjoyment there is a universal pool of emotions: desire, fear, greed, love, kindness, sympathy, compassion, envy, jealousy, etc. The intellect requires thoughts, which it draws from a vast world of ideas.

People who are dissatisfied with their lives and who want to feel something special and extraordinary often criticize Vedanta as merely an "intellectual" path. Usually they say that spirituality is about love and the "heart." It is, but not the way they think, as we will see later, in chapter 13. Even if the heart is extremely sensitive it cannot feel you because you are subtler than your heart. You feel things through your heart. You are prior to what you think and feel. We are not for or against feelings or thoughts; they are a simple fact of life. But it is wrong to say that Vedanta is intellectual knowledge because no concept can describe you, everything that is. That is not to say that the intellect, which is just a function in consciousness-awareness, is not intimately involved in self-knowledge. So the idea that it should be transcended or discarded is not correct either. Without it you cannot gain freedom.

If you seek freedom only because you think you are not free—which you do—then you should dismiss your search for the truth as "intellectual" and be happy as you are because the idea that you are bound is purely an "intellectual" notion as well. An ignorant intellect may be the problem, but ignorance is not the only option for the intellect.

The final result of Vedantic inquiry is not intellectual knowledge "of" the self. The knowledge "I am actionless, ordinary, unconcerned, unborn awareness" destroys the notion "I am a limited personal entity subject to suffering" and itself disappears, leaving you as you always were, free of concepts and free of experience itself.

The Self Is Not an Object

The self is not an object. For it to become an object there would have to be another "you" to experience it, but it is a matter of common sense that there is only one "you." The self is also indestructible. It is non-dual awareness. So it is impossible to split it into two conscious parts and get one part to experience the other part. Even if you could split it in two, both parts would have the same nature and nothing would be gained because the experience of both parts would be the same. Furthermore, even if it were divisible, who would divide it? Since it is not an agent it cannot divide itself. Finally, experience seems like it is a matter of a conscious subject experiencing an inert object but consciousness is everything, the subject and the object, and it is never inert. It is always just non-dual consciousness. Even when ignorance apparently turns the self into subject and object, neither the subject, the experiencing entity, or the objects are actually conscious, so the subject does not experience the objects, although it certainly seems to. The subject—the experiencing entity, which thinks it is conscious—is actually an object known to you, witnessing awareness. So what is experience? Experience is always only awareness experiencing itself. Duality is not involved. As we shall see, duality is only a belief.

So it seems that as far as self-knowledge is concerned, God made a mistake. If God wanted us to know who we are, It would have given us a suitable means of knowledge. This is why you often hear the refrain "Oh, the self is a great mystery! It is beyond everything. No one can know what it is. It will forever remain a mystery!" People get quite romantic about the unknowablity of God. It seems to turn them on.

Everyone Knows Objects but No One Knows the Subject

It must have been a big job to create the world in six days. After creating "fish and fowl" over which we supposedly have "dominion," it seems the Creator saved the best for last, i.e., us. When It should have been out partying on Saturday night in anticipation of Its day of rest, It stayed up late creating us.

Perhaps It had the bodies on an assembly line with the brains stacked nearby and as the bodies passed It inserted the brains. But because it was late and poor God was exhausted after six days of hard work, It accidentally put the brain facing out towards the world of objects instead of inward toward the self and, well, the rest is history: everyone knows objects but nobody knows who they are.

We are fortunate, however, because there is a holy man in India—Kalki by name, an Avatar guy—who can save us from God's mistake. For $5,000, he will reverse your brain and you'll get to know who you are! A lot of eager souls took him up on the offer, it seems, as he now has a huge golden temple. Evidently, the market for brain reversals is growing because it seems his son got in the business too. It is good news for the unenlightened because the price of enlightenment seems to have dropped recently owing to an increase on the supply side.

If the instruments we have are not suitable for knowing the self then how are we going to know it? It seems that consciousness wanted us to know because a very long time ago it revealed the Science of Self-knowledge—Vedanta—for precisely that reason.

Vedanta Is Not a Philosophy

The first thing we need to know about Vedanta is that it is not a philosophy. Philosophies are the contentions or beliefs of an individual or groups of individuals. Marx and Engels came up with the now defunct philosophy called communism, which was meant to correct the problems of capitalism. Existentialism was all the rage in Europe in the last century. Where is existentialism today? Philosophies don't last because they are cooked up by people to serve the intellectual needs of the times. When times change—which they do—the philosophies are no longer relevant.

It is very important to appreciate the fact that Vedanta does not come from human beings. Human beings have limited understanding and on top of it they always have an agenda, usually to save or destroy the world in some way or the other. If it is not world domination or world saving, they seem to be perennially inclined to sell you something, convince you of something or to get you or your circumstances to change. They are not objective.

It Is Not a Religion or a Spiritual Path

Humans cook up philosophies and religions. Vedanta is not a religion either. It is not the result of the experiences of mystics. It accounts for mystic experiences but it is beyond mysticism. It is not a spiritual path. It is the knowledge behind all religions and spiritual paths.

Before we proceed, you should know that it is not necessary that you believe these statements. They are difficult to swallow because we have the vanity to suppose that because we see ourselves as "the roof and crown of things" that everything meaningful comes from us. In any case its origins are reasonably unimportant because it does what it purports to do: it sets you free. If you properly expose your mind to Vedanta, you will see very clearly why we say that it is not a religion or a philosophy or a spiritual path invented by human beings. We say it is *apurusheyajnanam* which means *not from a person*.

It Is Not Channeled Information

It is not channeled either. People, with all their biases, prejudices, beliefs and opinions are like old pipes; a lot of gunk accumulates in them. So when knowledge flows through them it inevitably gets polluted. We are the greatest polluters on earth. Yes, we have some knowledge, but knowledge and ignorance sit side by side in the human mind and unfortunately most of us do not know the difference.

We don't want a means of knowledge that's made up of ignorance and truth. How will we separate them? Undiscriminating people swallow one with the other. You will not get free this way. Read the books of almost any modern teacher. You may find truth there, or some version of it, but the author's beliefs and opinions are usually so tightly woven into and around it, like vines wrapped around a tree trunk, that you swallow both and end up confused. This is not the way to freedom. The words of prophets and mystics should always be suspect.

It Is Revealed Knowledge

People experience truth. But it does not come *from* them. It comes *to* them from "outside." It is *seen*. It is *heard*. It comes from an objective source, from beyond us. Revelations have been an intimate part of human experience forever. Just as an objective body of scientific knowledge about objects has built up over the centuries, an objective body of knowledge of consciousness has developed too.

A good example of this kind of knowledge is Einstein's "discovery" of the law of relativity and gravity or Thomas Edison's discovery of electricity. To discover means to uncover something that was present but previously unknown. Relativity, gravity and electricity describe how the world works according to the laws of physics, not according to Einstein or Edison. Gravity, relativity and electricity do not care if you believe in them. They operate the same way whether you understand what they are or not. Self-knowledge is always here, right in front of our noses, but because we are blinded by duality, we do not see it.

It is very important that we trust knowledge, not people. People are not bad; they just tend to be ignorant, particularly on the topic of who they are. Ignorance is something that hides or veils knowledge and in the process allows wrong knowledge to happen in the form of projected beliefs and opinions, biases and prejudices. Because we don't know who we are, we take what we think and feel to be the truth, but personal truth is unreliable.

Humans have studied fire since the beginning of time. At some point it became clear that fire has a certain nature and behaves according to certain laws. Because of the knowledge of heat we can send rockets to Mars. Anyone who understands the knowledge and has the resources can send a rocket into space. There is nothing personal in it. In the same way, millions have had revelations of the non-dual nature of reality for thousands of years. The knowledge from these experiences has been extracted and put together in such a way that a science of consciousness—the self—developed.

One difference between modern material science and Vedanta is that one is focused on objects and the other is focused on the subject, consciousness. Additionally, knowledge gained by material science is constantly changing because the field of investigation is in a state of flux and the means of knowledge, the human mind, is conditioned by ignorance: the more we know about objects the more we don't know. The knowledge that Vedanta brings, however, does not change, because the self does not change. So self-knowledge is always good. Another difference between Vedanta and material science is that the purpose of self-knowledge is freedom from existential suffering, whereas the goal of material science is purely knowledge of the material forces playing in the field of consciousness and how to use those forces to obtain certain desirable objects. The gain of desirable objects, as we know, does not remove suffering. It is tantamount to suffering.

It is important to know, however, that Vedanta has no quarrel with material or psychological knowledge gained through impersonal means, i.e., experimentation. In chapter 6 I introduce knowledge of the Causal and Subtle bodies gained in the last fifty years, which, I believe, contributes to Vedanta as a means of self-knowledge.

It Is Knowledge of Everything

Vedanta covers everything: the cosmos, the psyche and pure consciousness-awareness, whereas material science covers only the cosmos, and psychological science covers only the psyche. Neither material science nor psychological science understands the relationship to each other, much less to consciousness, because their fields and methods of investigation are mutually exclusive. As human beings we are a combination of consciousness—some say spirit—and matter, and exist in a complex world of laws and forces, so to understand ourselves we need a complete means of knowledge.

Vedanta is not just about realizing who you are beyond the objects appearing in you. To be sure, this knowledge is the essence of Vedanta, but you cannot live as awareness in the world of objects unless you know the objects for what they are *and* how awareness and the objects—the experiencing individual and the field of experience—fit together. Vedanta is the knowledge of three orders of the one non-dual reality: (1) pure awareness with* and without† the capacity to create, (2) material objects‡ and (3) the individual§.

Without putting too fine a point on it, at this stage we can say that individuals are small bundles of desiring willing consciousness with various values and priorities. We need to understand them as they are. They find themselves involved in a world of gross and subtle material objects that are subject to impersonal forces and laws. If individuals don't understand the structure of the objective and subjective worlds in which they live, their knowledge is incomplete and their suffering will not abate.

The third aspect of Vedanta is pure consciousness with and without its capacity to create objects. It is called *Isvara* in our tradition, but if you insist on a Western word, you can call it God. We don't like the word *God* because the crazy ideas people have picked up from religion make it difficult to understand. You can't say a lot about consciousness apart from the objects appearing in it because, although it is the most important piece of the existential puzzle, it is very simple and subtler than the subtlest object. We can say much more about consciousness in its role as creator of the individuals, the individuals themselves and the objects with which they interact.

To be free I need to understand myself as everything, not just as awareness isolated from the objects appearing in it. Enlightenment is not an experience that sets me free; it is complete knowledge of myself as awareness *and the objects appearing in me*. It takes time for self-knowledge to become complete because ignorance is terribly persistent. You have to hear the teachings over and over and chip away at the ignorance little by little.

Many people have realized who they are in some kind of experiential way and claim that they are fully "cooked," but we do not call this enlightenment. These fully cooked people are actually half-baked, if you must know, because they have only partial knowledge of reality. It is only in the land of the blind that the one-eyed man is king. Many do not live righteous lives and seem to enjoy confusing seekers with outlandish views of enlightenment. If you don't understand the big

---

* Isvara

† paramatma

‡ jagat

§ jiva

picture—how everything fits together, how is it all the same and yet different—you are still unenlightened.

What Is Knowledge?

At the beginning of the teaching we need to get our terminology straight. When I use words you should know what they mean. Everyone agrees on what the word *tree* refers to but most do not agree on what the word *God* or *consciousness* means. *Knowledge* is a word we have been using so far without a proper definition.

Knowledge is something that cannot be negated, something you can always count on. Information is not knowledge. That General Motors stock is $43 today is not knowledge. It is only information because tomorrow it maybe $42. You can't count on it to be at $43 forever.

Knowledge is beyond experience. It trumps experience every time. It is extremely important to know that you can operate your life confidently on the basis of knowledge but that your confidence is always compromised when you operate only on the basis of knowledge garnered through your experience. Experience is valuable—life is experience—and most of us run our lives based on experience alone; we base our actions on how we feel, not what we know. There is no law against it but if you want to be happy you need to know that experience is unreliable. When you look at the diagram below you will experience the horizontal lines to be of different lengths. But if you measure them you will see that they are exactly the same. Knowledge says one thing, experience another.

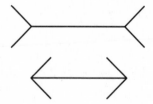

We take our interpretation of experience to be knowledge, but it is not knowledge. If you operate solely on the basis of your feelings—fears and desires—you will produce unwanted results because reality—the world in which experience takes place—does not care what you feel. It is an impersonal matrix of objects, forces, rules and conscious beings that behave independently of you. With knowledge as your guide you will not make mistakes because you will not find yourself in conflict with what is. For example, intuition is a particularly prized feeling among spiritual individuals, but it is unreliable. You may have a correct insight or intuition about a particular person or situation at one moment and find that insight or intuition contradicted by a different one later on.

When they send a space probe to Saturn, Saturn may be in the western sky, but they launch the probe into the eastern sky. Experience tells you to send it west but knowledge says east. After a while the rocket circles around in the gravitational field of Mars, increasing its velocity, and is then shot off in a southerly direction even though at the time Saturn is in the north. It stays on course as the planets continually change positions but years later it eventually enters the atmosphere of Saturn! If we used experience as a guide the probe would never get there. Isn't it amazing that after years a tiny piece of metal sent from a planet millions of miles away can suddenly start orbiting around a constantly moving object and collect data! Only knowledge makes this possible. Information, beliefs, opinions, feelings—all the human stuff—are not reliable.

We find ourselves in a cosmos that is made of knowledge. A tree is knowledge, a dog is knowledge, the elements are knowledge and human beings are just knowledge programmed to function in a certain way to serve the interests of the total. It is vital to our happiness that we understand the nature of reality. You can count on Vedanta. It is as good today as it was three thousand years ago because it is knowledge based. It's like the eyes. They do what they are intended to do. There is no need for a new eye. And if a new improved eye is needed consciousness will evolve it over millions of years. Likewise, there is no reason to invent a new teaching for modern people because we are what we have always been and the means of knowledge that has been setting individuals free for thousands of years is perfect.

How Does Vedanta Work?

Our normal means of knowledge work because there are objects that can be known. But since the self is beyond perception or inference it cannot be known as an object. Yoga and other practices give you experience of various subtle states of mind but Vedanta doesn't tout self-experience because, as noted above, you are already experiencing the self.

We don't need to prove that you exist either. Believe it or not some people in the spiritual world actually take it seriously when told that they don't exist. The

Buddhists have been saying it forever—there is no self, it is all void, emptiness, etc—and the modern Neo-Advaita crowd, God bless them, are not embarrassed to say it either. We say there is only one self, it is everything and it is never not present.

To be fair, perhaps they mean that the ego doesn't exist, but even it exists. It is not real but it is not nonexistent. There is no need to say you don't exist or to prove that you don't exist because that you exist is self-evident. You don't need a mirror to know that you have eyes because seeing, itself, proves the existence of eyes. And you cannot deny the existence of something unless it does exist. No thing is nonexistent. As soon as you think of it, it exists because objects are nothing more than the thought of objects. And as we have seen, experience takes place only in an apparently conscious mind as thoughts and feelings. So there is no such thing as non-existence, apart from the idea of non-existence.

But to know what you are, and to know what it means to be who you are, you need a mirror. My experience of myself is not a mirror for you. Experience does not transfer from individual to individual. If it did and I was in love, I could put you in love. Knowledge transfers. If you have a lighted candle and put the wick of another candle next to it, the fire jumps from one to the other. Vedanta is a mirror that reveals what you are and what it means to be you. It does this by stripping away the erroneous notions you have about who you are. It reveals you to you, using the unexamined logic of your own experience. The knowledge of you is in you and the experience of you is with you always, but something is still to be known, or you would be free.

You need the big picture. It is not available because you identify with beliefs and opinions about who you are that are not in harmony with your nature as everything. It is seemingly not available here only because you believe that it is only attainable elsewhere.

You Can't Study Vedanta

Vedanta is a means of inquiry that needs to be taught. The ego usually thinks it is an expert on everything relating to itself and does not take to the idea of teaching. Spiritual types deluded by the experiential view often cite Ramana Maharshi as evidence that no teacher or teaching is necessary for liberation. Perhaps a highly qualified soul could "get it" in one go but the chances are about the same as winning the lottery, probably less. Brainy types usually think they can get enlightened by synthesizing information from their study of the literature from various traditions, but this approach is equally ill-conceived. Reading or listening to someone talk about the self (Vedanta doesn't talk "about" it; it reveals it through a particular method) does not work because no matter how smart you think you are, you wouldn't be inquiring if you weren't self-ignorant. Ignorance operates as you listen and read, causing you to invariably misunderstand.

Furthermore, most seekers do not know the difference between knowledge and ignorance. They confuse their beliefs and opinions with knowledge. This means that I am not one to enlighten myself. I need an impersonal means of knowledge that is ignorance free and I need to have someone who has been set free by such a means to teach me. It should also be brought to your attention that someone claiming that enlightenment is experiential who cites her experience as proof of enlightenment and expects her words to be seen as scripture may or may not be enlightened but is not qualified to teach the self. Anyone can have a life changing epiphany and define it as enlightenment. To uncritically accept her teaching and instructions is to ask for trouble.

Generally people who are led to Vedanta have been seeking for a long time. It is not suitable for entry-level seekers. When a person gets to a certain point in life—when they are no longer in thrall to experience—they are led to Vedanta. Fruit plucked from the tree before it is ripe is never good. This is why we don't advertise. It comes when you are ready for it. We cannot teach those who are not ready. It is a waste of time for both the teacher and the student.

I sincerely and enthusiastically tried to set myself free full time for three years. I read all the books, went to India, hobnobbed with yogis and gurus, did many practices, yet I still flunked the enlightenment test and failed to matriculate. I got so fed up that I quit seeking and vowed (against all odds) to become a normal person. The very day I called off the search I met my teacher and it became obvious that I needed more than a technique. I felt very small and ignorant but at the same time it was terribly liberating to discover that a time-tested, impersonal means of knowledge and a respectable teaching tradition were available to me. To see self-knowledge working in another human being and understand that it had set him free was all I needed.

Listening

The first stage is listening. Usually, when you hear something you immediately begin formulating a reply in your mind. You hear the words and react impulsively but you do not actually listen to what is being said or where it is coming from. You cannot expect Vedanta to work if this is how you approach it, because Vedanta is much more than a few spiritual ideas aimed at your ego. It is a body of knowledge that needs to be assimilated in its entirety. It employs a particular methodology—superimposition and negation—that needs to be worked on you until you are capable of working it on yourself. In this stage you only have to keep your mind open, which involves setting aside your beliefs and opinions temporarily. It is not easy. But you need to let the teaching and the teacher do the work. Knowledge has its own power. It will do the work for you, if you let it. At some point the vision of non-duality will begin to form up in your mind and you will be able to work on yourself.

Reflecting

In the second stage* you are asked to look at what you believe and think you are *in light of what you have heard*, not the other way around. To reflect properly you need to surrender your idea of who you are to the knowledge of who you are as unfolded by the scripture. Normally, we retain the right to evaluate what we hear, but in the case of Vedanta this right has been ceded to the scriptures. You appreciate the fact that it, not you, is the authority. There are a lot of things you have got right and there are a lot that you have got wrong. So this stage is a winnowing process, a sifting, during which you discard your ignorance, based on an appreciation of the unassailable logic of Vedanta, which in turn is based on the unexamined logic of your own experience. Vedanta just plugs you into the deeper part of yourself, the part that knows, the part that sees, the part that contains and resolves life's dualities into the non-dual vision.

Assimilation

The final stage† is the result of listening and reflection. It is the complete assimilation of the knowledge that destroys the network of ignorance-based desires and one's sense of doership. It has a dramatic experiential impact insofar as one's life becomes free and peaceful and completely fulfilled.

---

* manana
† nididhyasana

Inquiry does not mean asking the question "Who am I?" Inquiry is the daily application of the teachings of Vedanta to the numerous, troubling self-doubts appearing in the mind in the form of the inexorable stream of fears and desires, likes and dislikes that disturb it. It is discrimination, disciplining the mind to think from the platform of wholeness, not from lack. It requires constant vigilance. We are not trying to kill or transcend the mind. If you find yourself in a human body your mind will be active from womb to tomb. It can be educated and purified but never destroyed. It is here at the behest of a power much greater than you and it is here to stay. In fact, it is not really "your" mind.

Normally the mind is your boss. It thinks for you and tells you what to do. The experiential notion of enlightenment is a clumsy attempt to address the issue of control, which is possible, but not by transcending or destroying the mind. Vedanta teaches what the mind is and why what it thinks is either in harmony with reality or not.

The teachings include a subsidiary body of knowledge, commentaries by great sages that resolve certain apparent contradictions inherent in the nature of reality—the seeming paradox presented by the appearance of duality superimposed on non-dual reality, and a brilliant method, superimposition and negation, by which self-ignorance is removed.

CHAPTER FOUR

QUALIFICATIONS

A Mature Human Being

It is good that teaching Vedanta is not a profession, although I do it professionally, because to make it lucrative uncomfortable facts should be avoided, one reason why Vedanta has never been popular. We teach only because we love the truth. Telling it does not involve "busting" a student's ego, even if that were a legitimate path, which it isn't. We are not here to figure out what is wrong with you and correct it. For that you can go to a psychologist. We reveal what is right with you and save you the trouble of trying to fix yourself. If some fixing *is* necessary, the truth will do the work.

Here is an unpleasant fact: qualifications are required for liberation. To my knowledge no modern teacher or teaching insists that seekers be qualified. If enlightenment is experiential, then presumably it can happen at any moment, like falling in love. So to stay in business all a teacher need do is suggest that enlightenment is a wonderful possible happening and exhort the student to seek it. But if it is a matter of knowledge and if ignorance is hard-wired—which it is—qualifications are required.

This is unwelcome news for seekers who have grown up in an age of instant gratification. Most valuable things require hard work. As far as self-inquiry is concerned, there are no shortcuts or quick fixes. You have to be committed. If a teacher tells the truth, he will attract qualified students. Quite a few are quickly set free by these teachings and the rest, understanding the value of Vedanta, relax as they work on the qualifications because they know that it is a reliable path. Those who don't understand its value hop from teacher to teacher, from one so-called teaching to another, ending up more confused than when they began.

Fishing in Germany

In Germany, you can't just dig a worm, put it on a hook and catch a fish. A cave man could but a modern German can't; he needs to be qualified. If you knew the rigmarole you have to go through to catch a trout there, you would give up fishing. A German friend told me that it takes almost a year to get a license.

Is it the inalienable right of every person to know the meaning of $E=MC^2$? $E=MC^2$ means: energy equals mass times the speed of light squared. But what does that mean? What is energy? What is mass? What is the speed of light? How do all these things fit together? Why should I care? I have no idea what it means—nor do you, most likely—because we are not qualified to understand. To qualify, one has to go to kindergarten, grade school, and high school and then get an advanced post-graduate degree in mathematics and physics. It takes about ten years to become a doctor or a lawyer. The medical and law schools are full of applicants. If people are willing to put so much energy into pursuits that don't even begin to address life's most important issue, much less set them free, why should seekers be unwilling to prepare themselves to understand who they are?

Because there have been enlightened and unenlightened people forever, there has been sufficient time to compare the two categories and discover the differences. The enlightened enjoy particular qualities of mind and heart that, irrespective of the material or social or educational circumstances, brought them to self-knowledge. It has also been repeatedly observed that where there is an absence of one or more quality, or where one or more is only partially developed, self-knowledge does not happen. Highly qualified people are quickly set free. The partially qualified take longer and it takes ages for those who are barely qualified. The unqualified never get it. We are not trying to scare you and send you off into the arms of the instant enlightenment gurus who say you can just "get it." If you get it, you will unget it just as quickly. These qualities are built into every conscious being and can be developed with understanding and practice.

We said that action is an inadequate means for liberation because it is based on the idea that reality is a duality and it does not resolve the issue of doership, but it is an adequate means to prepare the mind for liberation. Vedanta endorses it for that purpose. In subsequent chapters we unfold several practices that qualify the mind to understand. For lack of qualifications you should not walk away from the one teaching that will free you. By the end of this teaching you will be clear about who you are but if you have trouble assimilating what you have heard it is solely due to lack of qualification.

Some time ago I met a young man who had just graduated from one of the world's most prestigious universities. He had six-figure job offers from some of the biggest corporations in the world. He had spent the first twenty-five years of his life qualifying for a worldly career. He was exceedingly bright and I could see that he was really motivated to find out who he was. He turned down the job offers and entered the student stage of the tradition, which leads to the renunciation through knowledge, i.e., liberation. He spent three years getting the understanding and lifestyle in place that would serve to qualify him. This is a fine example of two of the most important qualifications: burning desire for liberation and discrimination. Everyone wants to be free but how badly do you want it? Will you walk away from worldly success without having tasted it… for freedom? Will you commit yourself no matter what it takes? In fact burning desire *is* discrimination. It means that you have clarity with reference to what you want in life.

Before we list the qualifications we should mention the two basic qualifications, which are actually the same, once more: the understanding that the joy is not in objects and that life is a zero-sum game. Very simply it means that you know that life is set up to teach you who you are, not to give you the objects— security, pleasure and virtue, etc.—that you think you want.

If you want things from life, go for it. There is nothing wrong with it. If fact, chase the objects well and welcome the disappointment that inevitably results. It is a great gift because it qualifies you to seek. Nowadays you see a lot of young people forgoing careers and families for enlightenment without having actually pursued either. It is not always a mistake but it can be a mistake because you can gain valuable skills in the world that serve well for self-inquiry. It often does prove to be a mistake, however, because without the maturity that comes from succeeding and failing in life, seeking can easily degenerate into just another worldly lifestyle, one that binds you tighter than the pursuit of mundane goals because it instills you with the vanity that you are pursuing something extraordinary. Over the years I have met many middle-aged people who fell into the open arms of cults or ran off to ashrams and zendos in their early twenties only to eventually discover that the desire for love or a family or meaningful work was not ameliorated by their spiritual pursuits. Many questioned the validity of the quest for freedom and called off the search prematurely, which is always a mistake.

By living life wholeheartedly as it is presented to you, you will inevitably realize the hollowness of worldly pursuits. The shallow billboard life that seems so appealing is only a whirlpool of desire and action. You want things and you do things to get what you want and whether or not you get what you want, the wanting and the doing never stops. The desires and the endless activities are quicksand, slowly sucking the stamina out of you, binding you ever tighter to the wheel of life. In this world there is a loss for every gain, a low for every high, a failure for every success. You cannot win. Only mature people understand this. The rest are like children, endlessly wanting stuff. They are not qualified to know who they are.

1) Discrimination

The first qualification is discrimination. We use it every day. It is a very valuable quality. On the basis of your likes and dislikes you chose to associate with one person and not another. You buy an apple, not an orange. The recent collapse of the housing market is due to the lack of discrimination. People listened to con men on the TV telling them they could get rich quick and have something for nothing. That markets grow endlessly is totally contrary to common sense. Things grow and shrink. It's also contrary to common sense that you can borrow your way to prosperity. You can collateralize debt, no doubt, but life is uncertain and when you take a chance, you can't guarantee that you won't lose money.

Worldly discrimination is choosing between two apparent realities but Vedantic discrimination is choosing between what's real and what is apparently real.

Definition of Reality

Most people define reality as what they are experiencing. The sun, the moon, the stars and what they think and feel is reality for them. But Vedanta has a different definition. It is: "what never changes." This means that you have a discrimination

problem if you think that life as we know it—your experience and the environment in which you experience—is real. We pursue objects because we think
they are real. If we knew that they weren't real, the pursuit would stop and our
relationship with the world would definitely become fruitful. Discrimination is
like waking up from a dream. When you are in it you think it is real but when you
wake up you enjoy a perspective that renders the dream events unreal.

Every conscious being is made up of two factors, consciousness and matter.
Matter changes. Consciousness is the part of you that does not change. It is more
than a part as we shall see, but for now we will call it a part. Everyone actually
knows that part. It is what was there observing your body and mind from birth.
It knows all the changes that happened to the body and mind up to the present
day. It is your consciousness or awareness. We call that part real. The part that
changes—the body and mind—is apparently real. You can never put your finger
on something that is never the same from one moment to the next. "Apparently
real" means that it is experienced but has no substance; it is not real. People suffer
because they confuse what is apparently real—their bodies and minds and the
world around—with the part that is real. The unchanging part is you, the self. If
you don't know this, you will say you change when the body and mind change.

There is nothing you can do about either part. It is the nature of the part
that changes to change and it is the nature of the part that doesn't change not to
change. If you confuse one with the other you will suffer because reality does not
care what you think or feel. For example, if you fall in love and you expect the
feeling of love to last, you will be disappointed because that kind of love belongs
to the body and mind. When the instruments of experience change, the love
changes. If you get angry or depressed because a love relationship—or anything
else that is subject to time—disappears, whose fault is it that the relationship
ends? It is your fault only if you have control over it. But you don't. What happens is not up to you. If you understand reality as it is, you will be happy because
you will not confuse your self, which is real, with the objects (in this case, the
experience of love), which aren't real.

Before we move on, it is important to know that the apparent reality, the part
of the self that changes, is not nonexistent. "Apparently real" does not mean nonexistent. We discussed this point earlier but it is important to repeat it because
if you think that it means nonexistent, you may be susceptible to a common
spiritual myth: that freedom is not possible if the experience of the world still
exists for you. The apparent reality, which is a duality, does not disappear when

you know who you are, as a dream does when you wake up. The changing part of the self always exists. You have to deal with it before enlightenment and you have to deal with it after enlightenment. There is an escape but it is not what you imagine it to be.

The discrimination that qualifies you for Vedanta is the knowledge of the difference between what is real and what is apparently real. A qualified person keeps this distinction in mind always and makes life choices based on it. Jesus' statement "On this rock I build my church" means that his life was centered on what is eternal, not on the shifting sands of time. If the rock of truth is the foundation of my life I can weather any storm.

An undiscriminating person stubbornly expects reality to conform to his likes and dislikes. Such individuals are not qualified for Vedanta.

2) Dispassion

The next qualification is dispassion. If discrimination is developed, a person will be dispassionate. Dispassion is indifference to the results of action, one's own and those that the field of existence presents.

A passionate person is always emotional about what has happened, what is happening or what is going to happen. She is attached to the results of her actions. When a passionate person doesn't get what she wants, she feels angry or depressed. If you are very passionate you may even get angry or depressed when the idea that you may not get what you want appears.

Although passion is considered a wonderful quality by the worldly, passionate people will be disturbed unless their passion is channeled into the search for truth. You don't have to dig around in your childhood to find out why you are an emotional mess. You can leave mom and pop out of it. You are emotional because you are not getting what you want in the present. A disturbed mind is not qualified for self-inquiry.

Dispassion is a sign of maturity. It is indifference to the results of your actions. How does the doer in you feel about this qualification? He is probably not happy with it because the doer is the undeveloped immature part of the psyche: like a child it wants what it wants when it wants it the way it wants it. Dispassion means that you don't care if you get what you want. It is a very rare quality because people's desires make them blind to one of the most obvious but almost always denied facts of life: the results of your actions are not up to you.

Dispassion does not mean that you don't want things and that you don't work to gain them. It means that you work patiently with a quiet mind and leave the results to life. You understand how silly it is to get upset about something over which you have very little control. This quality is absolutely essential for inquirers because you never know when (and if) you will be set free, assuming that you believe that freedom is for the person, which it is and isn't, as we shall see. If you are dispassionate you can do the preparatory work in the right frame of mind.

Another definition of dispassion is objectivity. The apparent reality has two aspects: the subjective and the objective. Money, for example, has an objective value; it can buy practical things that are needed to maintain life. In terms of the world it is real. But it assumes a subjective value if you think that it can remove insecurity. Projecting a subjective value on an object is called superimposition and appears in two forms: 1) mistaking an object for something else and 2) adding a value to an object that is not inherent in the nature of the object. The antidote to passion (for objects) is dispassion. You cannot make yourself dispassionate. You cannot make someone mature. Trying to do so is like prying a rosebud open to reveal its beauty before it is ready to flower. You need to live well with open eyes.

3) Control of the Mind

You don't control the mind by controlling the mind. If you think you are in control please tell me what you will think in five minutes. You do not control it, because your conditioning controls it. So what do we mean when we say "control of mind"? We mean that you understand that because the thoughts and feelings arise and subside on their own, they have nothing to do with you at all. Understanding this fact is control.

The meaning of your life is projected by your conditioning, your values. Feelings and thoughts have no power to disturb you apart from the way you interpret them. How you interpret them depends on your values. Your values are your point of view. If you examine your values, the bad values will fall away and the good values will come to the fore, changing your thoughts and feelings. Merely by observing it, you gain a certain mastery of the mind.

If your mind is not controllable, you should at least control your senses, the next qualification.

4) Control of Senses

Even if your mind is a mess and you can control your senses, at least your outer life will not be a mess. When your outer life is in line with the cosmic order, your inner life tends to follow suit. You can think and feel what you want, but once thoughts and feelings become actions, they are in the hands of the world and they will bounce back to you one way or the other. If your thoughts are not happy the world will not smile at you. It they are, it will.

Attachment to any sense organ can get you in trouble. If you don't like someone and say something nasty, not only will you worry about the outer consequences, you will feel guilty for violating the value of non-injury. If you eat, drink, or work too much, have a lot of sex, or watch too much TV, you will not succeed at self-inquiry. So you must restrain your organs, assuming that you cannot bring them under control with objectivity.

The most important sense to control is the organ of speech because it is through our words that both healthy and unhealthy emotions reach the world. It is not a coincidence that the organ of speech is connected to the fire element and the fire element evolves from *rajas,* one of the three basic building blocks of nature, about which much will be said later. Yes, *rajas* is desire and longing and it is also anger, thwarted desire. It is an intractable foe because it is a major source of psychological pain. When you cannot resolve the pain with reference to the vision of non-duality, you will try to relieve yourself of it in mechanical ways— physical violence, for example—and you will evolve speech habits that are self-insulting and injurious to others. The rules of communication require truthful and pleasant speech insofar as you want to succeed in life. It should be appropriate to the context that requires it and it should add value to the context as well. Just talking to talk is a sign of low self-esteem and a waste of energy. When you find yourself in the grip of anger, it is not wise to try to speak loving words. They will not come out properly. Just walk away from the situation.

5) Doing What Is Appropriate to Your Nature (*Svadharma*)

Failure to live up to this value will definitely prevent enlightenment. It is hard to understand and harder to accept because it seems to go against two of society's core values: doing good for others and bettering yourself.

Dharma is a very wonderful and complex concept about which much more will be said in chapter 9. It needs a lot of unfolding because the word has many meanings. *Svadharma* means *self-dharma*. Essentially it means doing your duty to yourself. It can refer to your essential nature—limitless awareness—or it can refer to your non-essential nature, the person you think you are. In the context of the discussion on qualifications it means doing your duty to the person you think you are. If you don't take care of that person, you will never realize who you really are.

The World Does Not Need Fixing

The Bhagavad Gita, one of the three pillars of the Vedanta teaching—perhaps the most important—makes an important statement. It says that to do the duty of another is "fraught with danger"; it is better to do a third-rate job looking after yourself than a first class job looking after someone else. Everybody wants to look good in the eyes of society and society defines virtue as "making a difference." It is a warm and fuzzy idea that often leads to mischief in that it easily translates into vain attempts to control and manipulate the lives of others according to your idea of what is good for them. Most of us are taught that it is noble to sacrifice for others. But since others follow their own natures irrespective of our wishes at the end of the day, is it any wonder that we feel frustrated, angry and resentful?

It may be news to you, but we are not here to save the world. The world is perfect as it is. The good and the bad serve consciousness perfectly. When you understand the big picture you will settle down and look after yourself properly. But when you have the special vanity that you know best—which is actually born of a sense of inferiority—and find yourself "helping" someone else, you are not actually doing a favor because you are creating a dependent person. The number one spiritual value is self-reliance. If you do the thinking for others and take care of their lives, they will not grow. This is not to say that legitimate and occasional demands to help should not be cheerfully responded to or that it is not the duty of parents to mold the lives of their children with love and good values. In the context of the quest for liberation, however, you should ideally avoid relationships that demand constant service, unless it is your nature to serve, a topic which we will consider presently.

They say that life imitates art. The soap operas are a good example of the svadharma problem because they glorify almost every bad value known to man, particularly manipulation. The victims are basically immature, none-too-bright people and the victimizers are do-gooders from hell. As they stab the victims in the back with smarmy smiles and warm embraces they claim it is for the victim's own good. "I am having sex with your wife and cheating you in business because I love you so much. You just can't see it because you are so stupid." The message is obvious: look after yourself. If you don't work out your own stuff, you'll never get freedom.

Should Is a Bad Word

The second meaning of *svadharma* is equally important. It means not trying to live up to an ideal. People imitate role models. Worldly women, I suppose, want to be like Angelina Jolie and men want to be like Brad Pitt. Spiritual people try to be like the Dalai Lamas, Ramanas and Amachis of the spiritual world. It is a big mistake to try to be anything other than what you are.

When you don't know that you are whole and complete, actionless awareness you either want your circumstances to be different or you want yourself, as you understand it, to be different—or both. Everyone thinks "I should be—I should do—" *Should* is a very bad word. Whenever you hear the mind thinking "should," press pause, think about it and hit delete. The road to liberation is not about transcending or denying your little self. It is accepting who you are here and now. If you made mistakes and did bad things, don't punish yourself by doing penance. Understand that if you knew who you really were you would not have done what you did and forgive yourself. Ignorance, not you, is to blame. Understanding this makes forgiveness possible. Then convert the desire to be different into a desire to know who you are, since you are pure and perfect and incapable of harmful actions.

My Relative Nature

Nobody comes here on her own. We all appear here once fine day at the behest of a power much greater than ourselves. We arrive programmed with a certain nature. After the basic biological stuff is sorted we differentiate into various types. The creation itself is a vast and complex, intelligently designed program that requires the contributions of many mini-programs or beings. The world needs thinkers, artists, business people, scientists, workers, saints, criminals, athletes, musicians, warriors, politicians, farmers, managers, administrators, accountants and so on. Plants and animals follow their programs faithfully and human beings are expected to follow theirs too. If they don't, they suffer.

However, owing to a self-reflective intellect and the desires and fears that self-ignorance engenders, the minds of human beings are not always attuned to their relative natures. In the old days, it was not hard to figure out what you should do. Your actions were more or less determined by socio-economic factors. Your father was a baker, you became a baker. But with the advent of technology and global prosperity it is not always clear what reality requires because options are seemingly limitless. To be sure, some people feel inclined to a certain path from childhood and unquestioningly pursue their dream. What should be done is never an issue for them, because they are obsessively driven by their programs.

If I do not know what my svadharma is, I do not know how to respond appropriately. Travelling the world as I do and meeting hundreds of people, I never cease to be amazed at how many people, even adults in their forties and fifties, are uncertain of what they should be doing. If this is the case, you can safely actualize your relative self by responding to the rules governing the immediate situation in a disinterested spirit.

Doing whatever is to be done at a given place and in a given situation, whether you like it or not, is svadharma. For example, it is a mistake to override your svadharma because of a need for security. Taking an unhealthy job just to pay the rent is not always the best course of action. Sometimes it is appropriate to resolve security related conflicts by taking a chance and following your heart (and perhaps suffering privation) or alternatively to perform the unwanted job in the *karma yoga* spirit, about which much will be said later. Karma yoga is the best way to qualify for liberation, irrespective of the type of activity you perform.

Through dharma yoga we master our likes and dislikes. Doing what we like is not always appropriate and avoiding what we don't like is not always appropriate either. To break the hold of your likes and dislikes you need to do what the situation requires and avoid doing what is not required. Exercising this understanding in every situation builds self-esteem. It empowers you and makes you feel successful because you have done what is right, not just what is expedient. The battle is over when you stand up to your desires and fears.

6) Single Pointedness

This quality is meant to correct two related and unhelpful tendencies of the mind: multitasking and too many interests. They are both born of greed and render the mind unfit for inquiry. The mind is curious. It is its nature to wander. If it does not wander you will not know anything. It is like a video camera, not a still camera. It is momentary, a series of energized images. But this tendency is not always helpful for self-inquiry.

Your mind needs the ability to stay on a given topic for a considerable period of time. The only topic for those of us looking for freedom is the self because it is the only free thing! The way to keep it in mind is to bring the mind back to the teachings over and over until the tendency to wander is curbed. Contemplate your desires and fears in light of the teachings until daily life conforms to the inquiry. One needs to see that inquiry is not just an occasional activity—or one among many—that is done when one is bored or unhappy.

All the qualifications are related. Seekers famously complain about their inability to focus on the self and are continually looking for new techniques to make focusing easier. Difficulty focusing is a values issue. Does anyone have difficulty focusing on sex? No, because it is highly valued. Failure to focus means that clarity about what you want, in our case freedom, is not the number one priority. When freedom is the number one value, concentration takes care of itself.

7) Forbearance

Forbearance is objectivity toward pain of all kinds without anxiety, complaint or attempt at revenge. It applies only to situations that we can do nothing about. In other situations you should act to change things if you can. Forbearance is understanding that people cannot be changed but giving them the freedom to be what they are, and setting up boundaries to take care of yourself.

This qualification creates a simple life. These days society is highly complicated and neurotic. Our sense of entitlement knows no bounds. We feel empowered to whine and complain from dawn to dusk about petty things. Our likes and dislikes are out of control. Luxuries have become necessities, our lives complicated and our minds shattered. These small things are not worthy of attention. My teacher used to call them "life's little pinpricks." Suffering them in good humor is necessary. If trivial things—body odors, unaesthetic landscapes, a messy room, dirty dishes, wrinkled clothing, incompetent or needy people, sounds from the street, a missed connection, a catty remark or a mistake on your bank statement—upset you, you need to work on this qualification.

I love my wife. My wife loves her mother. My mother-in-law does not love me for various reasons. She wants to visit her daughter on the weekend. I am stuck indoors because of an accident at work. We are going to have to spend two days under the same roof. Should I make a big issue of my bad feelings and react to hers or should I let the feelings slide? If I let them slide and treat my mother in law politely, I am a forbearing person. If I seek every opportunity to let her know how I "really" feel, I am not qualified for self-inquiry.

8) Devotion

The qualifications—dispassion, single pointedness, burning desire, discrimination, etc.— and devotion are intimately related, more or less different ways of looking at the same thing. Devotion is love of truth, love of knowledge. It means that my emotional power is squarely behind my quest for freedom. It is a positive value. I am not devoted solely because my suffering demands it—although it does; I am devoted to inquiry because I love truth.

I am always puzzled how parents can suffer so much misery at the hands of their children. I find it almost impossible to put up with my own needy mind for more than a few minutes so the only explanation for a twenty-plus-year commitment to the needy minds of two or three others—not to mention that parents often stay devoted to their children for as long as they live—can only be devotion. Devotion knows no pain. It is steady and deep and overcomes everything.

9) Faith

Some say faith is the number one qualification. The faith that qualifies you for self-inquiry is very simple and it is not blind. Vedanta says that nothing is wrong with you on any level. Even your self-ignorance is not your fault. The faith that is asked of you is the belief that you are pure and perfect, pending the result of your scripture-based inquiry.

Toward the end of the Cold War the Russians said "Trust us, we are destroying our nuclear weapons." And the Americans said "We trust you, but we would like to see for ourselves." Even if you believe you are bound, you should live as if you are free and see if reality doesn't support you one hundred percent. Experience may say it doesn't, but knowledge says it does. If you continually doubt, your doubt will compromise your ability to hear, reflect and assimilate the teachings. There is no happiness for doubters.

Studies of people who have faith in God have found that on balance those who believe in God are happier than those who don't even though neither the believers nor the non-believers know who or what God is. So you have to trust the teaching and the teacher.

10) Burning Desire for Freedom

One day a disciple asked his guru to talk about burning desire for freedom. The guru said, "Never mind. It is not important." The disciple was very intelligent and curious and not one to be dismissed so he asked again and again he got the same reply.

A few days later they were at the riverbank taking a bath. The bathing ritual involves dunking oneself three times in the water. On the third dunk the guru jumped on top of the disciple, put his foot on his back, grabbed his arm and held him tightly on the river bottom as he struggled to get free, releasing him just a second before he was about to drown. The disciple was very angry and was about to give his guru a good beating. The guru agreed to take his punishment but not before he asked the disciple this question, "What were you thinking when you were down there on the bottom of the river?" The disciple said that he definitely wasn't thinking, but the guru insisted that he was. They argued for a minute or two until the disciple asked, "Okay, what was I thinking?"

"You had one thought and one thought alone," the guru replied.

"What was it?" said the disciple.

"Air," the guru said. "Your only thought was 'I want to breathe.' Wanting liberation with the same intensity you wanted air is burning desire."

Everyone says they want to be free, but on this issue you need to be very honest with yourself. Is your desire, piddling, middling or burning?

A Qualified Teacher

So far we have a valid means of knowledge and a qualified student. You also need a qualified teacher. As mentioned previously you cannot teach Vedanta to yourself. Reading books and listening to unqualified teachers does not work. It is natural to begin your journey in this way but there is an obvious downside: your ignorance will cause you to interpret what you read.

An enlightened person is not necessarily a qualified teacher and a qualified teacher is not necessarily enlightened! If my teaching is nothing more than me and my enlightenment story—what I did, what happened to me—it is not going to work for you. My enlightenment and the conclusions I draw from it do not amount to a teaching because the problem is generic ignorance. The solution for self-ignorance is self-knowledge, and knowledge is not personal.

Walk the Talk

Enlightenment has no meaning apart from how you live. It is quite amazing in this day and age that the "crazy wisdom" idea still has legs. "Do as I say, not as I do," is not a teaching. What use is enlightenment if it amounts to nothing more than a license for the ego to indulge its cravings? It is quite sad that so many teachers have compromised themselves over the years and given truth a bad name over the most banal vices: money, sex, fame, or power. One imagines that the vices of the enlightened should somehow be more exotic.

When someone sits in front of you on a throne with hundreds of people staring at him and the "energy" is wonderful, you are tempted to imagine that they are very enlightened. In reality you know nothing about who they really are. A pleasing image and good feelings is all you require. A discriminating seeker is a fly on the wall and buzzes unobtrusively into the life of a teacher to see if he shines outside the limelight. Find out where the money goes. Listen to the gossip with discrimination; often where there is smoke there is fire. Public figures are always suspect. They often suffer low self-esteem and are clever at creating an image of themselves as caring souls, but a healthy dose of suspicion is warranted. The more "spiritual" they are, the greater should be your doubt. Like patriotism, spirituality is also a popular refuge for scoundrels.

We teach by precept *and* example. Only an extremely advanced, highly qualified person can get the knowledge from a rogue, if at all. Freedom talk is seductive and cheap, but who is actually free? When you meet a free person, you can feel it. There is a lightness, an unconcernedness, an ascetic simplicity to them that is unmistakable. They never have an agenda.

You should run fast when a teacher tries to recruit you. You should run twice as fast when a teacher tells you what to do. A teacher is someone who reveals the truth. If you see the truth, it will do the work for you. Who are you if your self-confidence is so low that you cannot figure out how to live your life? A teacher who asks you to surrender to him or her—or accepts your slavish personal devotion—is an immature human being, not a teacher, no matter how glorious she appears to be, as are you for offering it. You need be only a devotee of the truth—nothing else. If you are devoted to the truth alone, you will not be given a bad teacher.

A teacher who allows you to become dependent is not a teacher. He is power hungry. And a teacher who tries to hang on to you when you want to leave—tries to convince you that you are compromising your enlightenment—is a scoundrel. A real teacher will be happy to see you leave, knowing full well that life is the best teacher and that you will be back, not necessarily to him, but to the teaching. If the teacher is on the level and the teaching works—like Vedanta—you should feel more and more free of the teacher as the teaching progresses. A few weeks after I met my teacher he said, "Sit down and listen. We will have you out of here as quickly as possible because you are taking up valuable space that someone else can use."

A teacher who expects you to believe her words based on an epiphany you have had in her presence is not a teacher. A teacher who convinces you that your ego needs busting or that your mind needs to be destroyed is very dangerous. Fame does not a teacher make; groups of people can be as deluded as individuals. You will notice that the teachers around whom cults of personality develop invariably make the mind the enemy. Whenever a doubt happens, you are told that it is just "mind" and asked to dismiss it. If you find yourself with this kind of teacher and teaching, it means that he does not have a valid means of knowledge and is power hungry or needy. It is amazing how many popular teachers actually need your love. If you feel that a teacher needs you for any reason, head for the hills. You are asking for trouble. A true teacher is dispassionate and self-fulfilled and has nothing to gain by teaching you.

A teacher who teaches silence does not have a teaching. Silence is happy with ignorance. A teacher who teaches experiential enlightenment is not a teacher, because you are always experiencing the self; there is always only consciousness. Finally, a teacher who does not present the downside of his teaching is not a teacher. Many teachers, for example, tout *tantra* as a means of enlightenment. Perhaps tantra as it is conceived in its entirety is a useful indirect path for qualified people. However, sexual tantra—the most popular practice—barely deserves mention as it is only one of many techniques. Sexual tantra works as far as non-dual epiphanies go, if you are lucky. However, sexual tantra, which is a perfect setup for unfulfilled immature egos, has a glaring problem. The technique that gives you the experience of non-duality produces attachment to the technique! You become attached to sex, not the knowledge of non-duality, which should absorb your mind. Fixing the mind on the self is self-inquiry. Instead the mind is concerned with the next sexual episode.

It is the duty of a teacher to warn against attachment and offer techniques like karma yoga that destroy attachment instead of feeding it. Instead, unscrupulous teachers use this teaching to attract thousands and further their pursuit of fame and fortune, which usually leads to their undoing and to serious damage to their followers. Only Vedanta fearlessly points out the downside of everything to help you develop dispassion. Were we interested in attracting people, we would avoid informing seekers of the long list of qualifications enumerated in this chapter.

I understand that it may be difficult to hear this message, but keep in mind that these statements are in harmony with a teaching that has worked for thousands of years, that is as solid as the truth on which it is based. Your confidence is a valuable asset. Don't squander it on damaged goods.

I tout Vedanta because it worked for me and it has worked for many others since time immemorial, but don't think that you need Vedanta as I present it to get free, although you do need self-knowledge, however it comes to you. Vedanta is only a means of knowledge. If you are qualified and invoke consciousness properly, you will be set free, whoever and wherever you are—Vedanta be dammed. We do not look down on other paths, nor do we feel superior because our vehicle is beautifully efficient and others less so. Do what you will and seek as you see fit but don't discount these teachings.

At the expense of gilding the lily I repeat: the spiritual marketplace is a human institution, imperfect in every way. Because your options are limited, you find yourself in it by no fault of your own. You can wander in it for twenty-plus years and realize that the means available to you are faulty. And although it was not your intention and you had no idea how to seek when you began, you may have actually qualified yourself while you were there. All seeking is a mistake but it is a good mistake. We call it a "leading error" because it may very well indirectly lead you to where you need to be. Do not be surprised if Vedanta comes to you and you appreciate its beauty. Years ago in San Francisco I saw a poster with a guru's smiling face that said "Come to me when you are already happy." Whether the teacher was just fed up with unhappy people or whether he actually understood something, there is truth to it. Vedanta works when you are ready to stop seeking.

Finally, keep in mind that there are also teachers who know the truth, know they are the truth, and live dharmic lives but do not have a legitimate means of self-knowledge. It is not the kiss of death to associate with them; you can gain much. And do not lament if you have been used and abused at the hands of a spiritual teacher. Take it as a gift and don't give up. When the time is right the right teacher will appear.

The Grace of God

So I have a qualified means of knowledge, I am qualified myself and I have a compassionate teacher who wields the means of knowledge skillfully. Case closed, right? Wrong. One more factor needs to be taken into account—grace. Our enlightenment is meant as much as a service to the total as it is a personal liberation. God knows the needs of the total and caters to the needs of the total so that you will get your enlightenment when God wants it, not before. The conclusion to be drawn: expose your mind to the teaching at every opportunity, work sincerely and cheerfully on yourself and stop worrying about the result.

Before we teach the self we should review what we have learned so far. It is vitally important that you understand the complete logic of the teaching. You should go back and read the first four chapters again, but let's review what has been said so far because repetition is the best way to cement the knowledge.

A Short Summary

I know the joy is not in the object. I know the joy is in the subject, me, the self. I want to pursue the self directly so I can enjoy the fullness that comes from knowing who I am rather than taking temporary bits of happiness from objects and situations. Therefore, I become a seeker of liberation.

The experiential approach exhorts you to do practices that are meant to get you enlightened. The pathless path of knowledge is based on the idea that you are already free but don't appreciate this fact. If you don't understand who you are, you need a means of knowledge that will reveal it to you.

The experiential approach is unworkable because people have limited desire and knowledge and their actions produce limited results. They want a limitless result—freedom—but cannot perform actions that produce limitlessness.

The way out of this conundrum is to apply the doer to a task that does work—inquiry. Inquiry works because the result of inquiry is knowledge, not action. Knowledge sets you free because you are already free. The knowledge that I am free, that I am whole and complete, *is* freedom *assuming it negates the doer and renders the doer's conditioning unbinding.* Once it is firm, self-knowledge doesn't require maintenance. Experience requires constant maintenance, so seeking never stops. Once self-knowledge is firm, the compulsion to do stops and you don't do what you do for happiness, you do what you do happily.

We said knowledge requires a means of knowledge and that our God-given means are inadequate because the self is not an object of knowledge. So consciousness, not people, revealed and evolved Vedanta, a proven means. It removes the lack of clarity about your wholeness, your completeness. Knowledge sticks only in a prepared, qualified mind and it needs to be worked on you by a qualified teacher.

CHAPTER FIVE

Awareness, the Self

I always start teaching with a chant from one of Vedanta's source texts. It is a description of you.

> *Om Brahmanandan parama sukkadam kevalm jnana murtim*
> *dvandvatitam gangana sad drisham tatvamasyaadhi lakshyam.*
> *Ekam nityam vimalam achalam sarvadhi sakshi bhootam*
> *Bhavatam triguna rahitam sad gurum tam namami.*

The self, pure awareness, is limitless bliss and unending pleasure. It is beyond the dualities of the mind. It is the isness that sees, the isness that is known through Vedanta's statement "You are That." It is the one, eternal, pure, unchanging witness of everything. It is beyond experience and the three qualities of nature. I bow to that self, the one that removes ignorance.

Is this what your mind is telling you about who you are? Undoubtedly there is a voice inside that has another opinion. It probably says something like this: "I'm a frightened needy little worm, munching my way through the experiential garbage heap of the world, looking for fulfillment. Life is tough and I am lonely, fearful, depressed and driven by my desires most of the time. You say I am fine but I don't experience myself this way."

We all know this voice. It is one protagonist in the inner war between the truth of who we are and what we think we are. The teachings can't resolve that war; you have to resolve it by contemplating the meaning of the teachings. Vedanta is your ally. It reveals the non-dual truth of your experience and stands by your side, ever vigilant.

It affirms your identity as unborn, eternal, actionless, unconcerned awareness. It shows you that you are the goodness beyond good and bad, that the beauty of this creation—the sun, moon and stars—is just a pale reflection of the beauty of your own self. Vedanta says that because you are awareness-consciousness you are everything that is. Therefore you need to know yourself as everything. And, for those still longing for some kind of experiential enlightenment, Vedanta unequivocally states that what you seek—the self—is beyond experience.

Vedanta is concerned with a single topic—identity. You would think the teaching would start with the topic of the self and stick to it exclusively, but there is a lot more to self-inquiry than just saying we are awareness, which in itself is not a complex topic. It is a subtle topic, however, one that does not yield to imprecise and clumsy thinking or necessarily lead to a simple solution like asking 'Who am I?' It is also not straightforward owing to the fact that experience seems to contradict it, setting up a natural resistance to the assimilation of the teachings. And since the problem is ignorance and ignorance is hard-wired, you cannot just walk in off the street backed by an epiphany, awakened by a quick read of a popular book on non-duality, or primed by the gushing testimonials of friends and expect to "get it" immediately. If you do, you will unget it as quickly. Many with Einstienian IQs never crack the code. Self-inquiry is a unique pursuit.

A successful teaching like Vedanta needs to patiently set up the context in which self-inquiry becomes meaningful. This involves clarity with reference to your goals, getting a precise understanding of the nature of enlightenment, eliminating erroneous notions, appreciating the need for a means of knowledge and seeing to your qualifications, before you even begin to inquire. And you should know that the topic of the self—which in one sense is the only topic—sits roughly in the middle of the whole train of logic that constitutes the vision of non-duality, meaning that although it is the first, last and only word, it also isn't.

The statement "it is and it isn't" typifies the teaching. For example, there are many obviously contradictory statements in the texts. What does "It is bigger than the biggest and smaller than the smallest" mean? "Sitting still it runs faster than the mind." "The mind is the self but the self is not the mind." There is no quick and easy answer until a careful unfolding of the teachings resolves apparent contradictions and makes explicit what is implicit.

Imagine that you are out in nature on a path and you meet a stranger. Before any words are exchanged, what do you experience? You see a body and you see consciousness. If there is no consciousness, the body will not be vertical. It will be rotting away on the ground, food for worms. Consciousness appears as the spark of life that animates the body. You don't "see" it with your eyes but you know it by inference, which is just as good as direct experience since knowing it is nearly all that is required. We say "nearly" because simply knowing it indirectly as an object is not quite enough. It is truly known only when you know what it means to know it in terms of your experience of duality.

Usually when you walk into a room and someone is in it, you immediately introduce yourself; neither person sits and stares at each other without speaking. In terms of self-knowledge this presents a problem because the way we are conditioned to interact—which reveals what we know and what we don't know—demands that information about our respective identities be exchanged. You can't really function in the "real" world without knowing *who* you are dealing with. This information may come indirectly by inference or directly in the form of statements about the self. I seriously doubt that you have ever met a complete stranger who introduced himself or herself as non-dual, ordinary, actionless, unconcerned, limitless, unborn awareness. These are the words that most accurately identify the being sitting in the body in front of you, but that is not what that being says.

I Am Not My Story

The situation is a bit more complicated because even though the self did not actually come from anywhere, one of the first details to emerge in conversation is where it came from. Even though it is unborn it speaks of a mother and a father. Even though it is free of everything it seems to think that it is tied to a place, a dwelling, a spouse and offspring. Even though it is not a doer, because there is nothing other than it, it tells you that it does a certain job. Though nothing ever happened to it, it can regale you ad infinitum, usually ad nauseam, about all the things that happened: "my mother did this; my father did that; and then I...." It has a story to tell.

And that story is somehow meant to add up to the consciousness that is in front of you wagging its apparent tongue. The story is meant to be "me." But is there an equals sign between me and my story? If you added up all the things that happened to "you" over time—and what you thought about them—would they all equal you?

If all those words about you referred to something real, their referents would be available for experience here and now. Reality—awareness, meaning you—is always present. But none of these things are present apart from the words that supposedly represent them. They are not glued to your body for people to touch. They do not hover around you like a cloud of mosquitoes for observation. They are simply words coming out of you that disappear immediately into thin air.

I Am Ordinary Awareness

To extract an identity from a series of happenings, real and imagined, does not work. My story, my idea of who I am, is not me. If you want to know who you are, subtract your story. What is left over is you, one simple awareness—conscious being. There are not two of you, three of you or ten of you. There is just one ever-present, ordinary awareness.

We are at another important point in the teaching because everything we have read and heard, particularly the shallow testimonials of the plethora of so-called enlightened beings that flood the spiritual marketplace with their books, videos and websites, have convinced us that what we are seeking is some kind of mind-blowing, amazing, life-transforming experience—something that is supposed to turn us into enlightened super beings and give us lives that we can only dream of. Without the hyperbolic spiritual porn that passes for knowledge these days, the gargantuan spiritual world would shrink to the size of a small pea and the modern gurus would have to hang up their hats and get day jobs. The idea that self-realization is something special—it is, but not in the way you think it is—is the greatest imaginable impediment to enlightenment.

The persistence of this myth is due solely to the fact that the egos of those seeking it are so bored, lonely, and generally disenchanted with life that they will chase only something they think is: Incredible! Fantastic! Unbelievable! So the fantasy of the extraordinary self—the TRANSCENDENTAL self, the COSMIC self, etc.—survives, nay thrives, from age to age. If you hang on to the notion that you are going to experience something special and proceed with this inquiry you will be very disappointed because—sad to say—the self that you are, the self that you are going to realize—is totally ordinary. It is the awareness that is observing your mind take in these words, nothing more. It is not inaccessible at all. It is hidden in plain sight. It is always present and greatly unappreciated for no other reason than lack of understanding.

Thoughts, feelings, memories, dreams, perceptions, beliefs, and opinions arise and dissolve like mist in the early morning in this pure, simple, unchanging awareness that we are. Although *awareness* and *consciousness* are synonyms, I tend to use the word *awareness* because we almost invariably take consciousness to be the mind, i.e., the events that arise and subside in consciousness. Owing to its association with the mind, *consciousness*, which is often referred to as a stream or a flow of subjective experiences, is not as helpful a word as *awareness*, although in usage *awareness* often also refers to the mind.

The Most Obvious Thing

Here is a brilliant short inquiry from one of my friends, Christian Leeby. I fattened it a bit, but he gets all the credit.

"What is the most familiar experience to you? Shouldn't that be easy to answer? I know it's a rather vague question, but still, doesn't it seem like you should easily know what it is? Think about it. It shouldn't take more than a few seconds but it may take a long time because the answer is so obvious that most people don't get it.

When you experience something all of the time and it never ever changes it's almost impossible to notice it, like gravity. Gravity is pushing strongly on your body all of the time but you never notice it because it's always there. What's interesting about the most familiar experience to you is that it is also a constant like gravity, but you *can* know it. Although it never ever changes, you can be aware of it. So what is it?

The most familiar experience to you is that you exist. Every single thing you experience and know happens within the context of your existence. This is super obvious, right? But it doesn't come to mind because it's in the background and we don't think about it or appreciate it for what it is because…well…because it is always there. As you think about the fact that you exist right now, you immediately feel or sense or experience or know your existence in some way, don't you?

How do you know you exist? Well, you just know it, that's all. It's not because you see your existence, or hear, feel, or think it, or for any other reason. No other source of information is required. That you exist is the most important knowledge that every person has. It is obvious, fundamental, and ongoing. And you know it simply because you know it. Nothing new here; I'm just pointing out what you already know, all of the time.

There is one more very important fact about you that you need to consider. That you exist is clear, but what is the nature of your existence? What exactly is existence? Existence is awareness. These two words mean exactly the same thing. The most familiar experience to you is that you are aware. Existence, awareness, has to be there or you don't experience or know anything. Or you could say that existence or awareness has to be there, or you aren't there. Obvious, isn't it?

Some people in the spiritual world—most, in fact—seem to think that awareness is something special, something somewhere else, something to be discovered or realized or experienced in some mystical way. I am pointing out how completely normal and obvious awareness is to you.

It is one thing to understand that you are existence-awareness, but it is another to know what it means to be what you are. This will take a bit more time if you want to do it on your own, but if you listen to what I have to say, it will not take very long at all. What it means is that you are always full, whole and complete. This is what we mean by bliss. It means you are always satisfied with yourself. You will, of course, argue with me on this topic because your experience does not warrant that conclusion. Sometimes you feel positively dissatisfied. Before you stop listening, consider this: why are you not satisfied with dissatisfaction? The answer is because you are not focused on your existence-awareness, yourself. You don't feel satisfied because you just got what you want or avoided what you didn't want; you feel satisfied because you are at one with you.

There is something that obstructs your appreciation of yourself—your fears and desires! If you can lay them to rest you can be satisfied all the time. There are several solutions to this problem—karma yoga, for example—but the quickest one, if you are qualified, is self-inquiry. Apply the truth about yourself—the knowledge that I am whole and complete, ever-existent, actionless awareness—whenever a gratuitous fear or desire arises, and you will eventually knock them out. Every time you do it you will feel very satisfied because you are standing as you are, standing as existence-awareness, not as your silly desires and fears want you to think you are—a small, inadequate, incomplete little wimp.

It's like being in school and being told by the teacher to erase the chalkboard of your past. When you take self-inquiry to your mind you are erasing the old stuff. Take a few swipes with the eraser and you'll see an immediate difference, which is a wonderful thing with Vedanta. However, some of that chalk has been on there for a long time and needs many wipes and a bit of elbow grease. If you doubt that the eraser will work, it won't work, because you're not using it. Use it consistently and absolutely for sure, it will eventually work. That's self-inquiry.

Another terribly important point about enlightenment is to know that the idea that when you realize yourself you will discover something new is a complete lie. You will not discover or experience anything new. It will not fix your karma. If you're looking for something new—a special kind of experience—then you are just feeding your self-ignorance. In fact, when you realize the self, what happens is that you see that the most obvious and familiar experience to you— your existence-awareness—is what you've been looking for. That's why it's not a big deal and it is not an experience.

Our thoughts, feelings, and body are obvious to us. We all have them and we all know that they are separate from us. Our existence-awareness is super obvious to us now, but nobody ever told us that existence-awareness is different from them. So we assumed that our obvious sense of existence-awareness comes *from* the body. It doesn't. There's your body, your thoughts, your feelings, your ego, and then, standing quite alone, your existence-awareness. Although they are one because reality is non-dual, your body, thoughts, feelings and ego are different from you, existence. They are objects, like trees and mountains. You, existence-awareness, are what witnesses them. Awareness, the witness, is what you actually are.

Knowing this won't necessarily enlighten you, though it certainly could. But it is very important because it will keep your mind from getting all magical and spiritual about this mysterious awareness that everyone in the non-dual world is going on about. Even if you don't fully grasp it, be confident that the awareness you are thinking about is nothing more than that which is the most familiar experience to you—your existence.

It really is that simple."

A Second Awareness

Duality is a very tricky business. It is the belief that the one awareness is actually two or more. This is why you hear so much about the "higher self" and the "lower self," the "true self" and the "false self," the "real self" and the "illusory self." Duality is completely understandable and you should know at the beginning of this teaching that duality and non-duality are not incompatible, because they inhabit different orders of the one reality or, if you prefer, duality is a subset of non-duality. They do not contradict each other, just as a wave does not contradict the ocean. It is the ocean but the ocean is not it. We need not destroy duality. We need only negate it. If we experientially destroyed duality, we would have to invent a whole new way of living in the world. In fact there would be no world, as we know it, to live in. When you realize the truth of yourself, things on the ground are going to be the same as they were before your liberation, but they will also be different in a very good way. Paradoxes abound.

The "second awareness" is reflected awareness. Later on when we unfold the teaching of the macrocosmic principles we will discuss it in detail—it is quite technical—but now we need to briefly explain it to make it easy to understand why seeking enlightenment is not straightforward. It is not something you would figure out on your own. If it weren't for Vedanta it would escape your attention altogether.

The second awareness is like the moon and the first awareness is like the sun. The moon has no light of its own. It is a dead planet. The sun is a radiant fire shining in all directions, generating light from within itself. On a full moon night it is quite possible to make your way on the earth. If a child comes out at night it will see the moon and think that it is actually shining. It is shining but not with its own light. It reflects the light of the sun.

When *Maya*, the creative force, about which much will presently be said, is operating, the self appears as an individual with a Gross, Subtle and Causal Body. The Gross Body is well known. Not to put too fine a point on it, the Causal Body is your conditioning. It motivates your actions. The Subtle Body is the person you think you are. It is reflected awareness. And like the moon it is not actually conscious, although it is taken to be conscious because it is virtually impossible to separate the light shining on it from the reflective surface on which it shines. To further obscure the truth about the Subtle Body, it is the place in you where experience takes place, where all your feelings and thoughts happen. When Subtle Bodies (people) say "I think" or "I feel," it is not true, because awareness, the "I," does not think or feel. Subtle Bodies don't consciously think or feel, because they are not actually conscious. Pure awareness, like the sun, reflects off the Subtle Body, and the thoughts arising in it are illumined and known. If you take awareness away from the Subtle Body, you cannot see thoughts arising in it. In deep sleep awareness does not illumine the Subtle Body so there is no "you" there.

Before we continue, you will notice that we are starting to introduce some technical terms: Gross, Subtle and Causal Body.* If you are serious about self-inquiry, you should start to think about yourself in our scientific language to help you make the transition from the person that you think you are to the impersonal awareness that you actually are. Once you have made the transition, you can jettison the language.

Thinking of yourself as a person is a big problem. In fact it is the only problem. In a way, it is a shame that I have to tell you this because you may very well toss Vedanta and head off in search of a more warm and fuzzy teaching. It may be just too scary to let go of your story. It has been with you—in fact you think it *is* you—for as long as you can remember. You cannot imagine life without it. Actually, you need not worry—you can keep your personhood if you wish, because it does not cancel you. You cannot be cancelled. You have a much more illustrious identity, one that easily accommodates any story.

It is your thinking that creates *your* reality and, to the degree that your story is not in harmony with *the* reality, which is obviously impersonal, you are going to suffer. Thinking of yourself as impersonal, ordinary awareness, the knower of the person that you are so attached to, may seem a bit precious and unnecessary, but I assure you it isn't. As we supply the logic to back up our assertion about who you are, it will make more and more sense.

In any case, when pure awareness is under the spell of *Maya*, it becomes fascinated with the subjective events appearing in the Subtle Body, identifies with them and fails to realize that it is merely experiencing an inert reflection of itself. When you don't know this, you try to do the impossible: connect with yourself or realize yourself. It is not possible because reality is always only awareness experiencing itself. Awareness is "realized," meaning that it knows who and what

---

* *Sthula sarira, suksma sarira and karana sarira*

it is without the aid of words. It is self-aware. It is self-existent. It is free of the notion of subject and object that ignorance seemingly imposes on it.

Ask yourself this: what are you doing to be what you are? You are not doing anything to be what you are. You can't do anything to be what you are because you are what you are. Enlightenment is not knowing *that* you are. It is knowing *what* you are and what it means to be what you are.

I Do Not Die

When you take yourself to be the Subtle Body you are prone to certain beliefs that do not jibe with who you actually are. One of those beliefs is that you are born and that you die. This belief consciously or unconsciously influences everything you do. You believe that time is running out and that you need to get everything you want before you die. If you knew yourself as you are, you would not be interested in cramming desired experiences into your small life before you die because you would understand that you are immortal.

Awareness is unborn. If this is true—and you need to follow our inquiry to see if it is—then a lot of problems are solved. If you are not born, you do not die. Of course, you believe that you do, but where is the evidence that you die? Yes, we know the body dies but it is clear that you are not the body because it is known to you. To have knowledge of death you would have to be there to observe it. If you are there to observe it, it is obviously something other than you. In fact the body and death are only thought objects appearing in you at any moment. The body is not a solid object "out there" nor is death an event waiting to happen. They are just words that have no meaning apart from the reality that ignorance of your nature lends to them.

I Am a Partless Whole

It is not enough to know that you don't die, although it's a good start. If you are a miserable person it will not be good news. So we have to tell you something else, perhaps the most important fact about you. You are whole and complete. You can't deny that you are aware. It is obvious. That you are the awareness that is aware is not so obvious, but if you take yourself to be reflected awareness, the Subtle Body, you will always feel a sense of lack. This sense of lack, which you think belongs to you, actually belongs to the Subtle Body. It is a feeling that causes you to chase things and to hold on to them when you get them. It is a problem because the things that you want are not under your control. Not getting what you want and losing what you value is the number one cause of suffering. But if you knew that you are always full, you would be relieved of suffering. So it is very important to know that nothing can be added to you or subtracted from you. If you are not made up of parts, how can anything be added or subtracted?

Subtle Bodies often spend their whole lives trying to get themselves "together." It is a futile task for this reason: the awareness that you are has no parts. It very much seems to be an assemblage, but it is not. It is a partless whole. When you understand this fact you will stop trying to fix yourself because no glue can hold you together. You are already together.

During those moments when your mind is quiet you may have noticed a steady "current" of bliss, an unexplained feeling of satisfaction, a sense of self-confidence unconnected to anything you have accomplished. That experience is going on all the time in you. It is you experiencing the fullness that you are. It is hidden from you because you are distracted by the mind's agitations.

I Am Not a Doer

I have to tell you another important fact about yourself: you are not a doer, because you are non-dual. Non-dual means that there is only you. If there is only you, you cannot move from one place to another. Movement can apparently take place within the scope of your awareness, but awareness can't move. It may seem to move when Maya operates but it doesn't.

You are everywhere. If you journey to the end of the cosmos you will find that you are already there when you arrive. This fact is as important as the others because the burden of doership hangs heavy on the back of the one who does not understand who she is. A doer is someone who does actions to enjoy the results. The doer is not a real person. It is an idea that afflicts awareness when it does not know that it is the ground of being. When it thinks it is a doer it suffers all manner of unpleasant and pleasant emotions because the results of its actions are not up to it. The most common emotions the doer suffers are fear, desire and anger. So if you would like to be free of these feelings, self-knowledge is for you.

I Am Not Unique in Any Way

Another very important fact: you are not unique in anyway. But wait! When you think about it you are totally unique because there is only you, reality being what it is. It is so cool to understand this because most Subtle Bodies are afflicted with the notion that they are one among many billions of "others." Consequently, they work day and night to distinguish themselves, to be seen or heard. It is a great relief to the status conscious Subtle Body when it learns that there is no one to compare itself to.

No Need to Be Pure and Holy

Another benefit of being a partless whole is that the desire to be pure and "holy" disappears. Pure means partless. Everything in the apparent reality—life as we know it—is impure, meaning it is made up of parts. Purification is a process of removing various contaminants—parts—that are not in harmony with the nature of the thing to be purified. For example, what is called pure alcohol is not actually 100% alcohol. It can be purified up to 99% but some impurities will remain, no matter how hard you work to remove them. One of the most salient characteristics of Subtle Bodies with spiritual inclinations is the desire to be pure. Much effort is wasted on this work—although if you take yourself to be a Subtle Body it may be useful to purify some of the dross for reasons we will shortly discuss—and much frustration is encountered because you can never get to 100%. And when you are caught in the purification game you are just as frustrated at 99% as you were at 47%. That 1% becomes a glaring limitation, like the pea under the mattress of the proverbial princess.

I Don't Change

Next you need to know that you don't change. You don't become anything other than what you are...ever. This, too, is a saving and liberating knowledge because most of us are always striving to become something that we aren't. We don't like ourselves that much and would prefer to be a more, better or different someone. The desire to change one's situation is built into the Subtle Body and the desire to be different from what one is, is also built in.

Here are several important words that apply to you: unconcerned, untainted, unaffected and associationless. This means that whatever happens does not affect you in any way. Awareness is that element of you that never changes. It is not modified or validated by good experiences or invalidated by bad experiences. It validates itself.

I Can't Become More Aware

Seekers often believe that through self-inquiry they will become more conscious, more "aware." It is a myth. When you know who you are this desire disappears because you understand that you are the awareness that neither grows nor shrinks.

I Reveal Myself to Myself

You are self-effulgent, effortless awareness. You reveal yourself to yourself without the aid of a body and mind. You can be likened to a light bulb that shines steadily even though it was never switched on. It is a bulb that is not connected to the electric grid. It is its own self-generating electric grid. It cannot be turned off. If you know who you are and someone asks you who you are you can truthfully say "I am the light."

The Real and the Apparently Real

You, awareness, are what is. Reality is one but it appears as a duality. This duality is made up of you and the objects appearing in you. The objects come and go, but you don't come and go. Because of this they are called "apparently real." You are always present. You are "what is." We use several analogies to help you understand this point. If you have a lump of gold you can make it into a bracelet or a necklace or a small figurine. If you melt down the bracelet or the necklace or the figurine, the gold seems to change but it doesn't change. The gold is "what is" and the ornament apparently exists. It is a bracelet...until it isn't.

What a valuable understanding! Subtle Bodies are congenitally bedeviled with the notion of becoming something because they are always in a state of flux. Think about it for a minute. The "you" that you take yourself to be now is not the same you that you took yourself to be some time ago. And it will not be the same you tomorrow that it is today. That you is constantly melted down in the furnace of time and is reconstituted as something else. That you is non-essential and you are essential, the "part" that observes the changes, the part that can't be removed. When we say that knowledge is not negatable we mean that it always exists. It does not change. You can see why self-knowledge is your saving grace, your complete security. You cannot be negated because you are existence itself. You are what is. And you are everything that is, the gold from which all ornaments are fashioned.

We started this chapter with the idea that non-dual awareness does not mean anything without a context. Where there is only one there is no meaning. Years ago when I was wandering around India being "spiritual," I met a person who showed me a book on the self. It had no title and nothing was written on the pages. In itself it made an important point, but I thought that it also was a good symbol of the modern non-dual teachings. They tell us about the self all right, but they leave out the context. They say that there is no body and mind, no world, no you. No, no, no, *ad nauseam*. We say it too because it is ultimately true. But it does not constitute a teaching. Negation does not mean denial. If anything is not clear in this short chapter on the self, it will become increasingly clear as we now discuss the waves.

CHAPTER SIX

Beautiful Intelligent Ignorance

A tsunami is a very big wave. Before we get to the topic of ordinary waves—me and you—we need to discuss the big wave in awareness we call the creation. Just as non-duality doesn't mean anything apart from duality and we don't mean anything apart from the creation, awareness does not mean anything without Maya—Beautiful Intelligent Ignorance.

Before we proceed I need to tell you that so far I have been careful not to introduce too many technical terms but this is about to change. If you are serious about liberation and you are convinced that Vedanta can set you free, you will need to understand the science of your nature in depth. You are not complicated, but certain subtle aspects need to be understood before Vedanta can work its magic on you. So take your time and memorize the meaning of these words because success depends on it.

Before objects appeared, there was only non-dual limitless consciousness. There are no divisions in it, no parts. Something that is limitless can be anything. If it can't apparently be something other than what it is, it is limited. This is why scripture says that consciousness is all-powerful. In a way it is not correct to say it is powerful because power implies duality. But it is precisely with reference to duality that the statement about its power becomes meaningful. The power to create, which is inherent in consciousness, is called *Maya*. It is a word whose many meanings you need to know because it is the key to solving the riddle of existence.

The first thing we need to know about Maya that it is *only* all powerful with reference to the creation. We need to take a small verbal detour because most of us think of the Creator as God. You are free to use whatever word you want to refer to the Creator but if you want your understanding to line up with reality you need to know that God or Maya does not imply otherness, as we shall see. The popular notion of God as a SUPERBEING sitting somewhere outside the creation making it all happen is an understandable but primitive personification of the truth. It is true that Maya creates and sustains and destroys the universe, but not remotely. It is right here in you, right now, creating, sustaining, and destroying the objects that are forever appearing and disappearing in you.

The second thing to know is that while Maya is the cause of the whole creation, it is only a tiny flyspeck in awareness. It does not hide awareness. This may be an upsetting idea for the doer, calling into question attempts to discover awareness by removing the stuff that separates the seeker from it, unless that stuff is ignorance. If you have stuff to get rid of, it does not exist apart from your knowledge of it and your knowledge of it depends on consciousness because you cannot have knowledge without consciousness, so you are definitely something other than your stuff long before you try to rid yourself of it. If you know who you are, your stuff is relatively unimportant. In a way, however, it is good news if you are qualified because if enlightenment is the removal of ignorance about who you are, it is a relatively simple matter, assuming you have Vedanta and a skilful teacher at your disposal.

Appearances to the contrary notwithstanding, non-duality says that the world and everything in it—including us—is awareness. Maya creates in a very interesting way. If you want to make cheese you need to subject milk to a certain process. During the process milk no longer retains its nature as milk. It becomes something else altogether. If you want to get the milk back you cannot. So if awareness—let's call it Isvara in keeping with our tradition—becomes the world in this way, we can't know it as it is, because it no longer exists!

The dualists don't think that creation happens this way. They think that God stays put in heaven and creates from there, never getting sullied by what It creates. We agree that Isvara is not sullied by Its creation but we don't accept that the creation hides Isvara so that the only way It can be known or experienced is to die and go to the heavenly place where God sits. We don't accept it because we know that Isvara creates in another way.

We know this because the whole creation can be destroyed without disturbing anything except ignorance. To introduce you to this idea slowly, first consider the deep sleep state. When this state is operational there is no world whatsoever and you are perfectly fine; you are full of bliss. It is important to understand this to dissolve your resistance to the idea that you might end up like a zombie when Vedanta removes the world for you. The next idea to consider is the dream state. In the dream state you are there and a whole world appears in you. Your dream ego functions in that world as if it was a real world. In fact there is no "as if" for you because you actually take the dream to be real. It is only when you wake up that you see that it was a dream.

Isvara's creation is a dream creation. It is there as long as you are in it but it disappears when you wake up. Some people have experiences in Isvara's dream of life—this passing shadow—that wake them up, but this kind of awakening is subject to a cruel irony. You awaken in another dream—the dream that you are awake. Liberation is much more than waking up. It is waking up from the waker *and the waking up* because the "you" that woke up never slept. And this waking up is not an experiential awakening. It is not an awakening at all. It is simply self-knowledge.

The Macrocosmic Mind and the Three Gunas

So Isvara's creation, the macrocosm, is a projection, a dream. From Isvara's point of view it is a lovely dream, beautiful and intelligent. We call Isvara's dream ignorance, not because Isvara is ignorant but because it is such a wonderful dream that it hides Isvara from us. We are fascinated by it and think it is real. Isvara is awareness plus pure *sattva*. Pure sattva is awareness in the form of a special substance that makes knowledge possible. The whole creation is intelligently designed. It is made up of knowledge. Isvara is awareness with all the knowledge that makes the creation possible. Isvara is tree knowledge, animal knowledge, people knowledge, matter knowledge, mind knowledge—knowledge of everything. But knowledge is not enough for a creation, so Isvara needs a substance to transform into all the objects in the creation. Because reality is non-dual awareness, the substance from which the forms are shaped has to come from Isvara too.

a creates *Tamas* out of its own self. Tamas is matter. It is not conscious
n't transform itself. And knowledge alone is not capable of transforming
matter into forms so, realizing the need for another power, Isvara dreamed up
Rajas. Rajas is the power of desire. It allows Isvara to create and destroy the
forms in the creation according to knowledge.

This whole thing happens in the mind of Isvara in an instant, before one object appears in awareness. It did not take Isvara billions of years to think about
whether or not It wanted a creation and a few billion more to cook up the idea
of Maya. Once It had Maya figured out it did not labor for untold more millions
of years on the sattva-rajas-tamas idea and then proceed over many million more
to evolve the subtle and gross elements, bang the gross world into existence, and
wait until the conscious beings appeared and went about their funny dance so
It could have a good laugh. The creation is a thought and like a thought, it takes
place instantaneously. It may take a while to get your mind around this idea because it is completely contrary to the narratives foisted on us by both science and
religion, but once you rigorously expose your mind to Vedanta, you will understand what it means when we say that creation is a thought—a projection—in
you, awareness.

You may be surprised to know that the three gunas are not the whole story
of the creation. We are just getting started. Remember, this all "happens" before
there is a you and a me and a world.

The idea of the Five Elements also occurs to Isvara at the same time that the
idea of the gunas appears. The elements are Air, Fire, Water, Earth and Space.
We need not consider how they relate to the gunas because we are only interested in liberation and this topic is not directly related to it. When we think of
the elements we think of material tangible things. But the mind of Isvara is pure
formless intangible consciousness so to transform Itself into the material tangible world an intermediate step is required. The first objects to appear are subtle
elements in their pure form—they are called *tanmatras*—which combine and
recombine according to a certain formula (*panchikarana*) to evolve the tangible
material elements.

As if this was not enough to keep in mind, Isvara came up with the whole
mandala of existence too. If you have had time to think about it you cannot help
but appreciate the creation as an orderly and intelligently designed matrix, a
*uni*verse of physical, psychological and moral laws.

The Three Bodies

The gunas and the elements all exist within a basic pattern, unseen gridlines that structure the whole field of consciousness that is the creation. I call it the mandala of existence or the *dharma field*.

Although it is one beautifully designed, intelligent mandala, it is divided into three "bodies" arranged in a very logical way. These bodies belong to Isvara in its capacity as the Creator. *Isvara* outside its capacity to create is bodiless and is known as *Paramatma*, pure uncreated consciousness. The word *body* in Sanskrit—*sharira*—means "that which is subject to change." We also have three bodies that correspond with Isvara's bodies. In fact our bodies are just Isvara's bodies believed by us to belong to us. Before we reveal the identity of *jiva* and Isvara it is important to distinguish their respective natures. Its knowledge is limitless, ours is limited. Its power is limitless, ours is limited. Its desire is limitless, ours is limited. So far we have been talking about Isvara's Causal Body, brought about by Maya. It is the ideas that lie hidden in consciousness that make everything that we experience possible. Because it causes the creation it is called the Causal Body. There is more to it, as we shall see when we get down to the microcosmic level, but for now this is enough.

The Subtle Body is made of sattva. It is reflective. It reflects pure awareness. You cannot see pure awareness or the Causal Body. The Causal Body is unmanifest. It exists *in potentia*. You can't say what it is although you can infer its nature from its effects. And it should be noted at this point that inference is a valid means of knowledge. The Subtle Body is the place where the Causal Body becomes known in the form of your thoughts, feelings, experiences, perceptions, memories, dreams, desires, fears, etc., which you think of as your life. Isvara's Subtle Body consists of all the apparently conscious beings in the creation and the thoughts that animate them.

The Gross Body

The Gross Body is...well...the gross body. Like the Subtle Body, we know this one well. Isvara's Gross Body is all the matter in the creation. It is made of tamas.

Two thirds of this mandala is experienceable, one third hidden. The Causal Body is hidden. It is important to know that this whole structure is inert. It is not conscious or alive. However, it seemingly springs to life when pure consciousness illumines it. It becomes a spinning whirligig of energy, maintained by the law of karma, which again was cooked up by Isvara before one event actually happened.

Although it seems as if the Creator's dream is real because it spins and dances as if it is real, it is not actually real. What a joke! It is like a merry-go-round with its brightly colored horses going up and down, around and around, as cheery music plays. What fun! But it is not alive at all. It is just a machine, seemingly living. It exists, no doubt, but it is truly a dream. The realization that life is a dream is usually a big shock. When it happens you are well on your way to liberation. The self—you, awareness—is real (satya) and Maya's projection—the world—is apparently real. We have a technical term for what is apparently real that you should remember: *mithya*.

It is quite the fashion nowadays to claim that you are enlightened. People say "I am awareness" as if it were some kind of special status, as if it were the last word in all matters spiritual. We say "Big deal, who or what isn't?" It is totally easy to be awareness because there is no other option. You may define enlightenment as the realization "I am awareness" but this is only one half of the knowledge. The other half—what makes self-knowledge meaningful—is the knowledge of mithya, the apparent reality. We said liberation was complete knowledge, not partial knowledge. Complete knowledge is the knowledge of satya *and* mithya.

When we talk about liberation we mean one thing and one thing alone: the discrimination between satya and mithya, awareness and the objects appearing in it. To understand it better we need to go back up to the causal level and talk about Isvara and Maya again. Because of the three gunas, Isvara has three powers: the power to veil (tamas), the power to project (rajas) and the power to reveal (sattva). These powers—energies if you wish—pervade Isvara's Subtle Body.

When the world is projected, Tamas covers the Subtle Bodies of all beings. This is why we don't know we are awareness and why we accept the fictitious identity that mom and pop dream up for us. We look out through the organs of perception and see a world, and at that moment Rajas projects the idea that what is seen is reality. So basically, we come into the game of life with a stacked deck. We don't know who we really are, we take the person we are told we are to be a real person, and we assume the world we see is real. It would be very funny if it weren't so sad. But what to do? This is what we are dealing with. From birth onwards we are trying to sort out this problem. When a little sattva, the revealing power, creeps in we start to question the whole illusion.

Superimposition

We live in ignorance of the nature of reality because of these two powers. Our whole life is confused. To use Vedanta terminology, we "superimpose." We don't know what is real and what is apparently real. We take ourselves to be the Subtle Body and identify with all the stuff that arises in it. Along with superimposition come certain beliefs that keep us firmly locked into our confusion. For example, as we pointed out in the beginning, we think the joy is the object. We think we can get what we already have by doing something. We think that the things that make us happy should last. We can't understand why good and evil sit side by side. Actually it is not quite fair to say "we superimpose." Superimposition is unconscious. It happens before we appear so you should not feel that you made a mistake. Of course you do, but that is one of the ironies of life. That very uncomfortable feeling of global guilt, unexplained guilt, free-floating anxiety—the Christians call it original sin—is the result of superimposition. It is not your fault. Unfortunately, it becomes your problem until you remove it with discrimination.

A very nice story in our scriptures explains superimposition. It will help to cement this concept into your mind. A weary, thirsty traveler sees a village at twilight and proceeds to the well to get a drink of water. He reaches down to grab the bucket sitting beside the well and spots a big cobra coiled next to it, its hood up, ready to strike. He freezes, full of terror. At that moment a friendly, bearded old man appears and asks what's happening. The traveler implores him to get a stick and kill the snake. The old man takes a look and laughs. "That's no snake," he says, "it's the well rope coiled up next to the bucket."

What happened to the snake when the traveler received the knowledge? It disappeared! It did not have a real head and tail and scales and so forth. It was just a projection. And when you understand that it is a rope, you cannot see the snake again. It has been destroyed by knowledge. You can understand how you made a mistake and took the apparent for the real, but you cannot make the snake return. This is what we call firm knowledge. Once self-knowledge takes place, you will not accept yourself as your story, and you are freed of it.

The most interesting part of the snake and rope story, apart from the fact that it illustrates how the creation is a product of ignorance, is that this incident took place in twilight. Humans live in a twilight zone. If the man had come to the well in midday when the sun was shining brightly, he would not have seen a snake. If you have full knowledge of reality you cannot mistake yourself for the Subtle Body, the person with the story. If the man had gone to the well in the dead of night, no snake would have been perceived. When you are totally ignorant, like an animal, you cannot have a doubt about who you are. Only when there is twilight, when knowledge and ignorance sit side by side, can you superimpose individuality on the limitlessness of your own self. In the twilight of Maya's projection, the apparent reality, it's difficult to tell what is happening and it is easy to superimpose.

Another interesting aspect of this story is the symbol of the friendly old man. He represents Vedanta. Vedanta is your friend. It is inquiry. It strips away the projection that is causing your suffering by revealing your nature as awareness. When you see the underlying reality your existential fears go away. Not immediately perhaps—the effects of ignorance remain for a while; but they gradually fade away as the knowledge does its work.

Superimposition causes suffering. We want to be free of it. There is no point thinking that some kind of special experience will take care of this problem. Because the ignorance and the projection are hard wired, disentangling you from the objects appearing in you is hard work. It is hard work because the confusion seems so natural. We have lived undiscriminating lives since childhood and now we are asked to question the very assumptions on which our identity is based.

On a day to day level, how does superimposition work? It is very simple. There is not one person who has not said "I think, I feel, I do." All three statements are fine examples of superimposition. Why is it ignorant to make such statements? Because there is only one non-dual "I" and it has no body and mind, so it does not think or feel or act. The thinking feeling and acting belong to mithya, the apparent reality. They belong to the Subtle Body, not to awareness. You, awareness, are always free of the Subtle Body. When we say that you are free we mean that it is something other than you. It is something other than you because it is known to you. You are not what you know. What you know is you, but you are not it. You are the knower.

The Subtle Body is where experience takes place. It does not take place in awareness. It appears in awareness like a dream appears when you are asleep, but it does not affect awareness in any way. When you think that something happened to you it means that you lack discrimination. You have confused yourself with the experiencer, the Subtle Body, which is affected by experience. Liberation is not about making the experiencer "detached," as many people believe, setting it free. The experiencer is always attached to experience. Liberation is the understanding that you are not the experiencer and that you are awareness, the non-experiencing witness. When that is clearly understood, suffering stops. Suffering is the mental and emotional disturbances you add to the events that make up your life.

The Subtle Body – "Me"

Before we continue I need to tell you that we are going to pretend that the Subtle Body and the world in which it lives is real because that is where we find ourselves. It is to Vedanta's credit that instead of just dismissing it as unreal and telling us to transcend it (how you transcend something that is not real is not clear), it patiently comes into our dream and leads us out of ignorance step by step.

Just as there are several facts to know about the Causal Body, there are several things to know about the Subtle Body. These functions do not belong to Maya or to Awareness. They belong solely to the Subtle Body. Maya instantly projects the creation and covers it with Ignorance. Awareness is the part of you—which is not a part—that doesn't change. It effortlessly illumines the activities of the Subtle Body. Maya and Awareness are very simple. The Subtle body is more complex, more mechanical.

Doubt

The first function built into the Subtle Body is doubt. When something happens you immediately have a doubt about how to respond. Everybody has doubts. We have doubts about where we're going to live, what we're going to do, whether we'll find love and who we are.

Isvara was actually very kind because It must have known that when It appeared here as a Subtle Body—a living being—it would need protection. In a dream, nothing lasts and nothing is what it seems to be. To function in this dream you need to question things. Someone who takes things at face value and does not ask questions is asking for trouble.

For example, if you are lonely and want a Mr. or Mrs. Right to share your life and you get on a dating site and read the profile of a prospective mate, you are a complete idiot if you think that what the profile says is true. There may be little bits of truth cleverly strewn here and there, definitely some exaggerations and probably a few outright lies. In these intimate personal games people lie because they are full of fears and desires and the truth is not always appealing. They want to get something so they present themselves in the best possible light. It is quite "natural," but woe to the person who takes it seriously. Yes, you should trust but you should also tether your camel.

When you turn on the TV and the pitchman says I've got the deal for you, it actually means I've got the deal for me. Most of us think it is important to trust implicitly, but it is a mistake. Doubt is good in all matters samsaric, up to a point. But it is important not to fall in love with your doubts. A love affair with doubt is dithering. Ditherers are never happy. You need to be able to resolve your doubts.

Resolve the Doubt and Act

To resolve a doubt, you need information. Where is the information going to come from? Isvara to the rescue again! It evolved the intellect. The intellect is the Subtle Body in its determining, discriminating, inquiring function. The Subtle Body is very supple; it can do a lot of tricks. Its job is to ferret out the relevant information, make a determination, tell the ego—the doer—what to do, and generate the emotion appropriate to the action so you can respond properly to the situation. It is your duty, your dharma, to respond appropriately to whatever happens.

But where is the information going to come from? Someone just said "I love you." Your intellect can't just get out a smart phone, go on the internet and google "What do I do when someone says I love you?" You respond according to your programming. If you have never been in this situation you will probably hem and haw and get flustered and not say anything. If you have been in this situation and you want to encourage said suitor, you will say "I love you too." Actually you may not have been in that situation and still say "I love you too" because you saw a similar situation on TV or this is what your friend said when it happened to him. In either case conditioning came to the rescue. If you don't love her but want to take advantage of her, you will lie because that is what you are programmed to do. Your programming is stored in your Causal Body. We will discuss programming presently.

So the intellect has the knowledge of what to do. The knowledge the intellect retrieves from the Causal Body instantly transforms the Subtle Body into a doer—the doer is actually just a thought—and produces the emotions required to stimulate the active organs—hands, feet and speech, etc—causing the body to do or say something. This produces a new situation that requires a response and turns the wheel of life over once more. From morning to evening, day after day, year after year it goes on. It is just Isvara impersonally operating the Maya dream. You can do very little to change it and changing it presents various problems too, but it can be changed. We will talk about what you can do presently. In fact the rest of the book is about what you can do. But you need to know that if you are qualified, the knowledge alone will be enough. Unless you are ready to surrender the doer you will be caught up in this monotonous cycle forever. This is why we need to discuss Isvara both with and without Maya. Once you understand how it works you can easily surrender the doer.

As we will see presently in chapter 10, on discrimination, the point of discussing the Subtle Body and identifying the thoughts, feelings and karma that belong to it is to indicate that all of this stuff stays with the Subtle Body. It does not belong to you, awareness. Vedanta is not just passive knowledge, the knowledge that stops the seeking; it is the skillful application of knowledge to the Subtle Body that reveals the blissful fullness of awareness. You will need to apply the knowledge not only to stop the tendency to seek, but you will undoubtedly need to discriminate once you have stopped seeking because the effects of ignorance— gratuitous desires and fears—remain. When the weary traveler realized that the snake was actually a rope, it took a few minutes for the uncomfortable emotions to disappear. The intellect, which in a normal, unevolved person is busy discriminating between various objects, is now given the task of discriminating the self from the objects appearing in it.

If you have understood what we have said so far, you have either been set free by the knowledge or you have the knowledge needed to set yourself free. You can put the book down and get on with enjoying life as it is or you can meaningfully start your spiritual work. The first option is unlikely, however, for a particular reason, which we will take up now.

The Seeds

Each Vedanta teaching is as important as all the others but the topic of vasanas is very important because it identifies both your allies and your enemies in the battle of life. When you are ignorant of your fullness, you pursue objects that you feel will complete you. You go for certain things and you shy away from certain others. Fear and desire motivate your actions. When you act from a feeling of lack (fear) and the desire that springs from it, the action leaves a very subtle trace. When you are acting you do not realize that the action has unseen results beyond the immediate experience. The unseen result is called a *vasana*, a simple Sanskrit term that means *fragrance* or *trace*. Like the aroma emitted from a flower, the actions you take carry on unbeknownst to you. My teacher used to call them "the footprints of your actions." You are walking down the pristine beach of life leaving tracks in the sand. They are behind you so you don't notice them. But they are not actually gone. They come back to you later. In the meantime they go to the Causal Body. The Causal Body is called the "seed" body because it causes you to think and feel and act.

For example, you have sex and really enjoy it. When it is over physically it is not over. Nobody who had sex and enjoyed it did it only once. You may go about other business for a while but when you find yourself in a certain situation, you want it again. If sex completed you, you wouldn't be interested in it again. But you are interested because you still feel incomplete. The desires for objects that lie hidden in you and spring out from time to time are your vasanas. This applies to fears as well. If you have a bad experience, you will avoid that kind of experience like the plague. To make it very simple, we can say that your vasanas are your conditioning, your tendencies, the objects and activities that you are attracted to and repelled by.

Everything that moves in the apparent reality is driven by vasanas. Vasanas are not inherently good or bad. They are the seeds—the knowledge—that drives the creation. Isvara invented them. Nothing stirs in the creation without a vasana. A vasana becomes a good one when it drives you into pleasant circumstances and it becomes a bad one when it drives you into an unpleasant situation. Drinking alcohol is a very nice vasana for certain people. It is a very painful vasana for others.

A vasana is the momentum from a past action, the tendency to repeat it. It is purely a technical term. I make this point to counteract the idea that vasanas are only negative. The belief that they are all negative has given rise to a frustrating enlightenment idea: enlightenment happens when all the vasanas have been removed. Enlightened people have vasanas. If you are alive you have vasanas. When the vasanas pack up, you die.

Nothing is right or wrong about repeating a particular pattern of behavior. Certain habits are good and others are not, depending on what you are trying to achieve. As discriminating inquirers we are interested in the psychology behind our behavior, not the behaviors themselves, although certain behaviors are completely off limits—those that violate universal norms: injury, deceit, theft, etc. The basic psychology operating behind most of our unhelpful behaviors is fear, a sense of lack.

A vasana for food is natural. It is Isvara maintaining the body. I eat to live. But when I feel emotionally upset for any reason and I use food to calm me, the vasana becomes a problem because it masks my real motivation. I now live to eat. If my mind is clear I can understand that I am using food to solve a problem that cannot be solved by food and I can look for the solution elsewhere. But if my mind is not clear and food works—always only temporarily—I will repeatedly use food to manage my emotions. When a vasana is repeatedly repeated, the behavior associated with it becomes binding. When I keep responding habitually to life, boredom sets in. It is not pleasant to behave like a robot when you are actually a conscious being. At this stage the vasana-driven habit becomes an obsession or a compulsion, which finally morphs into an addiction. We call these states of desire and attachment "binding" vasanas. At this point you are not eating food; the food is eating you. In case you haven't figured it out, "food" represents any vasana-driven behavior meant to make you feel good.

Vedanta does not work for people with addictions and compulsions, unless the addiction has caused the person to "hit bottom." Hitting bottom means that there is no longer the slightest desire to defend the addictive behavior and there is a burning desire to be done with it. If a person has not hit bottom, he will not be open to the spiritual solution. He may talk freedom but persist in the behavior that masks the fundamental problem, absence of self-knowledge. This is why our scriptures say "Let not the wise unsettle the minds of the ignorant." It is a waste of time to lecture those whose minds are under the spellbinding vasanas because their minds belong to the vasana in play at the moment. For example, if you have a conversation with a drunk, it can all be very wonderful and meaningful at the time, but if you try to build on the relationship the next day, you cannot, because the sober person you are talking to today is not the drunk you were talking to the preceding evening. Actually, you were not talking to the person at all. You were talking to the alcohol vasana. And unfortunately vasanas are not conscious.

Dharma

A binding vasana is like a deep ravine or gorge in the Causal Body, the unconscious. Consciousness is forced to flow down it. If we stick with the ravine metaphor we can expand the meaning to include another important fact about ourselves, svadharma. We all exist in the mind of Isvara as conscious beings and within that designation there are human beings and within that designation there are many types. Each human type is a branch on the tree of samsara—Isvara's mind—and the roles it plays are the twigs.

As mentioned, svadharma means your relative nature, the type of person you are. Astrology and the Enneagram are attempts to describe various types of people. We have no quarrel with what these very soft "sciences" say about people—insofar as people are real—but we are not interested in the details. If your primary goal is to figure out who you are as a person, Vedanta is not for you, because although you do have a certain kind of conditional personal identity, knowing it doesn't solve the existential problems that you face. That you think of yourself as a unique person is the primary problem you face. Furthermore, without knowledge of the consciousness in which you operate, you are subject to any manner of problems.

However, if you don't know what your relative nature is, you will not behave in harmony with it and your mind will be very unsettled. If your mind is unsettled you will be unable to understand who you really are. So we need to know our svadharma, but it is not our goal. This topic is discussed in more detail in chapter 9.

In any case, a samskara is the result of the clustering effect of several vasanas. They are responsible for the roles we play and they make up the very fabric of our relative natures. Human beings are complex, unlike animals. Animals are more or less an aggregation of two or three rudimentary vasanas. They are programmed with eating, sleeping and sex vasanas and not much else, although animal lovers project all manner of amazing qualities on them. *Monkey* is a word that describes a certain program with a very limited range of behavior. If I am a monkey I will never behave like a dog. Dogs and cats and birds are other programs, samskaras. To stick with our valley metaphor, they are like a river in a small valley with a few feeder streams. A microbe is a samskara too. It is a very simple program, a tiny puddle of water with no feeder streams whatsoever. All of these beings follow their svadharma without question; they are true to what they are.

Your Nature – Svaharma

"Human being" is a unique program. Actually we are just animals with the ability to think. But in terms of our metaphor we are big rivers served by many large tributaries fed in turn by many smaller streams. What makes us so complex is intellect, the ability to think and choose.

This implies that something other than discrete vasanas condition us. Another doorway to this idea is this: why don't all newborns turn out the same way? One becomes a scientist, another a musician, a third a politician, etc. Some deeper force seems to be determining the choices we make and the actions that flow from them.

The creation itself is one vast program within which are millions of conscious beings stamped by Isvara with unique programs intended to serve the needs of the total. All conscious beings share one life. As long as every being follows its program, life works nicely. A tree puts out oxygen and consumes carbon dioxide and everything is fine. Birds follow bird nature and flies do what flies do and life goes on. Humans, it seems, have been given various natures according to the needs of the total and are meant to perform certain functions necessary for the smooth functioning of the whole.

In every system, something belongs but doesn't belong, a fly in the ointment, so to speak. Human beings are the fly in Isvara's ointment. That doesn't mean that we are "bad" and should be eliminated from the beautiful, intelligent creation. It just means that with ointment come flies. We make an otherwise beautiful but monotonous creation interesting because we have somehow been given intellect, self consciousness. Cows are not self conscious. They do not know they are cows. They are just consciousness, Isvara, in a particular body acting out a particular program. They are not going to write symphonies, teach the Vedas and invent airplanes and the internet. The intellect is responsible for culture and also makes it possible to choose one thing over another—"free" will. Of course we are not free when you look at it from Isvara's point of view, because Isvara creates and controls everything. But as apparent human beings in the apparent matrix of life we apparently have free will. Free will can be a blessing but it can also be a curse because it means that we can chose not to go with our relative nature and act out of an idea that is contrary to it. It means that we can break the rules if we so desire.

If you have the nature of an accountant and you try to become a poet it will not work for you. If you have the nature of a saint and you try to become a criminal it will not work. If you are a homosexual and you try to be heterosexual it will not work. If you have an entrepreneurial nature and you pump gas for minimum wage you will be going against dharma, your nature. To be happy you need to follow your nature.

Universal Values – *Samanya Dharma*

We call the creation "the dharma field." It is made up of physical laws, psychological laws and programmed conscious beings. The creation also has a moral dimension. The moral dimension is based on the non-dual nature of consciousness. This means that there is only one conscious being here, appearing as many, and that built into the creation are certain mutual expectations, all of which derive from the most fundamental dharma, non-injury. These universal expectations or values are called *Samanya Dharma*, about which more will also be said in chapter 9. I don't injure you, because I know how it feels to be injured. I don't lie, because I don't like to be lied to. I don't steal, because I value what I have and appreciate the fact that you value what you have.

Samanya dharma is built into our human program. It is a dharma that you violate at your peril. It is sometimes called "conscience." It is often argued that criminals don't have this programming, but they do. Every thief locks up his loot. Hit men carry guns to protect themselves. Actually there is no such thing as a criminal; there is one self taking itself to be incomplete and identifying with some kind of *adharmic* behavior. Adharmic behavior is actions that run contrary to the physical, moral and psychological laws operating in the dharma field.

Svadharma is Isvara and Samanya dharma is also Isvara. If you go against it, it will go against you. And this is not a battle you will win because Isvara is the will of the Total.

Situational Ethics – *Visesa Dharma*

Certain people seem to have a lock on dharma. It is very natural to them. In every situation where they are called upon to respond they respond appropriately; they rarely break the rules. Consequently, in general they are very healthy people. When you follow dharma impeccably, you accumulate merit and that goes with you everywhere in the form of a kind of self-assured glow, accompanied by an easy successful life. When you break it you have "bad energy" and are unhappy, and things never go well for long. The result of breaking dharma is called *demerit*.

But it is not always given to us to know what universal values demand. Life is not an ideal and situations come in various shades of gray. Sometimes violence is necessary. If you have a bad tooth, it is going to take a violent action to remove it. There will be pain involved. When an unpalatable truth will cause needless emotional harm, sometimes a white lie is the way to go. How we interpret Samanya Dharma is called *Visesa Dharma*. You could think of it as situational ethics.

Ordinary Dharma – Everyday Dharma

As if life were not complex enough, there are innumerable everyday dharmas: social, political, economic and legal rules. If you abide by them, in general you will not suffer. Contravening them is not the kiss of death but you will usually suffer in some way if you do. Sometimes, however, following man-made dharmas, which in general—but not always—are based on non-duality, can run counter to your svadharma, requiring considerable thought before venturing to act.

Body Dharma

The physical body is also Isvara. It operates according to the dharmas controlling the body. Insofar as the mind is required for inquiry and it is connected to the body, it is necessary to avoid actions that contravene the dharma of the body. Consequently, scripture counsels against actions that injure the body: alcohol, smoking, excessive exercise, etc. It also encourages habits that are conducive to health.

Appropriate Response

As you can see from this discussion on dharma, life in Isvara's apparent reality is not simple. It is in this reality that I am seeking happiness. We said that universal dharma and svadharma are built in but are not always available to influence my responses. When it is not clear how to respond to a given situation, we default to our conditioning, our vasanas, which may be dharmic, adharmic or some combination of the two. Our conditioning comes from the world around us. My life is just the way my conditioning interacts with what happens in the apparent reality moment to moment. If I have the good fortune to grow up in a dharma-oriented society, I will appreciate how my life fits into the world around me and I will respond accordingly. But if I grow up in a desire-oriented society, my desires and fears will basically determine how I respond. Very often the situations in which I find myself will require a response that is not in harmony with what I want. What do I do then? Do I go against the demands of the situation or do I conform?

Law of Karma – A Spinning Whirligig of Energy

Isvara's mandala of existence is a spinning whirligig of energy. The famous Buddhist word *anitya*, impermanence, is useful in certain contexts but simply does not do it justice. We have already pointed out that on its own it doesn't move. Yet, illumined by awareness, it springs to life. The movement belongs neither to awareness nor to the dharma field.

The movements that take place in the field—nothing takes place outside the field—are governed by the law of karma. Karma just means action. If something moves or changes, it is karma, a leaf falling off a tree, for instance. A thought is karma, a feeling is karma. If an action is initiated by a vasana in conjunction with a particular Subtle Body, that action will have an effect because everything is connected to everything else. There is nothing particularly hard to understand about the law of karma, except one thing. You can never know for certain what the result of a particular action will be, although in the material dimension of the dharma field the results are fairly predictable. If you apply heat to water, it will boil when it gets to a certain temperature. If you split an atom, it will cause a certain known reaction.

Karma itself is value neutral. It is just action and its results. It becomes meaningful only when we evaluate it. We like it or don't like it or are indifferent to it. There is no karma for animals because they do not evaluate the things that happen to them, in them and around them. Only in the minds of human beings does action become karma.

Karma is meaningful for us because, owing to ignorance of our limitless and complete nature, we want to gain certain experiences that we feel will complete us and avoid those that will increase our sense of isolation. Karma is suitable for creating something, getting rid of something, cleaning or changing something or getting something that one does not have. The problem, however, apart from the fact that objects obtained through karma don't supply lasting happiness, is that, as just mentioned, we never know when and if we will get what we want. If getting what we want is instrumental to our happiness, we are going to find ourselves subject to considerable suffering because many other *jivas*, or individuals, are competing for the same things and the supply of relatively valuable things is always limited.

Maya creates the three Bodies and deludes awareness into thinking it is a limited individual. In the following discussion, for all intents and purposes the Subtle Body is synonymous with the jiva. When you don't know you are awareness, you take yourself to be the Subtle Body. Before we take up the next topic, we need to look into the nature of the Causal and Subtle Bodies and their relationship to each other to determine how they impact on self-inquiry.

The Causal Body is an impersonal power of awareness that creates, controls, regulates and governs all the forces, processes and ideas that make up what we call reality. When an object presents itself to you—an event, for example—it triggers an instant, effortless and automatic reaction in the Causal Body. The Causal Body "thinks" but it does not think deliberately. It instantly takes the circumstance in the external world into account along with the individual's samskaras and provides the Subtle Body with apparently logical and definite information that determines the Subtle Body's response. Depending on the condition of the Subtle Body, the information is either clearly understood and deliberated on (sattva), instantly put into practice without thought (rajas), or ignored (tamas).

In nearly everyone the Subtle Body is not aware that the Causal Body is thinking for it, programming it to act. It assumes that the impulse determining its actions originated in it.

Unbeknownst to the Subtle Body, the Causal Body ties together disparate bits of information from the past into a seemingly believable causal narrative that comprises your identity and determines how you see the world. Because many forces impinge on us that require quick responses, the Causal Body also simplifies things for the Subtle Body, reducing the complex picture of reality to manageable formulas. It is not prone to doubt, like the Subtle Body. It uncritically selects information from a given situation and generates an immediate response. It has a flare for the dramatic, as it is prone to exaggerating the probability of unlikely and extreme outcomes. You cut your finger with a kitchen knife and find yourself thinking of a long stay in the hospital and perhaps even...death! As mentioned, it is the repository for the vasanas, which appear as the Subtle Body's likes and dislikes. It reads what are popularly called "vibes," the content of the Causal Body of others, and generates an immediate reaction in the Subtle Body. It unwisely urges the Subtle Body to interact with others on the basis of this information, which generally causes denial in the others, in that nobody likes unsolicited and unknown information about a part of themselves that they are completely unaware of.

The Causal Body is not bothered by a paucity of information; it concocts its narratives on the basis of the most flimsy evidence. It is in a hurry, so first impressions are quite enough for it. It is in love with appearances. It instantly cooks up reasons that evoke a range of positive and negative emotions on the fly. It is opinionated and overconfident and seems to know what is happening irrespective of the indeterminacy of a given situation. The Subtle Body is less confident, owing to its doubting function, and it will usually allow the dogmatic and hastily constructed intuitions of the Causal Body to determine its reactions.

The Causal Body looks like a memory because it recycles experience, but it has no memory. It is incredibly present and aware, as it is ever-present eternal awareness in its original form.

Because it is the source of desire and fear, it causes the Subtle Body to jump to conclusions. When you desire or fear something, you want to quickly rid yourself of the discomfort so you are prone to act on the basis of incomplete information.

The Causal Body is "intuitive." Whereas intuition is much prized by spiritual types, it is dangerous to trust it because it is wrong as often as it is right.

It also stereotypes and creates prototypes. Profiling is based on the Causal Body's ability to immediately recognize patterns. It is not interested in justice and noble Subtle Body ideals. It causes as much pain as pleasure. Its basic function as far as human beings are concerned is to provide the Subtle Body with a simple and handy survival manual as it tries to respond appropriately to the complex circumstances generated by Isvara. Another is to manage the individual's karma.

Much of the modern research into the relationship between the Subtle Body and Causal Body, which incidentally tallies with Vedanta's knowledge on the topic, is summarized in a brilliant book by Nobel-Prize-winning author Daniel Kahneman entitled *Thinking, Fast and Slow*. The Causal Body, which he calls "System 1," thinks "fast," and the Subtle Body, which he calls "System 2," thinks "slow." About the Causal Body he says "It continuously monitors what is going on inside and outside the mind, and continuously generates assessments of various aspects of the situation without specific intention and with little or no effort."

We have no choice about action. Awareness illumines the Causal Body and life happens. Activity is the signature of life. Isvara brings the jivas into an ever-changing dynamic field and whether or not they succeed depends on the appropriateness and timeliness of their actions. Because so much is going on, particularly these days with the tremendous stress produced by a greedy and ever-expanding population trying to survive on a seemingly shrinking planet, we are too busy to carefully analyze every situation and produce well considered and appropriate actions. Isvara designed the Causal Body to help us by simplifying things, providing seemingly useful answers to the problem of action. This necessary simplification process, the reduction of information to approximate and manageable data, is called heuristics in psychology. Although it is difficult not to, allowing the Causal Body to determine your likes and dislikes, moods, beliefs and reactions to events mitigates unfavorably for inquiry because inquiry is a deliberate action.

Maya produces a need to assign meaning to life, but there is no need for "meaning" if you understand reality as it is. Meaning is compensation for ignorance, but ignorance does not need to be compensated for. It needs to be known for what it is. The Causal Body is a sense-making organ. It makes us see the world as tidier, simpler, and more predictable and coherent than it really is. But this tendency conflicts with the truth and fosters overconfidence and a sense of invincibility in the Subtle Body.

The Subtle Body is "slow" insofar as it is that part of the self that can make deliberate calculations and comparisons, plan and choose and look at itself objectively. It is not "slow" when rajas dominates it; it responds almost as quickly as the Causal Body. It is too slow, meaning dull, to respond appropriately when it is dominated by tamas, but when sattva is present it can behave consciously and rationally. It imagines that it is in charge of its life, but because life is not easy it acquiesces and endorses the dominating impulses imposed on it by the Causal Body.

The Causal Body is the source of our tendencies and biases. For example, one of the most common biases is called the "anchoring effect." In a given situation it causes the Subtle Body to focus on the first impression when making decisions and to evaluate everything with reference to it. For example, the initial price offered for a used car sets the standard for the rest of the negotiations, so that prices lower than the initial price seem more reasonable even if they are still higher than what the car is really worth. If you go to a *satsang* and see a guru sitting on a stage surrounded by adoring devotees, you will assume he is wise and enlightened even though there is no evidence of wisdom or enlightenment. If you read the guru's books you will assume that everything he says is wise. The anchoring effect makes the Subtle Body far more gullible and suggestible than it should be.

The Causal Body's tendency to cook up a story to explain reality is called the narrative fallacy. The mind focuses on the most dramatic events and fails to take into account the myriad uninteresting factors that went into producing a particular outcome. For example, those of you who have read my autobiography will imagine that I had a fabulous life because of the many dramatic and bizarre events that happened. But 99% of it was filled with unremarkable events.

The Subtle Body is lazy because learning and understanding take considerable effort, so it would rather believe a plausible story than investigate things as they are. But stories are only explanations for things it does not understand. It tends to follow intuitions because they require less work—matching predictions to the evidence—and therefore feel more natural. Belief without investigation is dangerous.

Another pernicious tendency is called the availability heuristic. For example, if you have had a lot of bad experiences in love you will judge the uncertainty in a given present situation negatively because of the ease of retrieving the uncomfortable experiences from memory. If you have had three or four failed relationships and you meet a potential fifth partner, you will be extremely suspicious, even if the next candidate for your affections is a saint.

Another bias is the priming effect. You had a substandard meal at your favorite restaurant and decided not to return, even though, unbeknownst to you, the bad meal happened on the regular chef's day off. In a movie the hero wears a shirt with a Nike swoosh that you do not notice because you are absorbed in the plot. The next time you are shopping you buy a hat with the Nike logo.

An interesting tendency is the backfire effect. When it is in play you will increase the intensity of your belief in the face of reasonable evidence to the contrary. A devout Christian farmer in Wyoming found a dinosaur skeleton on his property, which most members of his church took as evidence of the Devil's work and intensified their belief that the world was created five thousand years ago. It is similar to the conservatism bias, a tendency to insufficiently alter one's opinion when presented with credible new evidence. Both of these biases are caused by tamas.

Drawing different conclusions from the same information, depending on how or by whom that information is presented, is a bias called the framing effect. The empathy gap is the tendency to underestimate the influence or strength of feelings, in either oneself or others. A belief bias is the tendency to see oneself as less biased than others. A confirmation bias is the tendency to search for, interpret, focus on and remember information in a way that confirms one's preconceptions.

The Causal Body can produce incorrect associations: you are a neat and tidy person and whenever you enter your wife's messy dressing room you think a negative thought about her. You take the clutter to be a character flaw even though she has a lovely personality and does not see the room as cluttered. You criticize her when she momentarily leaves the keys on the table on her way back to retrieve something from the room before going out to the office. Yet there is no connection whatsoever between keys and her character.

You are walking down the street and pass an acquaintance with a frown on his face who is deeply lost in thought and doesn't see you. You associate the frown with his feelings for you when the frown is related to his thoughts about a fight he just had with his boss. As a result your next meeting with him will be tense and awkward.

Because of its need for coherence, the Causal Body sees causal links where none exist. The previous evening you quarreled with your wife. In the morning she burned the breakfast toast. The toast burned because she was called to the phone. You became angry and created the story that she burned it because she doesn't love you. There is no actual connection between burned toast and anger or love. If there were, burned toast would cause anger in everyone. The anger was in you, and because of past experiences, burned toast provides an opportunity to relieve it.

Without describing them in detail, here are a number of additional functions of the Causal Body, drawn from Kahneman's research. It (1) links a sense of cognitive ease to illusions of truth, pleasant feelings, and reduced vigilance (tamas); (2) neglects ambiguity and suppresses doubt (tamas); (3) is biased to believe and confirm (tamas); (4) exaggerates emotional consistency (rajas); (5) focuses on existing evidence and ignores absent evidence (tamas); (6) thinks more than necessary (rajas); (7) substitutes easier questions for more difficult ones (tamas); (8) overweights low probabilities (tamas); (9) responds more strongly to losses than to gains (tamas); (10) no big picture: frames problems narrowly in isolation from one another (tamas); (12) is prone to exaggerate (rajas) the consistency and coherence of what it experiences; (13) ignores the indeterminacy of results of action (tamas); (14) sees patterns where none exist (rajas) and (15) stereotypes and thinks in categories.

Wikipedia lists 90 decision-making, belief, and behavioral biases, 26 social biases, and 47 memory errors and biases! As you can plainly see, obstacles to successful inquiry abound. Finally—and encouragingly with reference to self-inquiry—there is a bit of good news: the Causal Body *can be programmed by the Subtle Body*, or to use Kahneman's phrase, System 2 can "reset System 1 on the fly." Vedanta's methods for resetting the Causal Body begin with chapter 8.

You can see why we need to include a discussion of the Causal Body when we speak of discriminative wisdom, separating the truth from appearances. Self-inquiry is a deliberate and judicious Subtle Body function. The essence of inquiry is maintaining constant vigilance in the face of the daunting onslaught of proclivities and biases cascading down from the Causal Body. When you become aware of a particular bias, you are well on the way to neutralizing it. But self-inquiry is fighting these tendencies with the logic of the teaching until the Subtle Body no longer projects and denies, or at least until you are conscious of its influence on your mind and no longer act reflexively in response to it. Its purpose is to convert the Subtle Body to a thoughtful and rational, not an impulsive and emotional, instrument. Unexamined biases produce cognitive dissonance, i.e., suffering.

CHAPTER SEVEN

The Ordinary Person

The Individual and the Total

In the last chapter we discussed the macrocosm, Maya and Isvara, the Creator of the field in which awareness appears as objects. This chapter discusses the microcosm, jiva, the individual and its relationship to Isvara.

Definition of Jiva

The jiva is awareness with a Subtle Body. Jiva is an eternal principle, not a specific person. It is actually pure awareness, *Paramatma*.

The eternal Jiva has three levels of knowledge: (1) The jiva who thinks it is a person. This jiva is often called the doer or the human being, the one identified with objects. Humans who don't know about awareness are called *samsaris*, because they are completely caught up in the web of samsara, the apparent reality. (2) The jiva that knows awareness but does not know what it means to *be* awareness and is still controlled by its vasanas. It is sometimes called a self-realized jiva. Vedanta says it has "indirect" self-knowledge. (3) The jiva that knows it **is** awareness, what it means to be awareness, and whose vasanas have been neutralized by self-knowledge. This jiva is said to be a liberated or enlightened jiva (*jivanmukta*). *The Bhagavad Gita* says it is a person with "steady" wisdom who is described in the last chapter. I call it a self-actualized jiva, a jiva with "direct" knowledge. The liberated person, the self-realized person, and the samsari have a common identity as awareness.

The one eternal Jiva manifests sequentially as three individual jivas according to the state that it experiences:

1) As the waking state entity. In this state its mind is totally extroverted. It is hypnotized by duality. It chases and consumes experiences because it is controlled by its vasanas.

2) As the dreamer, the "shining one," awareness with a Subtle Body, *illumining* the dream state. The Subtle Body is turned inward in this state. Dream experience is vasanas manifesting. Both waking and dream state jivas are experiencing entities. In the waking state Jiva identifies with the doer so the doer is generally not seen as an object, although during an epiphany it is often objectified. In the dream state there is also identification, and the doer/ego may also appear as an object illumined by reflected awareness, the Subtle Body. The dreamer may see the waking jiva going about its business, walking, talking, eating, etc. The dreamer is similar in some respects to the waker but enjoys unique powers. These powers are inherent in the dream state and do not belong to the dreamer. The events appearing in the dream are just waking state events that have become vasanas.

3) As the sleeper in the deep sleep state. The sleeper is "almost enlightened" because it experiences the limitlessness and bliss of awareness but lacks knowledge of what it is experiencing owing to the absence of intellect in deep sleep.

The Subtle Body disappears in deep sleep state as does the Microcosmic Causal Body, the personal subconscious which belongs to the jiva and produces the jiva's karma. The deep sleep state is defined as a state with no mental activity. It is the same for everyone because the personal subconscious is dissolved into The Macrocosmic Causal Body when the waking jiva sleeps. Deep sleep is the presence of Tamas alone. Rajas and Sattva are dormant in this state. There is no sense of individuality in this state because the Subtle Body of the individual is not there to be conditioned. The Macrocosmic Causal Body, another name for Isvara, is the deep sleep state.

Although the nature of both the jiva and Isvara is awareness, both the jiva and Isvara are inconstant factors with reference to awareness. Jiva is inconstant because it changes from state to state and because self-knowledge removes the notion that it is a limited entity, revealing its nature to be pure awareness. Isvara in the role of creator is inconstant because logic and scripture—which is just science—informs us that it disappears at the end of the creation cycle; whatever is created will be destroyed. Isvara in the role of creator is eternal with reference to the jiva but not with reference to pure awareness, the constant factor.

The dream state has two aspects: waking dream and sleep dream. It is called the *pratibasika* state, the subjective state of reality. It is jiva's creation, a vasana-induced interpretation of reality. It is not created directly by Isvara although the raw material—the material elements and other jivas—on which jiva's interpretation is based belongs to Isvara. Ultimately both jiva's interpretation and Isvara's material is all Isvara, but to arrive at that understanding—which is tantamount to liberation—the jiva has to understand what belongs to it and what belongs to Isvara so that it can be free of both itself and Isvara.

Knowledge to Prepare the Subtle Body

The Subtle Body is the instrument of experience and knowledge. Awareness is not an experiencer or a knower. It becomes an experiencing, knowing entity when it is associated with the Subtle Body. A jiva does not know who it is because wrong knowledge brought about by Maya clouds and disturbs the Subtle Body to such a degree that right knowledge cannot establish itself. Therefore, it needs to be prepared to receive and assimilate the knowledge.

As we have seen, an individual jiva's fundamental problem is a scattered or a dull mind: extroverting vasanas focus panoramic non-specific awareness into a narrow beam of attention and cause it to hop more or less uncontrollably from one object to another. When our minds are extroverted we gain unsatisfying snippets of experience and diverse bits of knowledge but, lacking an overarching vision to integrate them, peace of mind eludes us.

Stage 1 – Ignorance

And when an individual has lived for long out of the knowledge of the light of awareness, a secondary problem develops: a structural distortion takes place in the Subtle Body which compromises its natural geometry. A healthy Subtle Body is conflict free because the three inner centers, the intellect, ego and the mind are united in the pursuit of a particular goal. But when the pressure of the extroverting vasanas becomes too intense and persists over time, inner conflict develops.

If you find yourself thinking one thing, saying something different and doing something else you can be sure you are out of *yoga,* union. You are not "together," to use a common expression. If you know something is wrong but you do it anyway, you are out of yoga. In a healthy Subtle Body, the intellect rules the roost. It stands apart, offers sage counsel to the doer and refuses to identify with unhealthy emotions. If it plays handmaiden to the ego or the emotions and provides them with clever rationalizations and justifications for adharmic behavior, it means the Subtle Body is out of yoga. Or if, believing that emotions are the problem, the intellect over-analyzes everything to such a point that it becomes paralyzed concerning action and loses itself, wandering in exhausting layers of mental abstraction, the Subtle Body is unhealthy. If you believe that feelings are more valuable than ideas and find yourself longing for love or more "meaningful" and "moving" experiences, your Subtle Body is unhealthy. If you act impulsively without concern for your feelings or the feelings of others, the Subtle Body is out of balance. If you stubbornly refuse to accept your lot, it means your Subtle Body needs work. If the war between your spiritual side and your material side is keeping you up at night you need yoga. And finally, if you are always trying to get a feeling of "connection" with people or your work, or anything else for that matter, it means you are out of yoga. Yoga yokes the three centers to the self.

Vedanta doesn't cook up a lot of fancy psychological terms for dysfunctional behavior and give you a nice complex to add to your problems. Nor do we send you off with a pocketful of pills to set you right. We proscribe yoga. Mind you, yoga is not for seriously disturbed individuals, schizophrenics, manic depressives and their ilk. Seeking is a more or less benign neurosis and yoga works well to cure it.

Conventional psychology pokes around in the colon of the past looking for clues to your bad feelings. Presumably, if you can discover the cause, it will cure them. But we say that negative emotions stem from a single cause: you are not getting what you want. The logic behind this statement is obvious: when you are getting what you want you feel good and you stop seeking. We do not chase objects when we feel good. We enjoy what we have. Please remember, "objects" means people, situations, feelings, thoughts—literally everything other than you.

I am going to take a small detour from the tradition at this point because there is one non-traditional idea that makes a bit of sense and helps to understand the subjective "self," the Subtle Body. When I say non-traditional I mean that it is not mentioned in the source texts. Actually it was cooked up in the last one hundred years and found its way into the Vedanta world but I will let it stand for now.

If the three inner centers, the mind (emotions and feelings), the intellect and the ego are out of yoga it stands to reason that there would be a dedicated yoga for each center. Therefore some say that devotional yoga corrects emotional problems by converting emotions into devotion for God, knowledge yoga corrects thinking problems by teaching the intellect how to discriminate between the self and the objects appearing in it and karma yoga takes care of the ego, the doer, by revealing the nature of action and converting the individual from a subjective to an objective view of life.

However, the texts only mention two yogas, or paths: action (experience) and knowledge. The topic of devotion is covered extensively but it is never considered to be a unique path because devotion is common to every willful endeavor and because all the rituals, including the mental rituals that evoke devotion, fall under the topic of karma.

In any case, the base yoga, the yoga without which no other yoga is worth a hill of beans, is karma yoga. It takes care of your bad feelings by purifying vasanas that extrovert the mind and cause it to pursue objects. Good feelings are not a problem for self-inquiry unless they are thought to belong to objects.

Karma yoga works on the ego. When an unenlightened person says "I," she means the ego, the doer. The doer is playing against a stacked deck. It thinks it is inadequate, incomplete, limited and separate from the objects that present themselves to it and it seeks to complete itself by obtaining said objects. When it gets what it wants it feels adequate and complete. This much we know. Its pursuit of objects is in terms of subtle and gross actions. Since *karma* means anything that moves or changes, action includes thoughts and feelings too.

THE DOER-ENJOYER

The doer's basic psychology is laughably simple: it does what it does to enjoy the result. When the desired object is obtained, the doer switches to enjoyer mode until the enjoyment wears off—as it does—whereupon it shifts back into doer mode and pursues other results that it hopes will give it pleasure and restore its sense of satisfaction. The doer, irrespective of the age of the body, is an eternal child. It wants what it wants when it wants it the way it wants it, or it gets upset. Depending on its perceived successes and failures it is either an eternal optimist or a grumpy pessimist. It does not know that there are no bad outcomes.

In the best of all possible worlds the doer's approach to life would not be unworkable but unfortunately samsara is not the best of all possible worlds. Even an infant, whose situation for enjoyment is more or less ideal insofar as loving parents constantly pander to his every need, often in an attempt to satisfy his own sense of incompleteness, learns very quickly that the world does not produce the object of his desires on demand. His reactions set the stage for predictable emotional patterns that dog him throughout his adult life.

Vedanta psychology depersonalizes suffering. Let's not pretend that any of us are unique psychologically. It is impossible to be unique because of the way Maya structures reality. Maya is lazy and very conservative. It does not invent a special psychology for every human. One size fits all; one Gross, Subtle and Causal Body functions the same way in everyone. Our psychology works for anyone because it applies to everyone. Getting the ego to accept this fact is another story altogether, owing to its sense of specialness. We don't say you aren't unique. It is true that no two snowflakes are alike, but they are all just snowflakes. Uniqueness gets you nowhere. It means nothing. It is pure vanity. We say you are snow.

The ego is little more than its desires and fears. Nothing is particularly wrong with it and (apparently) nothing can be done about it. Desire is a bad feeling. It is a statement of lack. Forget the romantic view. There is nothing romantic about wanting. It is the most boring and commonplace of emotions. Desire is suffering. The Buddha's whole teaching started with this fact.

Stage 2 – Desire and Fear

Desire is unconscious. You don't wake up in the morning and think "I should want something." You wake up wanting something. You plot your actions—your day—according to what you want or what you want to avoid. Perhaps you don't plot at all. Perhaps you are just mindlessly impelled to act. Desire is related to what you value. You desire what you value.

Desire and fear are the same thing. They are ignorance in action. My wife calls them the "terrible twins." I call them "incestuous bedfellows." They are always wrapped in a warm embrace. When I fear something, I want to avoid it. When I desire something, I fear I won't get it. For instance, the fear of dying is the desire to live. Desire is a single current of energy that is with us always. Seen from one end it is positive and from the other, negative. Fear is a negative desire and desire a positive fear. It only remains to be seen how to deal with it. As one of our premier texts says, "It is an intractable foe" although it need not be. Karma yoga is how we deal with it.

The desire-ridden ego faces many inconvenient truths, two of which stand out. In the first place, sadly it does not realize that it can remove the desire without having to foray into the dharma field to obtain the object meant to remove it. If you have doubt about the desirability of desire, Vedanta calls your attention to the fact that *an object is desirable precisely because it removes the desire for it, not for its own sake.* Second, it is regrettable that the dharma field, which is meant to supply the desired objects, is not terribly concerned with whether or not Mr. Ego gets what it wants when it wants it the way it wants it. In other words it is not a doting parent. It is quite fickle. It can fulfill your desire, ignore it or give you a good whack.

In the fullness of time it more or less gives me what I want if I act appropriately—or not—but the "fullness of time" and "more or less" are not concepts that a needy, wanting ego particularly appreciates. I want it and I want it now!

This situation sets the stage for a dysfunctional personality. An important fact about desire, which everyone should know but which many are loath to consider, is: desire alone is not enough to produce the object you want. Yes, it sometimes seems as if the wanting manifested the object, but it didn't, except indirectly insofar as it motivates you to do the appropriate action. Out of desire, actions are offered into the dharma field and then forgotten as they wend their way through it, interacting with the various objects—people mostly—obtaining in it. When the field produces a result, it seems as if you somehow have a powerful, magical connection with the field, but you don't. You have a logical, not a magical, connection.

Sad to say, the field is interested in you only to the extent that your actions contribute to or contravene the aggregate desire of the field itself. And what is that desire? It is to maintain the integrity of the field. Magical thinking is a huge impediment to self-knowledge and the spiritual world is rife with it. It is a caused by tamas—ignorance—and manifests as laziness. It is a quasi-criminal impulse, an attempt to avoid hard work by beating the system. It is a fantasy cooked up by an ego that has somehow convinced itself that it is special and entitled.

In any case, for karma yoga to work the ego needs to understand that the principle the field uses to deliver results is not the gratuitous desires of individuals for specific results but the needs of the total. If one's actions contribute to the needs of the total, action will generate a good result, and if they conflict with the ever changing needs of the field, it will deliver unwanted results or no results at all. Constant vigilance is required for success because the needs of the field are constantly changing. Failure to take the needs of others into account is a sure recipe for suffering. The essence of karma yoga is consideration for the needs of the field, meaning your physical and psychological environment.

One of the symptoms of excess desire is impulsiveness. Because complexity and uncertainty are the nature of the dharma field, a healthy Subtle Body is restrained and deliberate with respect to action. But when there is excess desire owing to an acute sense of insecurity, one often forays into the day completely unprepared for the very situations that one needs to resolve. You discover that you forgot your credit card when you get to the supermarket or two photos when you make an application for a passport. You were so eager to tick that item off your endless to-do list, a list that never shrinks no matter how fast you dispatch the chores that populate it, that you burst out the door unprepared.

Another symptom is an excessively refined sense of obligation. Yes, it is important to discharge your duties in a timely and appropriate fashion but if you find yourself saying that you "have to" or are "supposed to" do things that are not in any way required for the basic maintenance of life, you need karma yoga. This symptom is extremely common in so-called "developed" societies, where luxuries have become necessities. You may feel you "need" hard drives to back up your backup hard drives because you feel obligated not to lose a single stupid video clip, one you will never watch again. Or you can never throw away even broken and useless objects—waste not, want not! Your cabinets, closets and drawers are so stuffed with the flotsam and jetsam of the consumer society that you can't move in your own house. You can't stick with your list when you get to the supermarket; the impulse items cunningly displayed at every turn literally jump into your shopping cart. You think "Life's a bitch. I need to treat myself; I'm worth it." Or you don't even think, your hand just grabs an attractive package. If you feel bad because you "could have" gotten an extra t-shirt had you just stopped at the closeout sale on the way home from work when you already have thirty shirts, know that you need yoga. Obligation is just a fancy, socially acceptable word used by the insecure to dress up desire.

Stage 3 – Anxiety and Control

Anxiety is another form of desire and the constant companion of Mr. Ego for a simple reason: the results of its actions are not up to it. Why is the ego subject to anxiety? Because desire is unnatural. If something is natural it is welcome to stay. But something that is unnatural is always an unwelcome guest. This is why we know that bliss is the nature of the self. If bliss was unnatural you would immediately try to rid yourself of it when you start feeling good. You don't. You cling to it tooth and nail. But when suffering comes—even the pettiest irritation—you immediately try to get rid of it. Happiness is natural. Suffering is unnatural. If you are suffering, you don't know something important about yourself.

In any case I am anxious because the longer the field waits to give me what I want, the more I suffer. If I feel insecure and want my husband to tell me that he loves me, I am afflicted with anxiety. If the bills are mounting and my paycheck doesn't come for another month, I am afflicted with anxiety. If I don't care whether the bills are paid I will not have anxiety on that account. People can even become anxious over the idea that they are anxious! How can I get enlightened if I am anxious? When is my enlightenment going to happen?

One of the most obvious symptoms of this stage of the disease of ignorance is the issue of control. Anxiety breeds a need to control outcomes. In fact all negative emotions unconsciously tend to be manipulative, none as obviously as anger. Nobody likes conflict. Fear and anger are particular dominating energies that radiate far beyond the confines of the physical body. People in close proximity to an angry person, particularly those who are easy going or who have low self-esteem, will tend to accede to the demands of said person simply to avoid unpleasantness. To find oneself in a relationship with a fearful, angry person is to tread in a minefield. One small mistake and the whole field explodes with anger. Once an undeveloped and unloved individual sees the benefit of these emotions, she may take advantage of them and become consciously manipulative. Conscious manipulation of others is a sign that the natural structure of the Subtle Body has become seriously distorted.

Stage 4 – Anger

The fourth stage, anger, proceeds logically from the third. You will be pleased to know that you can stop blaming Mom and Pop, the church and the state, the media, or your big nose, etc. for your anger. The cause is very simple: the dharma field is not giving you what you want. When desire is obstructed, it turns to anger. It does not really require a big event—your husband runs off with his secretary—to trigger it; it can be something very simple—a driver who is slow to respond to a green light, or just the idea that you are not going to get what you want. Anger is very destructive, although it has its upsides too. In the right situations it can actually help you achieve what you want, although using anger in this way is not advisable owing to the long term effects on your health; the molecules of this emotion wreak havoc with the body. Not to mention what it does to your relationships with other conscious beings.

You will probably not have failed to notice that everything in life comes through others. Therefore it pays to develop loving positive relationships, at least with the people to whom we are beholden. But anger definitely needs to be managed. If it is not managed properly it will destroy you. Karma yoga is a stress and anger management tool.

Anger is not socially acceptable for obvious reasons: it is a violation of dharma, which is based on the mutual expectation of individuals. You don't want to deal with angry people and people don't want to deal with your anger. Anger is a violation of life's most fundamental dharma, non-injury. You may define violence in physical terms—fair enough—but anger is injurious both to others and to yourself. Non-injury as defined by Vedanta is in terms of "thought, word and deed." So imagining that you are somehow spiritual because you don't eat meat or beat your children, while showing anger to others—or even thinking angry thoughts—is definitely hypocritical. I find it extremely peculiar that angry people will behave with consideration toward strangers with whom they have no personal connection and yet dump their anger on family and friends with whom they have to relate on a daily basis.

DENIAL

Anger is not socially acceptable and it is not acceptable to Mr. Ego because it contradicts its own good opinion of itself. So what do you do with it? You either dump it on others, which doesn't work well, or you suppress it, which does. Temporarily. When an uncomfortable emotion is suppressed it becomes part of your "shadow," to use a term that has been in vogue since the days of Jung. In our language it retreats to the Causal Body, the Subconscious. The Unconscious—the macrocosmic vasanas—belongs to Isvara, the Total Mind. But the Subconscious is your own personal Causal Body, a little corner of Isvara's Causal Body—a *subset* is perhaps a reasonable word—where your personal karma is stored. Isvara is a wonder indeed! It is amazing because it keeps track of your actions and tailors the results of your actions to you, never confusing your karma with the karma of the other eight billion other individuals whose karma it manages. *Shadow* is a good word because shadows conceal, just as repression conceals your anger from you. It is "sub" conscious, meaning not known. Anger is rajas and repression is rajas but tamas is behind them both. Repression is rajas because it takes energy to keep the anger away from your life so it doesn't mess things up. Tamas is denial. Because you do not think of yourself as an angry person, you have to hide this fact from yourself.

What a mess we have already, only four steps into the convoluted psychology of the ego. Though the Causal Body "contains" good and bad vasanas, it is not a container in the usual sense of the word. If you have a jar you can stick valuables in it and bury it in the earth and nothing will come out until you dig it up and unscrew the lid. But the unconscious is not this kind of container. It is porous; what goes in comes back out. You can't see how it works—that is why I am describing it—but another sad fact is that nothing about you is hidden from the awareness or from the world because others can easily see your anger, but it is hidden from the Subtle Body, "you," the person you think you are, owing to tamas, denial.

But your subconscious is also a container in the classic sense because negative emotions accumulate. Every time you express one—believing that you are working it "out"—it works right back "in." You reinforce the vasana itself. So your tendency to get angry remains, even increases.

PROJECTION

How do you hide the fact that you are a dysfunctional person? Tamas helps you conceal it; then it teams up with rajas. Rajas projects. So you blame something or someone. It really doesn't matter who or what. What matters is that you believe that something other than you caused you to be the way you are so you can avoid taking responsibility for it. This is where the victim enters the drama, stage left. See how far away from our self we have journeyed, and we are still midway through the tragedy written by the greatest poet of all times: Madame Ignorance. Master Flaming Mouth has now become Mr. Poor Me, a victim of whatever. And it is little wonder that at every stage of this tragicomedy our self-esteem takes another hit.

When we talk about anger we are talking about the structural Subtle Body distortion that produces more or less nonstop existential suffering. Small occasional eruptions of anger in diverse circumstances are understandable and do not disqualify an individual for inquiry. But if a predictable set of circumstances produces an urgent need to have even small things a certain way, instead of taking care of the anger with karma yoga, you have a problem. Karma yoga—which we have yet to unfold—does not offer specific anger management techniques. It is a global approach, as we shall see in the next chapter.

Another symptom of this stage is extreme busyness, a hallmark of modern life. It goes undetected as a psychological problem because society considers it a virtue. Alcohol, drugs, sweets and fat-laden food are medications of choice when rajas is predominant. Irritability, insomnia and self-obsessed righteousness around the topic of action are symptoms of excess rajas. If you believe that things should be done a certain way and that the way that you do them is the only way, know for certain that your Subtle Body is firmly dominated by rajas. If you think none of this applies to you, think twice, *rajas* is always accompanied by an equal measure of tamas, denial.

COMPARISON – MATSARYA

As we have indicated when consciousness appeared in the form of (apparently) conscious beings and those beings became more complex, it eventually evolved the intellect, permitting them to make choices. It is wise to carefully consider all alternatives before one acts. But when the Subtle Body is conflicted, its discriminative function becomes perverted and it is delivered squarely into the hands of rajas (agitation and stress) and tamas, (inadvertence and sloth), further miring it in duality. Most animals evolve rudimentary pecking orders based on power. In these systems physical strength and aggressiveness determine one's place in the group. But humans have elevated the concept of status to a fine art.

When I was young I lived in the Philippines for a short time. I was color blind and thought Filipinos were too but before long I realized that one of the most important parameters for distinguishing one person from another was skin color. I soon came to realize that Filipinos—and later every group on the planet—calculated skin color in microtones. If you find your house in disarray for weeks because during a remodel you cannot determine what shade of peach you want for the dining room walls or you have to spend thirty minutes in the supermarket aisle to determine which of the eighty types of shampoo would best suit your hair, know that your Subtle Body needs a bit of yoga. If you find yourself evaluating your daily progress toward a fitness goal or a financial goal or a spiritual goal—am I pure and holy yet?—know that your Subtle Body needs a bit of yoga.

Comparison is a useful function but it can easily morph into less benign forms. Envy, a particularly dualistic and rudimentary emotion, signifies insecurity and low self-esteem. It is "I want what you have." A less honest, hidden and particularly insidious form of dualistic thinking is "I want to be like you." As this tendency ripens and produces more dysfunctional behavior it steps out into the open, becomes obviously rajasic and changes into a competitive spirit—"I want to beat you." And as it matures and enters its final stage it becomes totally tamasic—"I want to destroy you."

Stage 5 – Delusion

Because it requires a lot of energy, anger is difficult to maintain, although once you get conditioned to it, you feel empty without it. It is bad energy, no doubt, but it is better than no energy. When anger collapses it may feel as if you have suddenly lost your best friend. This means that the rajasic response has become a binding vasana. There is no better example of this psychological fact than bipolar disorder. Bipolar syndrome is rajas and tamas on steroids. I like the old term, manic depression, better. It is not a euphemism. Mania is rajas and depression is tamas. They always go together. To understand it one need look no further than the tiredness that comes after hard work. The mind and body can handle only so much stress—rajas is stress. Then tamas prevails. A manic person can remain active for weeks on end with virtually no sleep but when rajas has run its course he will stay in bed in a dark room day and night for equally long periods. Manic depression is a good example of an extreme structural distortion in the Subtle Body. It cannot be treated with karma yoga.

A successful person is a discriminating person, one who can make rational choices based on a clear knowledge of his or values as they relate to the world around, the dharma field. To discriminate effectively the mind needs to be predominately sattvic. You will recall that Maya has three powers: veiling, projecting and revealing. Sattva is the revealing power, the energy of knowledge. It can record experience as it is, evaluate it accurately, and make decisions that further the ego's agenda. But this is not possible in stage five.

When rajas has run its course, tamas takes over. Tamas is a veiling, concealing energy. It obscures the light of awareness as it reflects on the Subtle Body. It is responsible for confusion and delusion. Again we are not talking about the occasional dullness that comes throughout the day, a light cloud passing over the mind that causes your energy to temporarily flag. We are talking about a persistently sluggish apathetic feeling, characterized by an inability to make decisions and to do what is required on an everyday level. Suicidal thoughts appear when the Subtle Body is in the grip of structural tamas. When a jiva is in this state—keeping in mind the fact that the self is never in any state—you are near the end of a meaningful life. Usually, by this time you are in the hands of the medical profession or lying on a flattened cardboard box under the freeway with a needle in your arm. And while medicine may find some kind of legal chemical that excites the brain enough to irritate you to action and induce a goofy smile, you could be fairly said to have arrived at the state of the living dead. Your intellect is completely in the hands of tamas. When this happens, with or without meds, you lose your discrimination, enter into a state of advanced victimhood, and totally lose your self-esteem. The verse in one of our texts that chronicles this slippery slide to ruin concludes with the comment "...and the soul perishes." This state is commonly referred to as the dark night of the soul and usually signifies the beginning of inquiry.

Some symptoms of this state are helplessness, boredom, apathy, mistrust, suspicion, rebelliousness, defensiveness and vanity, a feeling that no matter what you do, nothing works. It is probably not necessary to discuss each in detail but know that you have more or less arrived at the end of your tether when a feeling of stuckness more or less pervades your life. Your habits chain you and your mind becomes rigid and stubborn. You have no confidence to deal with change but dig in your heels at every opportunity and resist common sense logic. If a habit that formerly brought pleasure starts to bring pain, and you stubbornly refuse to drop it and try something else, even if it is clear that the habit is detrimental, you have hit bottom. If you blithely ignore the messages of change that life sends and react negatively to anything perceived as a threat to your world view, you are ready for karma yoga. It is the way you manage and purify these emotions.

CHAPTER EIGHT

Karma Yoga

A Short Summary

If Vedanta is going to work for you, you need to change the way you think. And while the light may go on when you hear these teachings, a single exposure to them will not change your thinking patterns. The teaching should become your life. It should be with you every minute of the day. So you need to completely understand the big picture logic. Then, when you get stuck, you can bring up the road map and work out where you are and where you need to be.

We began with the statement that the joy we seek in objects actually belongs to the self and that seeking happiness in objects is a zero-sum game. The teaching about Maya reveals the psychology that causes us to seek happiness in objects. Objects, as you will recall, are anything other than the self. Maya makes the full and complete self think it is incomplete and dupes it into thinking that objects can fulfill it. This error constitutes the bedrock logic of samsara. If you can't see it, you are not ready for Vedanta and you are welcome to continue to pursue objects. If you keep chasing objects this logic will become clear as samsara grinds you down and forces you to accept it. The only way to win in samsara is to get out of it altogether. Every victory in the pursuit of objects is basically a defeat because it postpones the inevitable, the realization that the world is a dream. That it is a dream is very difficult to realize because Maya, like a wide-screen hi-definition TV, constantly projects beautiful sexy images that seem ever so real, exciting your fantasies. You can taste them, touch them, and smell them. So off you go, chasing experiences and accumulating vasanas. And your attention, which is just panoramic awareness reduced to a tiny pencil-like ray by Maya, becomes extroverted, riveted on objects. It is hard to miss the irony; you, the self, looking for yourself in objects, which have no self nature. What could be more absurd?

I am sorry to go on at length about this sad fact but we need to rub your spiritual nose in it because the basic truth of the apparent reality is completely counterintuitive. It "feels" wrong. Not much intellectual power is required to understand that life is just an unconscious process of stimulus and response. On its most basic level it is just you paying attention to the world's reactions to your reactions to the world. We call going from desire to action and action to desire *samsara chakra*. It is like being caught in quicksand—the more you struggle to free yourself, the deeper you sink in. One meaning of samsara is "whirlpool." When you get caught in it, you can't wiggle out. In fact the more you move the more surely you are implicated. The momentum of your past actions keeps you tied to this chakra, this wheel. When it goes up, you go up and when it goes down, you go down. You are only concerned with getting what you want and avoiding what you don't. It happened to me. I was the living dead, a complete robot, a puppet on the string of my fears and desires, mindlessly hopping up and down.

Before we show you how to get out of the whirlpool and get the self into your life, we need to add one more bit of unpleasant news. In the last chapter we mentioned that as the vasanas accumulate over time, a structural distortion takes place in the Subtle Body. In a healthy integrated person the three centers are yoked together and cooperate with each other to help the jiva achieve its goals. But when the vasana load is too heavy, the Subtle Body becomes distorted, their connection is broken, and inner conflict develops.

To get the self into the equation we need yoga. We need to take our conditioning into account because it keeps us out of contact with the self. I cannot understand how the modern teachers can tell you that you are not a doer and that there is no work to be done. Of course it is good for business because the ego wants to hear this message, but it is foolish advice. You are not happy for a reason, and the reason is that your conditioning keeps you tied to the world of objects. So you need to practice yoga.

How does yoga work? It removes the vasanas that extrovert the mind and develops vasanas that turn the mind toward the self so that inquiry can bear fruit.

Karma Yoga – No Bad Outcomes

If you know who you are, you will automatically act with the karma yoga spirit because you will be clear about what action and its results can and cannot do for you. So karma yoga is intended for people with spiritual vasanas who know that they are awareness but do not have full confidence in the knowledge. The lack of confidence is due to the veiling and projecting gunas, rajas and tamas, which cloud and disturb the mind to such a degree that it cannot enjoy the freedom that hard and fast self-knowledge confers.

Although it is common sense to a sensitive person, the source of this idea is the *Bhagavad Gita,* one of the three pillars of Vedanta. In the *Gita,* an extroverted person abandons his duty in the middle of a crisis and is taught self-knowledge on life's battlefield by his friend, an enlightened person. His mind is too agitated to permit him to assimilate the knowledge so he is encouraged to practice karma yoga.

Without karma yoga, self-knowledge will not stick. You may very well have non-dual epiphanies and feel that you are enlightened but without karma yoga the feeling will eventually be compromised and you will seek once more to regain your "enlightenment," such as it was.

You should also know that karma yoga will give you a happy life *whether or not you are seeking liberation.* Some people who are unconsciously in harmony with the spirit of the creation evolve karma yoga and practice it without knowing what it is. Before I unfold this teaching we must debunk another spiritual myth. Karma yoga is not selfless service. There is only one self and, in so far as it is doing anything, it is serving itself. As karma yoga is presented to Westerners familiar with the spiritual culture of India, it is little more than a clever ruse by gurus and their organizations to get free labor from unsuspecting spiritual neophytes.

If we are going to reduce our vasana load and turn the mind toward the self we need the karma yoga spirit. It is not a spirit you can successfully assume without understanding the logic behind it.

Karma yoga works on the ego, the doer. The ego is that part of the Subtle Body that acts to enjoy the results. It is also the part that owns action and its results. The words "I do, I enjoy, this is mine" belong to the doer. For someone seeking freedom these ideas are obstacles because they build unhelpful vasanas and obstruct knowledge.

People love to blame their childhood and their circumstances in life for their uncomfortable feelings. It is good business for the psychologists. My wife calls it woundology. I suppose the expectation is that if they understand what happened and what it did to them, they might somehow be relieved of the bad feelings. But Vedanta says that you need not look that far afield for the source of your emotional problems. The explanation, as we said in the last chapter, is very simple: *you are not getting what you want.* You do what you do expecting the result to make you feel good. When you don't get the result you want, you feel some form of anger (rajas) or disappointment that can lead to depression (tamas). All the uncomfortable emotions are generated from rajas and tamas. It is very difficult to argue with this logic because when you are getting what you want you feel great. Getting what it wants all the time is the doer's idea of happiness.

We do not say that you should or should not get what you want. You do what you do *to* get what you want. There is a strange notion in the spiritual world—popularized by the Buddha's teaching that desire is the cause of suffering—that you shouldn't want anything. But it is impossible to not want anything. It is not up to you. You come to earth full of desire and desire motivates you from morning until night, usually till the day you die. A human being is little more than what he wants. So we are all for you getting what you want. All we are saying is that getting what you want is not straightforward.

Karma Yoga, the Stress Buster

Anxiety about the results of one's actions is a fancy term for stress. If you ask people why they meditate, most will say "to remove stress." Meditation *does* remove stress but it does not remove the cause of stress. This is why people meditate unsuccessfully for many years. And it is the reason so many meditators abandon meditation in favor of some other approach. Karma yoga removes the cause of stress by exhausting the fears and desires that produce stress.

Results Not Up To You

Unfortunately, as we said before and never tire of saying, there is one small problem when you want what you want: the results of your actions are not up to you.

This is unwelcome information. Although it never goes away, about every twenty years spiritual materialism becomes an obsession in the spiritual world in the form of a teaching like The Secret. The sole purpose of this kind of teaching is to make the ego feel like there is hope. That, having been a failure in the world, it can take refuge in the fantasy that there is a special way, a secret technique, that permits it to control the results of its actions and beat the dharma field at its own game. It is appealing because most spiritual people—everyone, in fact—are lazy and do not like the idea of being controlled by anything. When you see through this idea you are actually ready to listen to reason.

If the results of your actions were up to you, you would have everything you want. So what are the results up to? The law of karma and the dharma field.

In the sixth chapter we presented a rudimentary outline of the dharma field. I call it the "mandala of existence." It is a vast field. It is comprised of all the material elements, the Gross Bodies and the forces and laws that control them. It includes the Subtle Bodies and all the forces and laws that control the psychic, psychological and moral aspects of the field, the macrocosmic mind. And finally, it is ultimately controlled by the Causal Body and the Law of Karma.

And who am I? I think I am a very minute flyspeck of limited consciousness in this vast complex ocean of dream consciousness. As part of the field I seem to generate actions, tiny ripples on the surface of life. My actions do not fly off to some other universe to fructify there. They remain in the field. The field behaves as if it is conscious because is it situated in consciousness, just as the snake in our earlier example is situated in the rope and seems to be alive when it is perceived in a certain context. So the field responds. It produces karma. Karma means that something happens. And the karma returns to the doer of the action, not always in obvious ways. Or, as they say, "What goes around comes around." It is expressed differently in the Bible: "As you sow, so shall you reap." Everyone knows about karma but almost nobody understands it.

To refresh your memory, the big question is: on the basis of what does the field return my action to me? You cannot say that the field does not return action, because my life is nothing but the happenings that the field of life brings to me. The field must be intelligent in some way because I don't get actions that belong to you. If you kill your spouse the police eventually show up at your door, not mine. If you drink alcohol I don't get cirrhosis of the liver. But what principle determines the result? *The field determines the result based on the needs of the field.*

Ignore the Dharma Field at Your Peril

This is a very difficult fact for the ego to accept because it only cares about the tiny part of the field that directly impacts on it. Some individuals are so ego-centric they can't even get along with their families much less their neighbors, employers, etc. This is very short-sighted because everything that comes to us comes from others. Even those who do look after their immediate circle of others still cannot control what happens because what happens to the people around an individual is conditioned by the people with whom she is connected, and that wider circle is affected by an even wider circle until the circle opens up to include everything. That "everything" is Isvara. From its point of view, no object in the field is more or less important than any other. This is bad news for me if I want something that does not serve the needs of the total.

Everyone knows this in one way or another. The religious people call it God. They say that everything is the grace of God. We more or less agree, but as mentioned, we *do* invest God with human and divine qualities and set It up outside the dharma field. The field itself is God. We don't say that only the good karma comes from God, we throw in the bad karma as well because we know that reality is non-dual. There are actually not two separate principles operating in the dharma field, although Maya makes it seem as if there are.

The Secret of Action

I understand that in terms of my happiness the field is all powerful and that dependence on it causes suffering. I also know that I cannot just walk away from it. The desire that is in me demands action and action causes desire. So even if I run off to a cave in India I have not solved my problem. My vasanas and my disturbed mind go with me.

What I don't understand is why action causes vasanas. The vasanas are caused by the attitude in play when I act. What is the attitude? The attitude is "I want. I don't want." In short, fear and desire motivate me. Although it is not my experience, it stands to reason that a different attitude may not produce the vasanas that tie me to action and its results. Is there such an attitude and what would it be?

Adults are not generally good examples, but children at play give us a hint. I was at the beach recently watching a group of children building a sand castle.

They worked happily for about an hour with their little buckets and shovels and then as soon as it was finished, they happily destroyed it and ran off into the surf for a swim. A few years back I was in London at the National Museum and observed a group of Tibetan monks making a large intricate mandala out of colored sand. Evidently they had been working on it for weeks and were, in a few days, about to blow it all away. What were they thinking? They were obviously uninterested in enjoying the mandala once it was finished. In both cases no binding vasana is created by such an action. What children understand intuitively and monks understand consciously is that action done in a certain spirit is liberating, not binding. What is that spirit?

Without too much introspection you have to admit that you do not want to die. People love life. One of my wife's relatives who had a particular type of cancer endured three chemotherapies and radiations before he succumbed. We want to live because life is beautiful. It is a great joy and privilege to be here, to be alive. Even a few moments in the embrace of the beauty of life and love is enough to cause us to endure great miseries.

Again, it does not take a genius to figure out that you did not give yourself life. You did not create the world around you. You did not create your body or your mind, much less do you perform the myriad unseen tasks that keep you alive. If you are honest you will have to admit that you created nothing. You appeared here one fine day and everything was set up, tailor made for your enjoyment. Who or what did this? Isvara, God, the dharma field, did. There is no other explanation.

Dharma Is Appropriate Response

When someone gives you a gift, what is the appropriate response? If you are cultured, you will say "Thank you," not merely to be polite but because you really do feel grateful. The body and mind can act only because they are blessed with the gift of life, and with them you can seek success here. It does not matter what you do. Billions of hands and feet are required by consciousness to maintain this amazing dream. They all belong to consciousness and are on loan to you. You are here for a reason and you have been given the powers necessary to do your dharma, your duty. You are required to respond. It is not *what* you do. Only *that* you do, that you *can* do, matters. How generous, how magnanimous is God!

How lucky I am to be here, to be alive! Each and every action that is done in this spirit, backed by this understanding, does not produce a vasana. So it is quite possible to de-condition yourself if you act in this spirit. It is also possible to recondition yourself, about which more will be said as we go.

If you study enlightened people you will find that they create no karma and are non-attached to objects. They don't create binding vasanas because, being whole and complete, being one with consciousness—all life—they know that they don't need objects to be happy. They are satisfied with the self alone and they are satisfied with whatever objects they have or don't have. They act, no doubt. Nobody is free not to act. But they act from fullness—from happiness— not for happiness from incompleteness.

That I am not enlightened does not mean that I cannot become reasonably free of karma and vasanas. No big enlightenment experience need happen to destroy all my desires. Desire survives all enlightenment experiences. Even if an enlightenment experience destroys the desire for everyday objects, it creates a binding desire on the spot because it is so wonderful that when it ends—as they all do because all experience is in samsara—you want it back immediately. Non-dual experiences can be dangerous drugs.

To rid myself of binding vasanas all that is required is a change in the attitude motivating my actions. Karma yoga is an attitude that you take with respect to action and its results that burns vasanas. It does not create them, except the vasana for karma yoga, which will eat itself when self-knowledge arises in the mind prepared by karma yoga. This teaching is designed to create the understanding that will motivate you to practice karma yoga, assuming that you want liberation. Saying "all that is required" makes it sound as if karma yoga were as easy as falling off a log. It is not easy if the idea that the joy I seek is in objects has become a binding vasana itself. So to establish karma yoga there is an immediate resistance from none other than the very person karma yoga is intended to liberate, Mr. or Ms. Ego.

Intelligent Ignorance

The ego is perhaps the most tamasic of the three inner centers. It resists change tooth and nail. It cannot be forced to do karma yoga. Karma yoga is like putting yourself on a diet. It requires eternal vigilance. When you go on a diet, your will power may be strong and you may very well be clear about your goal, but the fat person inside is not your friend. It will do everything it can to sabotage your efforts. For instance, you see a tasty pastry in the display case at the coffee shop as you sip your coffee. You know very well that it is not part of your weight loss program. You can tell the fat person that he cannot have it, but the fat person is cleverer than you imagine. He will convince the intellect that there are not as many calories in it as you think, that it is made of healthy organic flour and honey, which is so much "better" for you than that nasty toxic white sugar, that you deserve a treat because you have been so "good," etc. And before you know it the gooey sweet pastry will be keeping your coffee cup company. Ignorance is very intelligent. It will have its way.

The way to deal with Mr. Ego is to educate, not eradicate, it. This is why Vedanta, which is a pathless path, is superior to other paths. It does not tell you what to do. It does not tout fanciful escapes. It educates you, leads you out of ignorance. Once the logic is understood it becomes reasonably easy to do what has to be done. Karma yoga is dharma yoga, appropriate response.

Work Is Worship

So far we have explained the logic of karma yoga. But logic is only the beginning. Before we give karma yoga some teeth it is helpful to examine a recent misleading yoga notion. It is natural to think that different yogas are intended for different personality types. This idea was introduced about one hundred years ago by Swami Vivekananda, who could be said to be the father of "New" Vedanta or "Modern" Vedanta, the precursor to Neo-Advaita, the most popular iteration— dare I say corruption—of traditional Vedanta today. This fallacy is called the multi-path confusion and reveals a basic misunderstanding about the nature of the self. It arose about the time of Freud, hence its peculiar psychological bent.

To think that Vedanta and yoga should adapt to the times is a mistake be- cause people are fundamentally no different today from what they ever were: awareness plus three bodies. Vedanta addresses the core person, the universal person, not the conditioned person. Yes we have iPads and enjoy jet travel and live in complex societies but as the poet says, "There is nothing new under the sun." A human being is a human being. To add or subtract from the core logic or twist the teachings to make them fit with the experience of a specific human being or to conform to the times is not helpful.

The multi-path confusion claims that karma yoga is for active types, devotional yoga—popularly known as the path of love—is prescribed for devotional types and knowledge yoga is suggested for intellectual types. This "teaching" is patently absurd because every individual has an ego, emotions and an intellect. So to practice one yoga at the expense of the others only increases the structural distortion of the Subtle Body. All the centers should be harmoniously developed in tandem, yoked behind a single idea: I am whole and complete, ordinary, non-dual, actionless awareness. Additionally, when you understand the nature of reality you cannot distinguish between love, action and knowledge. Unfortunately, people identify with different aspects of the Subtle Body and develop limited identities based on the kind of activities their ignorance causes them to favor.

Karma yoga also is devotional yoga. It is simply love for one's self in the form of the creation. The love you have for life is not self-created. It is not "your" love. It is consciousness, which is love, loving in you and through you as you. In the case of karma yoga, the self, under the spell of Maya, thinks it is a person with love—which is just willing attention—to invest in objects, and because this does not work, the attention it invests in life in the form of action needs to be offered back to the creation in the same spirit in which it was given—to complete the cosmic cycle.

Consecration

Karma yoga is also knowledge yoga because to meaningfully worship life with my actions I need to appreciate the non-duality of reality. The love in me for objects is simply the self loving through me, misdirected toward objects. But is it misdirected? If I understand that reality is non-dual, aren't all the objects appearing in me—my life and everything in it—only me? Therefore, are not all the objects worthy of worship? Worship does not mean supplication. It is appreciative love. I am grateful for what I have been given, my self in the form of the creation, and I offer my actions to the creation with an attitude of gratitude.

Karma yoga unwinds the Subtle Body's grasping fearful orientation. This unconscious stance is there the moment an impulse to act arises and it is present with every thought, feeling and action. It is there when actions fructify, a constant silent companion. To shift a lifelong orientation to its opposite is hard work, a war with the ego. Consecration simply means thinking of the self, reminding yourself of your purpose here, invoking an attitude of gratitude to go with every action and then doing what is required without attachment to the results. When the impulse to act is met directly in this way, it is impossible to perform self-insulting actions or actions harmful to others. We cause injury only when we are unaware of what we do. Nobody can become more conscious because consciousness does not change, but we can become more aware of our limited orientation and the unwanted results it produces.

Aside from the flawed logic on which their views are based, the proponents of experiential enlightenment would benefit greatly from karma yoga. The experience of the reflection of the self in the Subtle Body can be made more or less constant, brighter and intense if rajas and tamas are purified from the Subtle Body by karma yoga. The more one practices karma yoga the purer the mind becomes and the more epiphanies take place in it, intensifying one's faith, assuming they are understood correctly.

A Gift from God

Life is nothing but the fruits of one's actions after they have wended their way through the dharma field. To complete our understanding of the karma yoga attitude we need to take what happens as a gift from God. A nice model for this idea is temple worship. A devotee brings an offering to the temple, hands it to the priest, who offers it to the deity and returns it consecrated. The devotee is free to do with it what he sees fit, usually distributing it to the beggars waiting outside the temple.

Peace of Mind

Taking what happens as a gift is fine as long as what happens is what we want, but what should I do when the dharma field gives me something that I don't want? Should I become angry and reject it? No, I should take it as a gift. Worldly people are happy when they get what they want and unhappy when they don't but karma yogis are happy when they get what they want *and* when they don't, because their goal is peace of mind, not the ephemeral joys that come from objects. How does this work?

The vasanas appear in the Subtle Body as likes and dislikes. Likes and dislikes, attractions and repulsions, fears and desires are the enemies of the karma yogi. Karma yoga is intended to neutralize them because they continually agitate the mind, making it unfit for discriminative inquiry. The dharma field is a university meant to teach us who we are. We do not matriculate until we have learned our lessons. It instructs by delivering the fruits of our actions. As my wife, Sundari, says, "A karma yogi knows that experience is a decaying time capsule meant to deliver knowledge." Results never last but the knowledge hidden in experience leads us to the self. So when something happens, irrespective of whether it is what we want or not, we are meant to welcome it and learn from it. In this way the likes and dislikes are neutralized and the dispassion necessary for inquiry develops.

States of Mind

Recently a friend recommended a "good" movie. But it was very disturbing because it involved senseless violence, even though the good guy—who was a very flawed human being—prevailed in the end. I did not sleep well and the Subtle Body was upset the following day. So far I have presented karma yoga as a response to external events but karma yoga also applies to states of mind. The feelings engendered by the movie were the unwanted results of my action. I could not know how my subconscious would respond to the movie. Should I get angry with myself for taking my friend's advice to watch it and add another layer of suffering to the existing layer? Or should I look at the film and my reaction to it from Isvara's point of view and accept it gladly? I have a choice. Karma yoga is discretion with reference to action and its results. It should be practiced on the good and bad feelings that appear in me as well as the events that trigger those feelings.

The Five Offerings

Karma yoga is not only right attitude; it is right action. Actions can be classified in terms of how well they serve to prepare the mind for inquiry. They are 1) sattvic: those that give maximum spiritual benefit, 2) rajasic: those that are neither beneficial or detrimental and 3) tamasic: those that are harmful and lead one away from the goal.

The third class of actions, adharmic karmas, are not recommended for anyone and are definitely prohibited for a karma yogi. Although they may bring a particular physical or psychological gain to the doer, they harm the animate and inanimate objects in the dharma field and bring the doer down spiritually. They are to be avoided at all costs. The second class of actions are not necessarily adharmic. They do not involve injury, except inadvertently, to oneself or others but are self-centered, compelling the doer to ignore the needs of others. They don't bring spiritual benefit—or very little, perhaps—nor are they necessarily detrimental but they are directed toward material ends.

The first class of actions, *sattvic* karmas, are necessary if karma yoga is going to bear fruit. They are giving karmas, not grabbing karmas. The more you give, the more you grow. You will remember that vasanas are created by a grasping attitude. Without putting too fine a point on it, they are undone when the opposite attitude is in play. Karma yoga involves actions that add value to every situation, offerings that contribute to the wellbeing of the dharma field. These offerings are discussed in chapter 8.

The intention of a karma yogi is to enshrine sattvic karmas at the forefront of her life, to see that rajasic karmas are relegated to subordinate status and to eliminate tamasic karmas. Of course it is impossible to eliminate tamasic actions altogether. Certain unavoidable situations will cause the doer to injure herself or others. She should always strive to do *sattvic* karmas because they bring about maturity and spiritual growth by neutralizing the agitation that is born from the inevitable contact with unholy situations and people.

CHAPTER NINE

DHARMA

Dharma Yoga

Because reality is an apparent duality, it is legitimate to look at the self from two perspectives. The absolute perspective—limitless, non-dual, unconcerned, ordinary awareness—is my "true" or "ultimate" nature, my Dharma with a capital D. Karma yoga is acting in accordance with my svadharma with an eye to realizing my true nature. Yes, it is true that if my knowledge of myself as awareness is not subject to doubt I will not practice karma yoga because all my actions will naturally be in harmony with my true nature. But if my self-knowledge is not firm I need to assume the stance of the self with reference to action and act accordingly. We call this "faking it until you make it." It is not really false to act as if I am the self because I *am* the self. It just "feels" fraudulent. So there is an element of awkwardness when I begin to practice karma yoga. It soon dissipates, however, as this yoga gradually produces an incredible lightness of being.

At the same time I have been blessed or cursed, depending on how you wish to look at it, with a relative nature, meaning that my samskaras give rise to specific tendencies and talents. I have loved books from an early age because I have an undying attraction to knowledge. I remember reading under the covers till three or four a.m. when I was very young to make my parents think I was asleep. I have read thousands of books and write prodigiously. When I was growing up one of my best friends was obsessed with money. Every summer he would pick up coke bottles from the side of the road and redeem them at the corner store for two cents and sell lemonade on the street when it was hot. He kept his money in Folgers coffee cans, which he buried in a canyon next to his house. He died recently and it seems he had accumulated a fortune. He had a business samskara, obviously. Some incline to art, some to science, some to sports, etc. Your predominant samskara is your relative nature, your svadharma.

Your svadharma, unlike Svadharma, is in samsara and is subject to change. So what lifestyle you followed yesterday, you will not necessarily follow tomorrow. If you act out your predominant samskara to Isvara's satisfaction, It will supply you with another svadharma. Some individuals are lucky—or not—in that they want to "be something" when they are only five years old—a musician, for example—and happily stick with it all their lives. But others live several lives and play many roles in one life. Others, it seems, never figure out what they are "supposed" to be doing. If that is the case, consecrate your actions to the dharma field, take what comes with a glad heart and don't worry about who you are on that level and what you are "supposed" to be doing.

In my case I never wanted to "be" anything. Of course it was all ego, but I thought I was wonderful the day I popped out of the womb and did not listen to anyone who had a different opinion. I just wanted to have a lot of money so I could chase women and travel the world. It was very strange because there were no business people in our family, but owing to this vasana, Isvara supplied the samskara necessary to realize my dream—the entrepreneurial archetype—and I made a lot of money. But once I worked it out—or perhaps it is more accurate to say that once it had run its course—I realized the limitation of money and that samskara receded back into the Causal Body and sits there today, more or less ignored. My next limited identity was seeker. I was not a seeker who fell in love with seeking like so many these days. It was more or less imposed by my suffering. But an epiphany activated the seeking samskara—or the seeking samskara activated the epiphany—and I embraced that dharma. When I got to India I realized that it was possible to do spirituality right because an infrastructure was available to serve that archetype. When I became a finder, a new samskara became active and when I worked that one out to Isvara's satisfaction, It supplied another one. Identities, dharmas, samskaras, roles and lifestyles are eternal. They come to the forefront at Isvara's beck and call and recede when they have been done well.

The self is straightforward. It is one thing only. It is simple and ordinary and ever-present. It is not the result of an action. It is always and already accomplished. But karma is not simple. It is "nuanced," to say the least. It is complex because so many factors go into the production of results. To know it is to know the mind of God. It is a field of laws that are not published in the newspapers or posted on the street corners. So when I act I need to take the field into account. But when I act, it is absolutely necessary to take my svadharma into account because if I don't act in harmony with it, I will reap conflict.

Who am I on the relative level? What kind of a doer am I? Isvara produces roles, dharmas, according to the nature of the dharma field at any given time. A long time ago you were probably a hunter or a gatherer because Isvara did not need money managers or real estate agents or scientists. All you needed to do was to throw a spear, catch a fish or climb a tree to pick fruit. Yes, there were individuals with spiritual samskaras (witches, shamans, priests) or artistic samskaras (storytellers, dramatists, etc.) and there were thinkers—the seers to whom this knowledge was revealed lived long before the age of agriculture—but basically everyone had the same nature with reference to action. Yes, the myriad tendencies that express themselves today were there in seed form, occasionally breaking out as visionaries, geniuses and mystics who opened up mankind to new possibilities, but the angst associated with action—what should I do with my life?—was largely absent. It was dictated by the situation.

As civilization "progressed" and agriculture developed, the need for new skills arose and Isvara supplied them. A person born during the age of agriculture had a few more options because life was more complex. Since the industrial revolution life has become exceedingly complex and promises to get more so. Abstracted from the physical, the fruits of man's actions have grown to astronomical heights today in the form of incredible, some would say obscene, wealth. With the rise of the nation state, this wealth, concentrated in the hands of a significant fraction of the world's population and administered by liberal democratic governments, basically eliminated hunger and physical insecurity. Few young people growing up in a "developed" economy have to worry about their next meal. The advent of peace and prosperity has had its downside, however: individuals need do virtually nothing to look after themselves or, should they wish to act, are presented with such a bewildering array of choices—like the dozens of brands of cereal on the supermarket shelves—that they have no idea what they want to be.

And insofar as doing is being in rajasic, materialistic societies, the modern world is saddled with a crisis of identity, the likes of which the world has never seen.

Seeking is a "world" that has its journeymen and its superstars and, like any other, its dharmas, rules. The problem with seeking as an occupation is that it ends abruptly when finding happens. Finding means the hard and fast understanding that being—which is happiness—is not related to doing. In short, "being" is not an occupation. This becomes a real problem for the doer, assuming it has survived finding, because now it needs a new job.

In any case, the dharma of a seeker is to apply self-knowledge to her mind. But there are various levels of seeking. If you are at the upper end of the evolutionary scale, meaning that your desire for freedom is burning, you have the requisite qualifications and have been blessed with conducive circumstances (a proven means of knowledge, the guidance of a qualified teacher and few tamasic karmas), you can seek properly. When you seek properly you do not listen to that voice in your head that asks you when you are going to get real and get a proper job. In other words you are in harmony with your svadharma as a renunciate. Karma yogis act in harmony with svadharma.

But if you are not one hundred percent committed to enlightenment you will have a conflict. You will listen as the doer ridicules your spiritual impulse. You will be torn between forgoing the possibility of success in the "real" world and spiritual success, which does not promise to pay the bills. I remember a conversation many years ago with my mother, who represented the "real" world for me at the time. I told her that I was "into God," just to keep things simple. She raised her eyebrows and said, "Well, James, that's all well and good but the Lord does not bring in the bacon." I told her that "the Lord" *was* the bacon, but it went over her head.

In any case, if you act in harmony with your svadharma—assuming you know what it is—you will have eliminated one source of conflict. You know if you are acting in harmony with it, if what you are doing in life "feels" right. If you act contrary to it, you will be unhappy. You will not know, however, that you are unhappy, because you are not acting in harmony with your nature. You will think it is because the results of your actions are not what you want. You will not see that the results Isvara is sending are in harmony with your assumed nature and not your svadharma. When you are not clear about who you are as a person, and you do not know you are the self, you will try to "be" someone that you think is interesting and attractive. Nobody tries to be a phony. People act inauthentically because their svadharma is hidden from them. The desire for identity is the strongest desire in the human mind and it will not be denied.

In general we say that you need to realize who you are as a person and be okay with that before you are qualified for liberation. Chapter 4 discussed the qualifications at length. This is why Vedanta says that you should stay in the world as the person you are and work out your svadharma with the karma yoga attitude. But what if you don't know what it is? What if you are just knocking about from pillar to post taking odd jobs, taking up one relationship after another, never doing meaningful work, growing older but no wiser?

In other words, why is your svadharma hidden from you? It is obscured by your fears and your desires. They extrovert you so much that you never have time to really get in touch with who you are on that level. They keep you looking for something in the world and sap your self-confidence to such a degree that you haven't got the courage to actually let go of your idea of success. You still really want security or love to come from the outside.

Or it may be that you have worked it all out already in some "past life" and that deep down you somehow know that you really are not anybody on that level. This is a situation that we find to be quite common these days. In the spiritual world these people are called "old souls." All that is left is to find out the truth of who they are. If you are in this predicament you are basically consigned to a lot of spiritual suffering because the infrastructure that is available in the West for freedom is undeveloped. The Western spiritual world is just paddling around on the surface of self-inquiry, trying to sort out what it is all about, pretending all the while that it knows what is happening.

And although you occasionally hear the word *Vedanta* bandied about these days, basically nobody, except those associated with Swami Dayananda, the Chinmaya Mission and the few who read my website and my books, have a clue about what it is. It is a shame because Vedanta can give you a provisional identity—karma yogi—that will take up the slack until you have realized your svadharma, your true nature. And once you are clear about who you really are, who you are on the relative level is no longer an issue. Your svadharma does not change, or if it does, it is okay with you because you know for sure that you are not a doer. The beauty of identifying yourself as a karma yogi—one of Isvara's premier limited identities—lies in the fact that your duty is clear and simple:

consecrate your actions to the field with an attitude of gratitude and take the results as a gift. And success in karma yoga brings an increasing sense of wellbeing as it neutralizes your likes and dislikes.

The next thing a karma yogi needs to know is that an action that does not involve a violation of dharma is okay assuming the action is sattvic or rajasic. The number one universal dharma is non-injury so any activity that does not involve injury to others is sanctioned. Obviously if you are looking at reality in terms of injury and non-injury then everything in the dharma field helps and hurts everything else. For example, I might be given a job as a painter. I am suited for it and I like my work. But it so happens the paint is toxic and harms the environment and may cause cancer or some other malady. What should I do? Of course there is no easy answer for this problem because of the nature of the dharma field, so you have to use your discrimination. It may be that you are suited to killing things—it seems Isvara needs killers because there have always been and will always be killers—but killing is obviously considered a proscribed action for karma yogis, unless, for example, you find yourself living above the Arctic Circle where there are no grocery stores and no vegetables and your survival depends on taking the life of animals. If you find yourself in this situation karma yoga applies; consecrate the action, do it mindfully in the kindest way possible and take the results as a gift. Our scriptures are full of examples of people who did very worldly jobs, even prostitution, in the karma yoga spirit and realized the self.

And finally, there are five prescribed dharmas for karma yogis.

1. *Worship of God in Any Form.* See the beauty of Vedanta! It is not a religion but it honors the religious impulse. You can be a Muslim, Christian or Jew and practice karma yoga.

One of the biggest problems with the Western non-duality world is its disdain for religion. Of course it is understandable from a certain point of view, insofar as unbelievable suffering has been inflicted on human beings in its name. But to abandon the religious impulse, which is just the self loving itself, because the church loses sight of the religious spirit from time to time is to throw the baby out with the bath. The desire to worship is as hard wired as the desire for identity. So choose a symbol of the self that is attractive to you and worship it regularly. Worship, which will be discussed later, invokes the self and produces a pure Subtle Body.

Here is a translation of a popular prayer; it should be sincerely spoken with great love daily:

> May all humans be well. May the great souls reveal the path of virtue to us. May there be perpetual joy for those who understand who they are. May all beings in all the worlds, terrestrial and extraterrestrial, be happy and free. May all beings be healthy. May they all have good luck and may none fall into evil ways.

This inexpensive and most extensive prayer travels instantaneously in consciousness to all dimensions of the creation, blessing every living being.

2. *Unconditional Reverence for Parents.* See the wisdom! Most of our stuff, positive and negative, comes from our parents. You can't blame them, because they picked up what they handed to you from their parents when they were too young to think for themselves. You have to take responsibility. As long as there is no resentment toward your parents and as long as you can see that they did their best according to what they knew and can see the gifts they gave and honor them in your thoughts daily, this is enough.

3. *Worship of scriptures.* The purpose of karma yoga is to gain a contemplative disposition so that you can assimilate the meaning of the teachings. But you should not think that you will start inquiry one fine day when you are contemplative. You should set aside a half an hour or an hour a day, or more, for study of Vedanta. You don't become contemplative all at once. You have contemplative moments throughout the day and insights all along. The progression from an outward turned mind to an inward turned mind is gradual. One day you will realize how clear and peaceful your mind has become, even in the midst of a busy life. Karma yoga is for doers who have a strong desire for freedom and who understand the value of knowledge.

4. *Service to humanity.* When someone wants something from you, see if you can't give them get what they want, *assuming it is a reasonable desire.* If you are helping others, at least you are not wasting your time indulging tamasic and rajasic habits. Service work cultivates sattva. It is difficult to practice service work because the ego can easily imagine that is it superior to those who only look

after themselves. So it is important to keep it simple—no big "save the world" ideas. Isvara presents opportunities every day to serve others. Service doesn't just mean doing what others want you to do, although it might include that. It means being open to others, not shutting them out. Serving others requires considerable mindfulness because ego, born of a sense of inadequacy and inferiority, looks for opportunities to feel special and virtuous. Service to others should be based on a recognition of the essential oneness of all of us. It is also wise because everything we need comes through others. Service-oriented individuals are generally well looked after.

5. *Worship of all sentient beings.* The appreciation of the oneness of everything should extend to include all life forms. Practice it by respecting the environment. Recycle. Be conscious of your carbon footprint. Go green. Vegetarianism is a good way to worship life.

Two More Dharmas

As you can see, the topic of dharma is very complex. Dharma as appropriate response. Dharma as rules. Dharma as duty. Dharma as true self nature. Dharma as reflected self nature. And now two more dharmas: *samanya dharma* and *visesa dharma*.

Samanya Dharma

With reference to my life, do I know best or does Isvara know best? In our scriptures there is a wonderful story about a warrior who is an incarnation of the self. He is an exceptional person in every way: kind, intelligent and very popular. His actions are always thoughtful and beneficial and he follows his svadharma to the letter. But nothing in his life goes according to plan. In general when things go wrong we usually blame others but should probably start blaming ourselves because often we make foolish choices that produce unwanted karma. But although he has acted mindfully in every situation, in harmony with his nature and the social order, at every turn things go "wrong." A few days before he is to be crowned king, an event which he, his wife and family, and indeed, the whole kingdom fervently desires, he is informed that he will not be king and will be exiled to the forest owing to an unfulfilled promise his father made to his stepmother. When he is told the "bad" news he is unperturbed, neither happy nor angry, and says,

"It is the duty of the son to obey the wishes of his parents," whereupon he goes happily into exile.

The idea, of course, is that there is particular order in society, a universal order that has been established by Isvara, the needs of the total. The family unit, which is the basis of society, functions properly when children respect the wishes of their parents, assuming that the parents follow the social order as well. The social order is based on the psychological order that evolves from the guna structure behind it. The purpose of this order is to bring all the apparently conflicting desires and fears of individuals into harmony so that the total functions properly. When conflicts develop, everyone suffers. And the psychological order is based on the non-dual nature of reality, the one principle—consciousness/love—behind everything. If reality is non-dual, it stands to reason that the number one value of all sentient beings is non-injury. What better testimonial to the value of non-injury than the timeless and universal obsession with security?

Because duality—the idea that my gain is your loss—is so ingrained, we all have fears for our safety, livelihood, etc. These fears can lead to various behaviors that cause injury to others. Non-injury in our tradition is defined as "non-injury by thought, word, or deed." So by following the value or dharma of non-injury— the moral law—we put our lives squarely in harmony with Isvara, the giver of the law. All universal values—truthfulness, charity, freedom, non-stealing, etc—are based on the principal of non-injury. I don't steal from you because I understand that you value your possessions and that I inflict emotional duress on you when I deprive you of them. I appreciate your feelings because I know that we are actually one; I would feel the same way were you to steal from me. Although it seems as if we are different we are actually the same, the non-dual self. I don't lie to you because it will cause pain to you. It should not be forgotten that lying causes pain to the liar as well because dharma is built in to every sentient being. It is often called "conscience." I don't deprive you of your freedom, because I value freedom above everything. Freedom, in fact, is the ultimate non-dual value because even when I am socially, politically and physically free of limitation I am inclined to seek inner freedom.

Dharma Yoga

Universal values are called *samanya dharma*. The problem with universal values is that that they are universal. They exist in an ideal realm, apparently abstracted from the exigencies of everyday life. They mean something only when they are interpreted and acted on by individuals. Interpreted values are called *visesha dharma*. Dharma yoga is squaring my life with universal values. It means that Isvara knows best. By "yoga" we mean to connect or join our actions with the will of the total.

See the downside for the ego! What happens when what I want is not in harmony with the needs of the total? A person brought up in a desire-oriented, liberal, materialistic, consumer-oriented society, infected with a strong sense of personal entitlement, will have a big problem with this idea. In America especially, the enduring popularity of the rebel archetype—a disdain for rules—is a stark testament to the difficulties we face when we practice dharma yoga.

If I am not keen on the idea of surrendering my will to the will of Isvara, I will be confused about the needs of the total. Some of this confusion is justified because sometimes the particular part of the dharma field that I inhabit is under the spell of *adharma* and it seems as if the needs of the total are evil. For example, a good law-abiding person brought up in Germany after the First World War could see the invasion of other countries and the concentration camps as the "needs of the total." And indeed, the defense of low-level citizens who were given the job of managing the concentration camps used the duty argument because they were conditioned to follow rules without thinking. But it is sometimes important to ignore the needs of the immediate total because its needs are adharmic. The ego, that part of the self that is under the spell of ignorance, is not above using clever arguments to avoid practicing dharma yoga, so it is important to define the needs of the total more specifically.

Guilt

The needs of the total are always manifest in my particular environment. I always find myself in a world of apparently sentient objects—jivas, and obviously insentient objects—matter. I use this environment to get what I want. At the same time, the environment has its own needs. If I am a husband and a father, my family represents the needs of the total. The family unit fits into a bigger picture. It is an expression of a universal need to live and be happy. If I come home after work and switch on the TV to unwind and ignore my children I am putting my needs ahead of my children's needs, which is a violation of dharma. The ego will justify it in various ways—"I sweat and slave all day turning the wheels of commerce to provide for my family and I deserve to relax"—but it will not really relax because dharma is built-in; I will feel guilty. Guilt is one of the most disturbing emotions and needs to be purified if the Subtle Body is to be made inquiry worthy. Guilt stems from violations of dharma.

Visesha dharma is a nuanced topic. We need to look into the meaning of the word *total* in this context because it is a relative term. In the case of an individual in Germany at the time, the society was the total. But German society was just one society in the world social order, which is controlled by Isvara. When the German total came up against the *total* total, the needs of the dharma field itself for freedom trumped German needs for power and control. When family dharma comes in conflict with the dharma of the society in which it lives, it will be disciplined because the needs of the total come first. The law of eminent domain or the illegality of polygamy is an example.

Which total should determine my behavior? The American government seems inclined to periodic wars. Should I pay my taxes and support those wars? Which wars are dharmic and which wars are not? You cannot argue that all war is adharmic because when adharma gets to a certain level it always comes in conflict with dharma. When adharmic forces in world culture get to a certain level of power, world war occurs and a reasonable balance between dharma and adharma is re-established. The dharma field never perishes, because it is eternal, but the forces of dharma and adharma are in continual conflict and therefore the human mind is always in conflict. Because all non-human living beings follow their programs implicitly there is no dharma for them. But, owing to free will humans can think and so they are subject to dharma and adharma. Understanding dharma and karma is indeed difficult because the line demarcating them is never completely clear. Sometimes good actions produce bad consequences and sometimes bad actions produce good consequences. Seen from the point of view of awareness there are no good and bad actions or consequences, only the eternal play of the dualities.

Visesha dharma, the application of *samanya dharma* to daily life, is fraught with difficulties because of adharma. But what is contrary to dharma at one time is not necessarily contrary to dharma at another. For example, a robber who sticks a knife in the abdomen of a stranger on the street is guilty of adharmic behavior. But a surgeon who puts a knife to the abdomen of someone with an infected appendix is following dharma even if the patient dies. Both are following their svadharma. It is the nature of those with criminal samskaras to rob and it is the nature of those with saintly samskaras to heal. But the value of the action itself depends on the context. You could argue that killing a man for money satisfies the needs of the criminal for his next meal but it does so at the expense of the life of another. It is not difficult to understand that the value of life trumps the value of the next meal. The point of this discussion, however, lies in appreciation of the fact that there is a continual tension between dharma and adharma insofar as our desires are concerned. This tension is resolved by the practice of dharma/karma yoga.

Dharma is intimately connected to karma because it does not mean anything apart from the actions that support or contravene it. To keep dharma alive, action is required. In any case it is not always clear how to dharmically respond to a given situation. Should I tell the truth and hurt someone's feelings or should I tell a white lie and feel bad because I violated the value of honesty? Incidentally, expressing one's feelings is sometimes dharmic and sometimes not, depending on the context. Particularly insensitive individuals with a strong moral sense often find themselves involved in very unpleasant situations because of their need to "tell the truth." How I feel is *a* truth. It is not *the* truth.

People whose minds are under the spell of tamas usually want a formula for life. Because their intellects are clouded they lack the discrimination to negotiate the dharma field. They want a black and white movie. But life is shades of gray; there is usually uncertainty as to which actions are right and which actions are wrong both in terms of svadharma and visesha dharma. Therefore, on the topic of action, discrimination is always required, the idea being that an inquirer needs to perform actions that have the most beneficial impact on the Subtle Body. Or, to state it negatively, to perform actions that have the least detrimental impact, taking dharma into account.

In a nutshell, dharma yoga is sacrificing one's personal needs for Isvara, the needs of the total, but only when there is a conflict. Do-gooders are individuals who look for opportunities to sacrifice. This does not qualify as dharma yoga if it is driven by a sense of moral inadequacy or insecurity, because it builds a sense of self righteous ego. Dharma yoga is a great opportunity to bring the ego to heel and erase its sense of otherness. However, if it is your nature to help, it is important to follow your nature.

A mature, cultured person is someone who is mindful of her own needs, but understands the need to maintain dharma as a service to the total. World literature is full of great statements about the importance of dharma and often portrays it as an epic struggle between mythic supernatural forces, but life is not a drama. It is just life. The practice of dharma yoga on a daily basis amounts to little more than the maintenance of traditions of civility or, to put it more prosaically, to observing good manners.

Spiritual practice is little more than resolving the persistent conflicts that disturb the Subtle Body. Conflict comes from not following your svadharma, from improper interpretation of samanya dharma and from anxiety for the fruits of action. Karma/dharma yoga resolves these conflicts. As the practice matures and the mind turns within and becomes peaceful, it becomes established in sattva, the light of awareness shines brightly in it and you will come to identify that light as your own self.

CHAPTER TEN

THE ROPES

The creation behaves according to certain laws and principles. Everything is intelligently designed and constructed to serve the needs of the total. It is apparently, not actually, self-aware. For the benefit of the seeming entities who take it to be real and want to be free of it we now unfold the teaching of the three gunas. The gunas were discussed on the macrocosmic level in chapter 6. In this chapter we will explain how they work in the human mind.

Before the creation existed, awareness existed. A power in awareness, Maya, manifested the universe out of awareness. Maya is both the material and the intelligent cause of the manifestation. The creation is made of energy. Although energy is one, it appears in three forms or gunas. Every object, subtle and gross, is created out of these three energies. To understand our world and the nature of our experience we need to understand the gunas.

I am sorry to introduce another Sanskrit word but there are no words in any language that are adequate to describe them. The most common word in English is *qualities* but it is not enough. Be that as it may, the gunas cause experience. In fact they are experience itself. They cause suffering and they cause joy. Knowledge of them is the solution to suffering.

A person who knows that she is awareness may or may not be interested in changing the nature of her samsaric experience. If she is not interested it is because she sits above the gunas dispassionately witnessing what happens, enjoying the bliss of awareness. But those who are not happy are very interested in the nature of their experience. It is dissatisfaction with experience that motivates the quest for enlightenment and most other endeavors.

Enlightenment—liberation—is for the mind. You, awareness, are already free. The bondage that you experience exists solely in the Subtle Body. The Subtle Body is the experiencing and knowing part of the self. Ignorance and knowledge reside in it. Ignorance is the belief that the self is a limited, incomplete, inadequate entity, a thinker, perceiver, doer. Knowledge is "I am limitless, non-dual, ordinary, actionless awareness."

Direct and Indirect Cause

As far as liberation goes we do not have to focus on the Gross and Causal Bodies. The physical body should be strong and healthy and one's environment neat, clean, quiet and secure. The Causal Body is the key to the whole riddle of existence, but nothing can be done about it directly because it is subtler than the experiencer/doer. It is understood by inference. It is transformed indirectly through the work done by the Subtle Body. This work is called sadhana, spiritual practice, the "means of attainment." While self-knowledge is the direct cause of liberation, practice is the indirect cause. It prepares the mind for self-knowledge.

There is a strange notion in the spiritual world that a seeker has some kind of choice over whether or not he follows the direct or the indirect path. The direct path is thought to be very easy and the indirect path is a lot of work. So most seekers want to follow the direct path. But the direct path is easy only if the seeker is qualified. If you are qualified Isvara will bring you to a direct path teacher. If you are not qualified and you go to a direct path teacher you will not understand or you will get an incompetent direct path teacher. So your qualifications, not your will, determine your path.

The fear that you will not gain enlightenment or that you will lose it once it is gained is solely due to the fact that the Subtle Body has not been properly prepared. The preparation of the Subtle Body is in terms of managing and neutralizing binding likes and dislikes. If they are not managed and neutralized, neither self-knowledge nor self-experience will be steady.

Firm self-knowledge can bring about an abiding mind, one that enjoys a steady experience of the bliss of awareness as it reflects on the Subtle Body. But seekers whose knowledge is shaky often experience the "firefly" phenomenon: the knowledge/experience of who you are blinks on and off as the mind changes, creating a destabilizing sense of frustration. It blinks on and off because the Subtle Body is not established in sattva guna. Seekers try frantically to get it back when the experience of wholeness and completeness deserts them. They worry endlessly when they are experiencing wholeness because they are not in control of the experience. What is in control? The gunas control experience. When the guna changes, an individual's experience changes. Therefore, knowledge of the gunas is essential for anyone seeking liberation through inquiry.

Not to put a fine point on it, I feel happy when sattva guna is predominant and more or less unhappy when rajas or tamas predominates. One of the meanings of guna is "rope." The gunas, like ropes, chain me to experience. It never ceases to amaze me how the proponents of experiential enlightenment fail to teach karma yoga, dharma yoga or the yoga of the three gunas. It can be due only to ignorance because if enlightenment is experiential—it is and isn't—knowledge of experience and how to control it is absolutely necessary.

When we say that enlightenment is experiential we mean that when awareness reflects on a sattvic mind it produces an assortment of experiences that are variously described as mystical, transcendental, out-of-body, non-dual, near-death, etc. These experiences are so unlike ordinary experiences and are generally so exciting and satisfying—but always puzzling—that they usually create a vasana for more. One problem with them is that the experiencer believes he is experiencing something that is beyond samsara, a wonderful something that is not subject to change, and develops a desire to "go there" to experience "it" permanently. But all experience is in samsara and subject to change. So there is no permanent enlightenment experience, only temporary enlightenment experiences.

No Quarrel with Experience

So far we have said that enlightenment is not experiential but that does not mean that Vedanta has a quarrel with experience. Life is the self in the form of experience and Vedanta is the science of the self, so Vedanta and experience are not enemies. You cannot be for or against experience because from the level of the apparent reality experience is all there is. And that we want to enjoy our lives goes without saying. In fact the whole purpose of Vedanta is not to give you a special "experienceless" experience but to take the suffering out of everyday experience so the self, operating as a Subtle Body, enjoys its life. Remember, the ego, the doer/experiencer, is the self under the spell of ignorance.

We quarrel with those who think that enlightenment is a particular kind of experience different from everyday experience. The logic was presented in chapter 2. But to refresh our memory, Vedanta says that reality is non-dual. If it is non-dual everything experienced and known is only awareness, which means that what you are experiencing at any moment is the self. If you don't like what you are experiencing then enlightenment is not going to help, except indirectly. If you don't like it and you want it to be different, then you need to do the actions that make your experience suitable to you. If you are going to change your experience you need to understand what experience is. And if you want to understand what it is then you need to understand the gunas because experience is nothing but the three gunas.

The Flow, Stuckness, and No Movement

Before we unfold the technical aspects of the three gunas teaching we need to consider three global kinds of experience: the feeling of flow, the feeling of stuckness and a feeling of no movement whatsoever, sometimes called "the zone." These are obviously not technical Vedantic words but are terms that help to make the guna idea more accessible. The feeling that life is flowing is obviously desirable for everyone, but it is particularly desirable for predominately rajasic individuals. Rajas is the mode of passion. It inclines one to activity. A rajasic person is goal oriented and wants results badly because his happiness rides on results. We already know that if the doer is in control rajas is not a problem but Isvara is in control of results and Isvara doesn't necessarily give you what you want when you want it the way you want it. So rajasic people are by definition emotional. They are high and happy when they are getting what they want and angry and depressed when they aren't.

Doership

Rajas is an interesting energy in that once you have operated out of this guna for a while, activity itself becomes a goal. You become attached to the idea that you should be doing something all the time and you feel guilty if you aren't.

Sometimes the compelling desire to act is so strong you perform self-insulting, silly and trivial actions simply because deliberate action or inaction is impossible. The most common justification for the state of mindless activity is survival. You believe that your activities are responsible for your survival. It is lost on you that if you weren't surviving, you would be unable to perform activities. This is not to say that action is bad as far as liberation is concerned, only that excess rajas mitigates against success in that success depends on the appropriateness and timeliness of your actions. When your mind is agitated, you do not act deliberately and skillfully.

"An idle mind is the devil's workshop," my mother used to say. Actually a busy mind is the devil's workshop unless it is busy inquiring, assuming your ultimate goal is liberation. People controlled by this guna are often plagued by boredom and suffer because they cannot relax. In the sixties they were called uptight, meaning stressed. They are victims of doership. Doership is not about doing. From womb to tomb you are active. It is not up to you. Doership is an identity issue, not an action issue. You think you are a doer. Doing happens, no doubt, but you are not doing it, either as the jiva or as the self. The gunas are the doer. If you are rajasic, you evaluate yourself in terms of what you have accomplished or failed to accomplish or want to accomplish. This leads to a psychological problem: inflation and deflation. You have an exaggerated sense of your self-importance when you are getting what you want and a sense of failure and depression when you aren't.

Usually rajasic persons think they are very clever because they accomplish so much, but much energy is wasted spinning their wheels. From a spiritual point of view they are not the sharpest knives in the drawer because they are so busy acting out their desires that they fail to dispassionately evaluate the results of their actions, which means that they make the same mistakes over and over. They tend to be stubborn and defensive. They vigorously cling to their doings and defend their wants no matter what. They find themselves in constant conflict with the world because they think their wants are more important that the wants of Isvara in the form of the wants of others. The feeling of flow is a situation where you are getting what you want. When Isvara does not deliver the desired result, stuckness, tamas, ensues.

You can identify doership by observing your language. If you hear yourself saying you are "supposed to," "have to" or "must" do something, doership is alive and well. You are not compelled or obligated to do anything, because you are actually free not to see yourself as a doer. Furthermore, you can consider life from the point of view of who you really are. If you do it will be clear that life is a dream and that you do not come and go because you are the ground of being on which actions take place.

If you know that you are awareness you are not concerned with being in or out of the flow of life because there is no sense of doership. If, however, you don't know you are awareness and are identified with the doer/experiencer/enjoyer entity, then you would obviously want your life to flow. If you want it to flow you will benefit by the knowledge of the gunas and how they work.

The feeling of stuckness is caused by tamas. It is a failure to see what has to be done in a given situation and a lack of will to accomplish it. Tamas is dullness, a cloudy energy. Tamasic people are lazy. They prefer to enjoy without doing. If you find yourself sitting endlessly in front of the TV with a can of beer and a huge bag of fatty chips, you are in the grip of tamas. Criminals tend to be tamasic in their thinking, although they may very well be rajasic physically. They would rather figure out ways to beat the system than to work for a living. Easy money is their holy mantra. This guna inclines one to sensuality and the pursuit of short-term pleasure. Alcoholics, drug addicts and gluttons are tamasic. How much effort does it take to get drunk? When you are drunk or stoned your problems seem to disappear. "Out of sight, out of mind." Tamasic people do not want to think. Thinking is hard work. They want to follow formulas. They cannot see the value of knowledge.

People in whom tamas is predominant want to feel. Feeling is easy. Tamasic people love sleep because it allows them to avoid unpleasant tasks. Eating large quantities of sensuous foods is an activity of choice for tamasic people. Sex is a big draw, although unfortunately it tends to involve a bit of effort. The narcotic post-coital effect is pure tamas. "Yum! Feels great." The short-lived success in the eighties and nineties of the famous sex guru, Osho, was due to the power of tamas. Tamasic people are loyal to a fault. Even today, long after Osho and his "path" have been completely discredited, many of his devotees stubbornly worship him and are enthralled by the tamasic way of life he espoused.

Because tamasic people continually indulge themselves they do not accumulate good karma. In fact they collect bad karma or simply spend whatever good karma stands in their account until it is gone. They are perpetually in debt, financially and energetically. Life is a huge weight, a millstone around the neck dragging them down. They do not grow. They don't stay the same. They devolve.

Tamas is inertia. It is the most destructive energy of the three, although rajas is a close second. To overcome it, you have to act. Rajas is about obtaining things and tamas is about keeping them. Even maintenance requires energy. You have to pay your parking tickets or your car will be impounded and sold. If you don't brush your teeth, they rot. If you don't love and serve your wife, she runs off with someone who does. Everything in samsara is sliding into the abyss as we speak. But when you are tamasic, you are too lazy to protect what you have. Nothing in your life lasts, so there is nothing to build on. You end up living hand to mouth. It wears you out. You become fatigued and overcome with a sense of failure. Depression sets in and your self-esteem plummets. In my day tamas was called the yuppie disease. This term has evidently been relegated to the dustbin because now a suitable euphemism has replaced it, ME. Tamasic people are messy, forgetful and prone to accidents and loss. They are perpetually confused. When the Subtle Body is predominately tamasic, the self, masquerading as the ego, feels totally stuck.

The third type of experience is the feeling of the zone. It is a very positive experience. It can be confused with tamas because nothing is apparently happening. It is the experience of clarity and bliss and is the third guna, sattva. Rajas is the mode of passion, tamas the mode of inertia and dullness and sattva is the mode of knowledge and bliss. Sattva is the revealing power, an energy that reveals awareness. By "reveal" I mean it makes awareness accessible as knowledge and experience. If you want to feel good all the time, produce a mind that is one hundred percent sattvic. Of course this is not possible, because sattva is supplanted by rajas and tamas as the gunas cycle, but with a little work an inquirer can create a predominantly sattvic mind.

Sattva is the feeling of peace and satisfaction. When you are satisfied the mind sits still. Such a mind is valuable for two reasons: it reveals the self to be nondual and it allows you to evaluate objects as they are. Whether you are looking at (the refection of) the self or at objects, you are experiencing through the Subtle Body so the energy dominating the Subtle Body at any time is of paramount importance for an inquirer.

These two benefits are not unconnected. If you just want to feel good you need not seek enlightenment, you need to cultivate sattva. You can never get a one hundred percent feel-good flowing life, but you can get pretty close if your mind is predominately sattvic because you can be objective about your thoughts and feelings and the external things that happen to you. If you are clear about what is happening in you, you can work with your stuff and creatively remove the obstacles to your happiness as they arise.

If your Subtle Body is predominately rajasic and tamasic, it is virtually impossible to gain self-knowledge, or if you do it will only be a frustrating flash of insight. Even if you are predominantly sattvic you will not necessarily gain self-knowledge, but you will be in a position to develop the qualifications, assuming a burning desire for freedom. So either way you have to address your experience, not deny it or try to transcend it. You must work with it creatively using guna knowledge, not out of beliefs and opinions born of mindless desires and unexamined fears. And if you are predominately sattvic you will easily assimilate the teachings of Vedanta. If not, not.

In any case, let's call the experience of sattva the experience of no-movement because a steady and clear mind reveals the self as unchanging awareness. A beautiful verse in the *Bhagavad Gita* expresses it this way: "The one who sees inaction in action is indeed wise." You know that the changes that are taking place in you and around you are only apparent changes. Or to use a saying much in vogue in the spiritual world, "Nothing ever happened." When the Subtle Body is sattvic you can act or not act; you are not compelled to act nor are you too lazy to act.

Although we have presented an outline of the rajasic and tamasic personalities we will not discuss the sattvic personality here. We will save it for later when we take up the topic of values. More can be said about the three personality types but Vedanta is not interested in personality analysis because the Subtle Body is not the self. We are interested only in how these energies affect the assimilation of experience and how the assimilation of experience, or lack thereof, relates to self-inquiry and the assimilation of the teachings.

The Assimilation of Experience

Experience is an unbroken series of inner and outer events and the reaction or response to them. The reaction of animals to experience is totally programmed. Humans have an advantage because they have the power to think. They can study their experience, extract knowledge from it and change it, freeing them to some degree from their programming.

Spiritual growth comes about through the proper assimilation of experience. Just as partially digested food inhibits the efficient functioning of the body, partially or improperly assimilated experience compromises the development of the Subtle Body. Because awareness illumines the body-mind entity, it is propelled along its life track to its ultimate destination: the realization of its non-separation from everything. As long as the meaning of life's experiences is unknown to it, the person is little more than an animal and cannot fulfill its destiny.

Like an animal, a human infant unknowingly lives out its subconscious tendencies. It grows physically, but it does not evolve. It has no control over the direction of its life because it has insufficient experience and knowledge to make informed choices. Once its intellect develops and it assimilates certain values, it can evaluate its experiences and begin to evolve.

The longer an experience remains unassimilated, the more problems it causes. Let us say that your father was an alcoholic and abused your mother, so that she fell into a lifelong depression and was unable to raise you and your siblings properly. Because you were the eldest, you ended up parenting your younger brothers and sisters. You did it because you had no choice. You developed a deep resentment toward your father for robbing you of your childhood and a deep sympathy for your poor victimized mother. In reality, she was not blameless, because she never stood up to her husband; she actually enabled his alcoholism in subtle ways. Nonetheless, you saw her as a martyr and loved her for it. Your father died, but your hatred lived on. You believed a grave injustice had been done and it colored your feelings toward men in general.

One day, a nice man wanted to marry you and in the excitement of first love, you agreed. You married, but as time went on certain things your husband said or did reminded you of your father. This brought up old feelings of resentment and rage. You began to pick quarrels with him for no reason. Your fears slowly got the best of you and you incorrectly imagined that these small things he shared with your father—a certain inflection in his voice when he was stressed, for example—revealed a selfish and abusive nature. You accused him of changing and said he did not really love you, which was not true. Your relationship deteriorated and your children started to become neurotic. You confided in one of your divorced women friends who came from a similar background and was holding a grudge against her ex. She showed so much concern for your plight that you fell in love with her, left your husband, abandoned your children and became gay. But after a while your new identity did not work, because you loved her for the wrong reason: she was not a man. Had your mother been the abuser, you may have hated women and loved men. We can make this story go on and on for fifty years or more, each tragic event unfolding out of the preceding event like clockwork, until it becomes impossible to work back to the beginning and discover the reason for the suffering and heal the wound.

Experience does not interpret or assimilate itself. The intellect interprets experience. It sits behind the mind and evaluates what happens. There is nothing wrong with it. This is what it is supposed to do. If experience conforms to the ego's desire, it gives the thumbs up and positive feelings arise. If life delivers experience contrary to its desire, it gives the thumbs down and negative feelings arise. How it interprets experience depends on acquired knowledge and ignorance plus three factors that are normally beyond its control. Two of these factors inhibit its ability to discriminate and one facilitates it. The factors over which the intellect has limited control are rajas, tamas and sattva.

Rajas and the Assimilation of Experience

How does rajas affect the assimilation of experience? Whether the goals are worldly or spiritual, and whether or not they are realized, the rajasic intellect is not concerned with the truth of experience, only with how a particular experience relates to the fulfillment of the ego's desires.

Rajas is always a source of frustration because everything gained is inevitably lost. An object gained causes attachment and an object lost produces grief, neither of which is conducive to happiness. Rather than accept the impermanence of life as a fact and be satisfied with what is, rajas causes the ego to continually seek fulfillment in new experiences. Even though the individual knows better, rajas can cause such a lack of discrimination that the individual will consistently repeat actions that produce suffering. It often generates so many actions in such a short time that the intellect can never determine which action was responsible for a given result, thus preventing it from learning from its experiences.

When a pleasurable experience ends, rajas causes disappointment because it wants the pleasure to continue, even though the intellect knows that pleasure is fleeting. If an experience is mediocre, it wants it to be better. If it is bad, it should end instantly and not happen again. If experience repeats itself over and over, as it does owing to conditioning, rajas causes boredom and produces a strong desire for variety. More-better-different is its holy mantra. It produces an endlessly active, time-constrained life of loose ends.

No matter how much is accomplished, the to-do list never shrinks. Rajas is a closet, garage, basement and attic overflowing with a confusing assortment of neglected and unused objects. It is a late tax return, a forgotten appointment, an unreturned call, a frantic search for one's keys. Rajas's aggressive, extroverted forays into samsara are inevitably accompanied by tiredness and insomnia.

When I was young my father, who was wise in many ways, used to say "You can't win." At the time I did not understand what he meant, but a life well spent and the teachings of Vedanta made it clear. Life is a zero-sum game, an eternal war within one's self in which neither side prevails for long. For example, when tamas appears in a person whose predominant guna is rajas a painful experience is inevitable. You have many things on your to-do list but your mind is so dull that every action becomes painful. You are wired but tired. It is not fun. And conversely, when you need to indulge your tamas and sleep, your mind is too busy. So you suffer.

Assimilation of experience takes place only when the mind is alert and present. Therefore, when rajas dominates the Subtle Body, the innate wisdom of the self, much less common sense knowledge, is not available to help the intellect accurately determine what is happening and resolve doubts. Resolved experience leaves attention fully present, so that it is able to meet the next experience without prejudice. Because life is an unending procession of experiences in this pressurized age, it is important to lay each experience to rest as quickly as possible, preferably as it happens. When you are so rajasic that your mind is totally wrapped up dealing with an endless succession of trivial daily desires you are too busy to look at your issues so they remain in the background and cause suffering.

Unresolved experience subliminally drains attention. Difficulty focusing on what needs to be done and avoidance of what should or should not be done are signs that the mind is excessively rajasic. As unresolved experience accumulates, the individual suffers existential constipation. She feels overwhelmed, stressed and unable to keep up with life's demands. Growth rarely comes through the easy attainment of desires, but an extroverted person is also denied the growth-enhancing benefits of assimilated unwanted experiences.

Tamas and the Assimilation of Experience

Tamas, the veiling power, inhibits the assimilation of experience as efficiently as rajas, but for different reasons. Under its influence, the Subtle Body, though seemingly quiet, is actually dull. Efficient evaluation of experience requires mental clarity, but when a torpid veil covers the Subtle Body, perception is distorted and assimilation is compromised. When the intellect is dull, it has difficulty connecting the results of its actions with the thoughts motivating them, causing uncertainty with respect to what has to be done and what should not be done. When the Subtle Body is predominately dull, you are negotiating the ocean of samsara in a rudderless ship. "Where should I go? What should I do? What's going on? I don't know. I do not want to know" are some signature thoughts.

A tamasic mind runs unthinkingly off conditioned patterns. Unlike rajas, it hates the new. Because creative thinking takes so much energy, the tamasic mind does not value inquiry. Therefore, it cannot gain control of events and is forced to continually revisit negative situations. Consequently, tamas is responsible for the feelings of helplessness that cause deep and lasting depressions. Tamas solves problems by denying them. When unwanted karma happens, it teams up with rajas to lay the blame elsewhere.

The undigested experiential backlog brought on by a tamasic mind causes the ego to dither and procrastinate. If you have a rajasic lifestyle and feel constantly exhausted, know that rajas is causing tamas. When tamas is particularly heavy, even small daily duties like brushing teeth, combing hair or taking out the garbage seem like gargantuan undertakings. Neglect is tamasic and is responsible in large part for the rampant emotional dysfunction seen in materialistic societies. Parents become so caught up in their own lives that children are neglected. Unloved children quickly develop low self-esteem and are unable to properly fulfill their roles in society.

There are no experiential qualifications for enlightenment, only the right guna balance. Samadhis, satoris, nirvanas and other non-dual, mind-blowing epiphanies can be as much a hindrance as a help. If the mind is predominately sattvic it can assimilate information carefully and quickly lay experiences to rest. If you have a consistent issue in your life—it can be love or food or recognition or power—it means you have an assimilation problem and your mind will be unfit for inquiry. Unprocessed experience can stay with you your whole life long.

I have a friend who was adopted. His mother gave him up to a good family for adoption when he was very young. He was loved and given all the advantages. But when he was told he was adopted, he developed a terrible complex. He was unable to assimilate that information properly. If he had been sattvic at that time then he would have realized that Isvara was great because an unfit mother had been eliminated and replaced with a good one. But his mind was tamasic and he took it to mean he wasn't valuable. That idea stuck in his mind for more than fifty years. It ruined several marriages and he did not find love until Vedanta came into his life, because of the thought that he was not worthy.

Upside to the Gunas

There is an upside as well as a downside to each guna. When it is balanced by appropriate amounts of sattva and rajas, tamas helps the psyche function smoothly. It clings to what is good and provides the patience necessary to ground ideas in reality. Finally, it is responsible for sleep. Insufficient tamas results in sleep deprivation, a major source of suffering, because the body and mind need rest. A restless mind cannot discriminate the self from objects.

Rajas projects and tamas obscures, but sattva reveals things as they are. When sattva is present, the intellect is clear and experience is seen for what it is. Unlike rajas and tamas, sattva is an indirect means of enlightenment because it reveals the self.

Sattva and the Assimilation of Experience

When rajas dominates the mind, desire interprets experience. When tamas dominates, fear interprets experience. Both obscure the truth. When sattva dominates, truth interprets experience.

Awareness shines on each of the three energies in the Causal Body. Its light, reflected on the Subtle Body, produces three distinct conditions. If I desire to experience the self and the Subtle Body is the instrument of experience, it stands to reason that I would want to have a sattvic Causal Body. In fact the chitta, the substance of the Causal Body, is consciousness and reflects it accurately. But if it is burdened with tamasic and rajasic tendencies the reflection will be distorted and inquiry will not bear fruit. If the Causal Body is dominated by rajasic tendencies, the self appears as dynamic energy, not radiant light. If the Causal Body is tamasic, I will have no idea of the self whatsoever. The conclusion is obvious: if I want to experience the self as it is, I should cultivate a sattvic mind. Experience of the self is not enlightenment, but it can lead to enlightenment if the intellect can assimilate the knowledge—"I am awareness"—that arises when the attention is turned within and the mind is sattvic.

Because reality is non-dual consciousness, the mind is consciousness. To gain a predominately sattvic mind, one capable of discrimination and the easy assimilation of experience, the proportions of rajas and tamas relative to sattva need to be changed. Enough rajas needs to be retained for motivational purposes and enough tamas preserved to ground one's ideas in reality. But the lion's share of the mind should be sattvic. A predominately sattvic mind will gain success in any field, worldly or spiritual, because it can discriminate properly. Enlightenment—*moksa*—is defined as discrimination. It takes place only in a sattvic mind.

How the Ropes Bind

Finally, these three energies are called gunas or ropes because they apparently bind the self, the indweller in the body, to habitual thoughts, feelings and actions. Each binds in a different way. Rajas binds by longing and attachment. Craving for things and attachment to things pressures you to become a doer and ties you up with karma. Furthermore, desire makes rule breaking tempting. If you push against the rules, the rules push back. Continual reaction to events is bondage.

Tamas binds by ignorance and its effects. When you are dull you cannot think clearly, so you are uncertain about what needs to be done and you tend to opt not to do what you should do or to do what you should not do. In the best of all possible worlds you would not be penalized for not doing something, however, life is not the best of all possible worlds. If you do not respond to life appropriately, you are blessed with suffering. Try not paying taxes or the mortgage and see what happens. Furthermore, when you are lazy you are prone to cutting corners, which does not make you a friend of dharma.

Although sattva is a necessary stepping stone to self-realization, it binds through attachment to pleasure and happiness. When the mind is sattvic, you feel good. When you feel good, there is a strong tendency to identify with the feeling. Actually, there is only one "I" and it does not feel good or bad, but when it is apparently ignorant of its nature, it thinks it is an enjoyer. The pleasure that one feels is always associated with an object and objects are experienced in the mind, so when rajas or tamas takes over, the pleasure disappears. By identifying with happiness, you are asking for unhappiness.

Sattva also binds by attachment to knowledge. Because sattva is responsible for knowledge and because knowledge is necessary for survival, it is easy to become attached to what you know or do not know. As we know, awareness is not a knower. It illumines the knower, knowledge and the objects of knowledge. It illumines the absence of knowledge. Therefore, attachment to sattva, not sattva itself, stands in the way of self-knowledge.

This is always a problem because the world does not necessarily conform to these ideals. In reality, existence is awareness and awareness is value neutral but a mind under the spell of the gunas is not value neutral. Sattva causes the individual to interpret reality in terms of "higher" or "spiritual" values; goodness, truth, beauty, for example. But Isvara's creation is not all sweetness and light. It contains everything in equal measure from pure goodness to unrepentant evil, from sublime beauty to wretched ugliness.

Incestuous Bedfellows – The Psychological Mechanism

The simple and universal psychology of the gunas obviates the need for psychoanalysis. You need not look to the past to explain your hangups and complexes. All stem from the same unconscious mechanism, denial and projection. Tamas causes denial and rajas projects. Where you find one, you will find the other. They are dynamic energies operating all the time. If you know who you are, the play of rajas and tamas rises to the level of consciousness and they lose their power to create suffering.

Many things about ourselves contradict our good opinion of ourselves: selfishness, arrogance, cruelty, dishonesty, envy, lust, greed, etc. We do not want to think of ourselves in this way nor do we want to be perceived in this way so tamas conceals them. Because the Causal Body is dynamic these qualities are continually seeking to express themselves. I cannot say that I am selfish or greedy so rajas projects the selfishness or greed or deceit onto someone or something else. It blames.

A Rudimentary Inquiry

There is a simple inquiry for dealing with denial and projection. When something is bothering you and it brings you into conflict with some object—the most common is another person, although you can imagine you are at war with the society, the government, the church, the corporations, the weather, the list is endless—you ask yourself if it is true that one of the hooks for these projections is actually responsible for your bad feelings.

Of course your ego is going to say that it is. The ego has a vested interest in its projections. Projections protect it and keep it in business. They bolster its self-esteem, its sense of rightness. It needs to think that it is innocent. Actually it is innocent insofar as it is actually self. Unfortunately, Maya has seen to it that it does not know the truth of its nature and it thinks it is a person because it is conditioned by society; nothing projects like groups of individuals. Societies have ready-made enemies at their fingertips. Hitler had the Jews, Stalin the petty bourgeois capitalists, the Christians Satan, whites the blacks, husbands wives and wives husbands. We need someone to blame. I cannot be the problem. But the truth is: I am the problem. There is no problem apart from me.

This method takes the ego into account and asks "Is it really true that...." Sometimes it is true that the world is out to get you. So you need to look at the facts closely and see if it is reasonable to assume that the problem lies elsewhere. If the problem lies elsewhere then redress lies elsewhere and you need to seek it elsewhere. Or you can relax because it is not your problem. But not all problems are caused by the world. In fact, very few problems are centered on objects. Even if an object is causing the problem, is it really a problem apart from the thought that it is a problem? If it isn't, then all problems ultimately belong to me.

In the third stage of this inquiry you go a bit deeper. You inquire into the reason you have the problem. You say "Who would I be without this belief?" This is the hard part because this is where you discover that the problem is essential to your identity. The answer always is "I would be happy."

The next step should be easy: drop the problem. But it is only as easy as it is non-essential to your identity. People who once drank excessively but who have been clean and sober for thirty years stand up in AA meetings and say with a straight face "Hi, I'm Tom. I'm an alcoholic." Tom's whole adult life has centered around the alcohol problem. It has provided him with an identity. And, oddly enough, "I am an alcoholic" is a projection, an idea—thanks to Maya—designed to keep him from appreciating his true nature.

Dealing with your issues is a tricky business because of the projecting power. A common projection designed to protect the ego is "I am right." When you are under the influence of rajas you do not really care about dharma. The ego needs the moral high ground; it needs to be right because it does not feel right about itself. So it makes you right and the object wrong. See duality in action. Actually you are not right or wrong. You are just ordinary awareness. But—again thanks to Maya—you need to enhance your sense of self-esteem, which is never what it should be if you do not know who you are. Exaggeration is another problem caused by rajas, which keeps you right and the object wrong. In every institution-alized relationship, like marriage, there are always unresolved issues that lead to conflict. If your husband occasionally forgets to take out the garbage one night, he "never" takes out the garbage. If your wife occasionally forgets to pick up your shirts at the cleaners, she "always" forgets.

And finally, if, heaven forbid, someone accuses you of projecting and/or deny-ing, you will, of course, deny and project. Endless indeed are the disturbances of a mind in thrall to rajas and tamas. Unless we understand the dynamics of this unconscious mechanism and gain control of it as it plays out, the Subtle Body will never become inquiry worthy because undigested experience will keep it endlessly disturbed.

Karma Is Unassimilated Experience

Karma yoga is an attitude with respect to action that neutralizes the unhelpful vasanas produced by denial and projection. If the vasanas are not neutralized by karma yoga and by an understanding brought on by an analysis of the causal mechanism, unassimilated experience will produce unwanted karma and the mind will remain extroverted and disturbed. Maya will continue to conceal the self and rajas will project the frustrating idea that there is an objective solution to the desire for completeness.

The Pain Body

One of the most popular formulations of this mechanism in recent years is Eckhart Tolle's "pain body." It is presented as a more or less organic entity that feeds on painful experiences, which is to say that pain itself becomes a vasana and then a samskara. There is no "entity" living in us that it doing this. It is purely an unconscious process that seems conscious because of the proximity of the Causal Body to the Self. The self is not the Causal Body—it is always free of the structures set up by Maya that appear in it—but the Causal Body is the self in its subtlest manifestation. Separating it and its effects from the self is the subject of the next chapter, but the sense that pain is conscious and seeks to renew itself is certainly understandable.

Pain has many forms, but our most fundamental pain is the pain of compulsive action because it strips us of our most precious asset: freedom to choose and act. "Stone walls do not a prison make, nor iron bars a cage." As we pointed out in the first chapter, all human activity is centered around an attempt to remove the sense of limitation brought about by ignorance-inspired desires and fears. We do not pursue objects for the sake of the objects themselves; we pursue them for the sense of freedom that ensues when attaining them removes the painful desire for them. The denial/projection syndrome that we suffer produces life's most fundamental duality, the painful feeling that I am separate from what I want all the while masking the simple fact that I am what I want. As I experience momentary freedoms and joys delivered at the hand of objects, I build a vasana load that eventually distorts the natural geometry of the Subtle Body and I am treated to the additional pain of inner conflict, which in turn motivates further vain actions that harvest additional painful experiences.

It should be clear by now that the raft of experiential solutions to this problem presented in the modern spiritual world are not going to work. How can a discrete experience of the self, a meditation technique or childishly asking "Who am I?" undo this built-in pain producing mechanism? It is impossible. Ignorance is hard wired in the neural networks of human beings and only consistent action based on understanding will bring it to heel over time.

How to Cultivate Sattva

The mind is a garden in which Vedanta plants the seed of self-knowledge, which eventually becomes a great tree. It will not grow in the toxic soil of samsaric consciousness. The logic of this chapter leads us to the conclusion that a sattvic mind is necessary for liberation. How to cultivate it? How to transform rajasic and tamasic vasanas into sattva?

Yoga practice is a commitment to adjusting the relative proportions of rajas and tamas with reference to sattva to produce an efficient, powerful and clear thinking mind. When yoga has prepared the mind, discriminating the self from the objects appearing in it can bear fruit.

You cultivate sattva by connecting your actions with the results. This is not always easy, because results have observable and unobservable effects. If you drink a bottle of wine you will feel stimulated (rajasic) and momentarily happy (sattvic). But the next day your mind will be tamasic and filled with regret. That you indulge yourself in this way shows that you are in pain. Pain motivates you and pain is the result of your actions. You cannot think clearly when you are in pain.

Discrimination is very simple. If something agitates or dulls you, it has to be renounced. You cannot just keep doing what you are doing and somehow expect your mind to become pure. And without a pure mind, the truth will not incarnate in you. At the same time you should take up activities that uplift and harmonize the mind.

But it is not easy because the ego uses its habits to manage rajas and tamas. Take away the habit and it is suddenly exposed to the very energy that is it trying to eliminate. It gets attached to things that are not good for it. It will come up with a million reasons why it can't let go. I was once lecturing a friend about his bad habits. He heard me out and said, "Well, Jim, it may be shit, but it is warm and it is mine." If you know very well what is not good for you and you go ahead doing it, you deserve to suffer. You are going against dharma. This is how Isvara teaches us. If you are going to grow you have to face the music. Because we have become a race of self-indulgent sissies, the gurus have a field day. They say either that you have to do nothing or that you can keep right on doing what you are doing and it will take you there. But you have to take responsibility for "your" projections even though ultimately they do not belong to you. When they are fully owned the mind becomes resolved and will naturally respond according to dharma.

Stuck in Sattva

But you have to be careful. The more pure your mind becomes the greater is the danger that you will develop a spiritual ego. The ego is that part of the Subtle Body that owns actions and the results. It associates with the sublime feeling of sattva and says "I am pure. I am holy. I am spiritual." It can become extremely vain and obnoxious in a smarmy, loving way. The practice of discrimination is not intended to improve you or make you pure. You are already-accomplished-awareness and as pure as the driven snow. A pure mind, a pure heart is not the goal. It is only a means to an end. It is the field in which Vedanta can establish the vision of non-duality. The vision of non-duality destroys the ego's sense of ownership and establishes self-knowledge as the doer. There is no purifier like self-knowledge.

Sattva Plus Vedanta

If the vision of non-duality is established in a pure mind, experience is processed as it happens. Things come up and I respond appropriately. I see the big picture and see where I fit into it. Everyday happenings are laid to rest, leaving space for old stuff to come forth and offer itself into the fire of self-knowledge. *Our goal is to make this teaching the interpreter of our experience.* We need to trust the teaching and let it do the work. Once you see how it works, you will not go back to interpreting reality from your personal standpoint. Your life will flow effortlessly because the doer will have stepped aside and let the truth take over. It is like being on a magic carpet, floating here and there. Nothing gets in your way. You are like water, flowing around every rock.

By now the relationship between action and knowledge should be clear. Action purifies you and knowledge sets you free. In a way you could argue that action is even more important than knowledge because unless you have done the work, the knowledge cannot destroy your ignorance. In the next chapter, The Vision of Non-Duality, we discuss Vedanta's signature teaching, the discrimination between awareness and the objects appearing in you. The teaching of the three gunas will appear again in a different context.

But before we move on we need to consider how it is possible, but difficult, to achieve enlightenment through yoga. So far I have used the word *yoga* to mean an action or actions done to obtain a certain result. We know that the self is ever-free and already accomplished, so yoga does not work for liberation. However, it may lead to liberation. Although the modern world sees yoga as calisthenics, and indeed there is a branch of yoga that is purely physical, in the Vedic world the word *yoga* generally refers to *Astanga Yoga*, the yoga of the eight steps or "limbs." It is a path of meditation leading to various spiritual states of mind.

Leading Error

Here is a quotation from a 14th-century Vedanta text called *Panchadasi*:

> A person saw a ray of light emitted by a diamond and another saw a ray coming from a candle. Both believed that the rays were coming from a diamond and went to obtain it. Though both took the ray to be a diamond, one found a diamond and the other didn't. Mistaking the ray of a candle for a diamond is called a "misleading error," an error that does not lead to the goal. Taking the ray of a gem for a gem is called a "leading" or "informative" error because it leads to the goal. If someone thinks mist is smoke and sets out to collect charcoal and finds charcoal, the mistake is a "leading" error or a coincidence. Meditation on or worship of awareness may also lead to liberation.

Meditation

Meditation is an action. Although some meditations insist that the body be positioned a certain way, meditation is actually an act of mind. We call it a *manasa karma*. People who take up meditation believe that the technique will produce the experience of enlightenment. This is why you see enlightenment touted as a "state" in the yogic literature. The meditator wants to achieve a certain state like Samadhi or Nirvana. We know this is not possible because reality is non-dual awareness. Non-duality means there is only one "state" and you are it. The gunas are three different states created by Maya out of non-dual awareness. However, meditation may inadvertently lead to liberation. Therefore it is called a leading error.

One of the best examples of a leading error is the experience of Ramana Maharshi, one of India's greatest sages. Here is a description of an experience he had that delivered self-knowledge to him:

I felt I was going to die and that I had to solve the problem myself, there and then. The shock of the fear of death *drove my mind inwards* and I said to myself mentally without forming the words, "Now death has come, what does it mean? What is it that is dying? This body dies." And *I at once dramatized the occurrence of death.* I lay with my limbs stretched out still as though rigor mortis had set in and imitated a corpse so as to give greater reality to the inquiry. I held my breath and kept my lips tightly closed so that no sound could escape so that neither the word "I" nor any other word could be uttered. "Well then," I said to myself, "The body is dead. It will be carried stiff to the burning ground and there reduced to ashes. But with the death of the body am I dead? Is the body 'I'? It is silent and inert, but I could feel the full force of my personality and even the voice of the 'I' within me, apart from it. So I am spirit transcending the body. The body dies but the spirit that transcends it cannot be touched by death. That means that I am the deathless spirit." All this was not a dull thought. It flashed through me vividly as living truth which I perceived directly, almost without thought process.

"I" was something very real, the only real thing about my present state, and all the conscious activity connected with my body was centered on that "I." From that moment onwards the "I" or "Self" focused attention on itself by a powerful fascination. Fear of death had vanished once and for all. Absorption in the Self continued unbroken from that time on. Other thoughts might come and go like the various notes of music but the "I" continued like the fundamental *sruti* note that underlies and blends with all other states. Whether the body was engaged in talking, reading, or anything else I was still centered on the "I." Previous to that crisis I had felt no perceptible or direct interest in it, much less any inclination to dwell permanently in it.

This is a typical self "experience." It, or something like it, happens somewhere to many people every day. There is a vast literature of these kinds of experiences. The first thing we notice is the statement "the shock of the fear of death drove my mind inwards." The mind was previously facing the world. Now it is looking inwards. An inward turned mind need not be the result of a trauma, although traumas often drive the mind inward. An epiphany that happens in this way may be a fortuitous event; it was in Ramana's case because it led to self-knowledge. But it is not as useful as the gradual cultivation of an inward turned mind through the consistent practice of karma and *jnana* yoga. This is because the mind introverted by chance or a radical technique invariably returns to an extroverted state because the extroverting vasanas are only temporarily suspended by the epiphany. They are not destroyed. No discrete experience of the reflection of awareness in a sattvic mind can undo lifetimes of ignorance.

Experience is only a decaying time capsule meant to deliver knowledge. What did Ramana learn from this experience? This is important because it reveals the nature of Ramana's mind very clearly. Ordinarily, when we have intense experiences involving great pleasure or great pain, our emotions take over and cloud our appreciation of the experience. We either get so frightened we cannot report what happened accurately, or we get so ecstatic we cannot report what happened accurately. But Ramana stayed cool. He was dispassionate, the number one qualification for self-knowledge. He says, "Now death has come, what does it mean? What is it that is dying? This body dies."

Vedanta is concerned with meaning. It is "the knowledge that ends the search for knowledge." Here you have an inquiring mind, one not fascinated by the experience, one seeking to understand the experience. And using logic he draws the right conclusion: "This body dies." Already we can see by implication that he knows he is other than the body. He has completely objectified it. Then he dramatizes it "to give greater reality to the inquiry." The rest of his musings up to "it is silent and inert" are further confirmation of his understanding that he is not the body.

Next we come to the realization of the self. This is the positive side—what happens when the world is negated. He says, "but I could feel the full force of my personality and even the voice of the 'I' within me, apart from it." The word *personality* is quite interesting. I don't know if this was an accurate translation of Ramana's words. But he probably meant the Subtle Body. It is often referred to as the "embodied" self or individual. The self is unembodied, but seems to be embodied when you look at it through the body.

So now he is aware of the dead body and the Subtle Body and "even the voice of the 'I' within me, apart from it." You see the whole structure of the self in this experience. Then, he concludes correctly, "So I am spirit transcending the body." He has answered the "Who am I?" question, which up to this point he had never even considered.

Most meditators and those blessed—or cursed as the case may be—by accidental epiphanies who experience the reflection of awareness in a sattvic mind lack discrimination. Ramana, it seems, was highly discriminating even though he was a mere lad of seventeen and had no idea of the self before this experience. Discrimination, along with dispassion, sits at the top of the list of qualifications. See the logic: "So, I am spirit (awareness) transcending body."

And next, the icing on the cake; he describes self-knowledge. "All this was not a dull thought. It flashed through me vividly as living truth which I perceived directly, almost without thought process."

When you have any experience, the knowledge of that experience arises in the mind. This knowledge needs to be grasped, owned, if you will. In this case, he witnessed the knowledge "flashing vividly through me as living truth." This should quiet the people who say that the mind has to be dead for enlightenment. The operative words are "almost without thought process." This means there was thought.

Many people have these kinds of experiences but do not realize that they are "spirit transcending body." It is this knowledge that is called liberation. Why is it liberation? Because thinking you are the body is a huge problem. It makes the world and everything in it seem to be real. But to the self, the world appears as a kind of dream, so all the experiences you have in it cannot bind you. In the next statement he addresses this issue of what is real. He says, "'I' was something very real, the only real thing about my present state, and all the conscious activity connected with my body was centered on that 'I.'" This is knowledge. The "I" is real. The body-mind entity is not "taken to be real." And you will notice that he says "my present state." This means that "he" was not "in" the state of meditation or samadhi. He was the awareness of it. We know this because it appears as an object known to awareness.

So whether attention is driven inward unintentionally and the reflection of the self is experienced in a happenstance moment or it is experienced more or less at will through meditation, the "ray of a diamond" is meaningful only if it brings the knowledge. Experiences never last but knowledge is eternal.

Obviously we are arguing for the gradual cultivation of the mind through the yogas discussed so far: karma/dharma yoga and the yoga of the three gunas. It is not that we want you to go to a lot of trouble for your enlightenment—heaven forbid!—but the logic of existence, the way the vasanas are formed and the way they are ameliorated, demands patient, hard work. If you are not willing to commit your life to it, it is better to forget it and settle for the frustrations of normal life rather than the frustrations of a life of inquiry.

But let's assume that you have really had enough suffering and you have a burning desire for liberation and you have been living your life as karma yoga. You are also interpreting what happens correctly in light of your nature as awareness. You have managed the gunas properly and created a very still, pure mind. Your attention is fixed on the reflection of the self. You think you are a person meditating on the self but you are actually the self meditating on your reflection in the mind.

Before we get to the point, it is important to know that meditation, holding your attention on the reflection of the self, burns vasanas very quickly—not as quickly as self-knowledge, but much more quickly than karma yoga. It burns them because a vasana needs to be meditated on or acted out to be recycled. If you don't think about it or perform actions connected to it, it burns up in the meditation.

Finally, before we return to the relationship between meditation and self-knowledge, it is also important to know that meditation is one of the most pleasurable experiences known to man because the mind is not troubled by the vasanas. Meditation does not mean struggling with the vasanas, waiting for them to clear before you feel peace. It is locking attention on the reflection of awareness. If you are meditating only for peace, for relief from vasana-induced stress, you will undoubtedly miss the real meaning of meditation. The real meaning is the knowledge, as Ramana says, "I am spirit (read awareness) transcending body." This knowledge in the form of a thought is called the *akhandakara vritti*. It can appear in whatever language you speak and the words can vary but the knowledge is "I am whole and complete, non-dual, ordinary, actionless, unconcerned awareness." Ramana somehow "intuitively" understood the value of this knowledge and it seems it became his primary identity at that time or maybe later during his stay in the caves. This is why, along with Vedanta, he said, "By knowledge alone is the self to be gained." Virtually nobody gets enlightened through meditation because they meditate for experience, not for knowledge. They do so because they do not understand the value of self-knowledge. But meditation can be a leading error. Inquiry can develop and you may appreciate the value of the thought "I am limitless awareness" when it arises.

A Short Summary

The purpose of all the yogas is to convert an extroverted mind, a disturbed and dull mind, into a contemplative, inward turned mind. A contemplative or sattvic mind is not totally free of rajas and tamas; it is just not dominated by them.

The transition from an extroverted mind to a contemplative mind, one that is committed to discriminating awareness from the objects in it and taking a stand in awareness, is not always smooth. Even when you begin your practice, the mind will have moments, sometimes days or weeks on end, of clarity and joy as it basks in the reflection of awareness created by your practice. Then it may slowly become active and dull as old rajasic and tamasic habits attempt to reassert themselves. You cannot be too vigilant. My teacher used to say "Eternal vigilance is the price of freedom." The gunas are Isvara's circadian rhythms. They not only go through complete cycles on a daily basis, they operate globally too. Just because a habit no longer seems binding, don't assume that it is gone for good. It retreats to the Causal Body and often lives to fight another day. You can quit smoking for months, even years, and one day find yourself puffing away once more.

When sattva is predominant it seems like you are enlightened or moving quickly toward your goal. When tamas and rajas predominate, it seems as if you are backsliding. We are aiming for a predominantly sattvic mind, but it is frustrating if you think enlightenment is a state of permanent sattva. There are no permanent states. If you are in the habit of nervously evaluating your progress on a daily or even weekly basis you are asking for heartbreak. This is why Vedanta is not really useful unless you are qualified. A qualified person who has properly assimilated the knowledge sees himself as the self, understands the nature of the mind, and works doggedly and cheerfully on it, not allowing the fluctuations of the gunas to try his patient resolve.

As practice matures, the mind enjoys increasingly global periods of sattva undisturbed by the daily ups and downs of rajas and tamas. The greatest impediment to happiness is the notion that the ego should have direct control of its experience. The tremendous popularity of drugs, alcohol, sex and extreme sports testifies to the prevalence of the desire to instantly feel good. As mentioned in the last chapter, it does have a certain degree of indirect control, as samskaras are slowly transformed by the practice of karma yoga and modifications of behavior.

The transformation of the Subtle Body is unpredictable. Certain negative patterns can take many years to neutralize. Others may dissolve in a trice. One of the most important qualifications is forbearance. I spent thirteen years patiently eradicating a particular vasana. In the old days of reduced expectations, people were disciplined. In this age of instant gratification and entitlement, discipline is a bad word. We want our enlightenment and we want it now!

This from an anguished seeker:

> I know there's nothing to get or achieve, I know that the only thing I need is a clear understanding of who I really am. But, how is it possible that if I know all these things, I am back in my old habits? Why am I that same old sad person who gets affected by what other people say or think of me? WHY? It seems so hard. Why can't I just see myself as awareness? If I know that that's the true ME!!!!!!!!

We sympathize, but what can we say? There is tremendous opportunity for mischief when a person suffers. Whenever there is a natural disaster, the scammers come out of the woodwork like noxious parasites. Many modern teachers feed off this kind of misery. "I have just the deal for you! Buy my special blend of eleven magic yogic practices for radiant health and instant enlightenment now!" Or as the Neo Non-Dualists mindlessly intone: "There is nothing to do except listen to me say there is nothing to do. Just get it." There are no quick fixes.

Respect Isvara

Isvara—the gunas—can be your best friend or your worst enemy. It is up to you. It is not particularly pleasant to be the one to deliver this news, but life is a terribly conservative force. It abhors change. See how long it takes a species to adapt and evolve. And when the pace of life speeds up beyond the organism's capacity to evolve, it becomes extinct. Will the polar bears survive global warming? The ice will go, humans will invade their habitat and it will be history. Can a rhino evolve a hornless snout in the face of the overweening ignorance of sex crazed Asians?

We have only one life to set ourselves free. It is definitely possible but only when we are armed with rugged determination and a clear understanding of our animal nature and the laws that govern our environments. If you are willing to let go of your attachment to the way things are, maintain dispassion in the face of suffering, and embrace the truth of your limitless identity irrespective of how you feel in the moment, you can succeed. If you respect Isvara it is easy. If not, not.

CHAPTER ELEVEN

The Vision of Non-Duality— Knowledge Yoga

Relative Knowledge

Relative knowledge can be negated. For example, in terms of our physical world—the planet earth—the law of gravity is a constant. It applies everywhere. But it is not knowledge because there is no gravity in outer space. It is "negated" when we include space. It is "relative" to the context.

We call the structure of the apparent reality *knowledge* because it is almost as good as self-knowledge. This knowledge is to Maya what gravity is to the earth. It consists of twenty-four *tattvas*, constant principles operating in the apparent reality: the five elements, the five physiological systems, the five senses plus the five organs of action, mind, intellect, ego and the Causal Body, sometimes called chitta. As long as Maya is manifest they are always present and can be counted as knowledge. When we speak of self-knowledge we don't just mean knowledge of the nature of consciousness, we mean understanding these factors and how they relate to the self and to each other. When you understand how the apparent reality functions you are freed of it. This knowledge is tantamount to knowledge of pure consciousness because it negates the apparent reality. It doesn't negate you, obviously. It reveals you. Knowledge of cosmic principles is relative knowledge because it is good only as far as the creation goes. But it is almost as good as self-knowledge because with reference to the life of a jiva it is eternal.

Finally, information is the lowest grade of relative knowledge. Information is extremely short-lived knowledge and of no use for inquirers. Yes, it is knowledge that it is 4:20 in the afternoon but 4:20 knowledge is not knowledge at 4:21.

Absolute Knowledge

Self-knowledge is "absolute" knowledge. It cannot be negated. This means that there is no time or place when the self is not present or not eternal. Therefore you cannot negate self-knowledge. Self-knowledge is obviously not personal knowledge because the person comes and goes, is born and dies. What is self-knowledge? It is knowledge of you. It is impossible to find the time or place when/where you do not exist. You cannot negate you.

Vedanta—knowledge yoga—consists of both relative and absolute knowledge. It is both the knowledge you need to prepare yourself for enlightenment and the knowledge that sets you free. See how carefully the teaching has unfolded the preparatory knowledge: motivations, the nature of enlightenment, the need for a means of knowledge, the nature of the means and the qualifications required, the importance of a proven teaching and a proper teacher, the nature of the pure self and the nature of the self as Isvara, the Creator and the giver of the results of action, and finally karma/dharma yoga and the nature of the forces operating in the human psyche. We are not cheerleaders trying to get you all fired up, asking you to chant "I want enlightenment and I want it now! Rah, Rah, Rah! Gird your loins and stride onto the field of enlightenment and instantly slay your miserable ego!" We expect you to appreciate the value of knowledge and be inspired to pursue it no matter what.

There are two kinds of self-knowledge: direct and indirect. Indirect knowledge is: "the self exists." This statement implies that it is not me. It means that the self is an object known to me. Most modern teachers, out of ignorance, tell us that they are experiencing the self, as if everyone else wasn't, and that the experience is enlightenment. This means that their knowledge is indirect because it separates the experiencer from the experienced, which is pure duality. Indirect self-knowledge is better than no knowledge but it does not resolve duality. Duality produces suffering because it causes desire and action and makes me result-oriented when I don't need results to be happy. It causes seeking.

Direct knowledge—I am the self—solves the problem if it is properly assimilated because it destroys desire, frees me of the need to act and stops the seeking.

Seeking Stops When the Knowledge Is Firm

The whole point of seeking is to stop seeking. It is easier said than done because seeking has its own beauty and romance. It becomes a vasana. But after a while it loses its cachet and produces exhaustion. You want that needy voice that craves enlightenment to shut up. You just want to wake up, kiss your wife, have your cup of cup of coffee, stir the oatmeal, read the paper and be happy for no reason.

Seeking stops when the knowledge is firm. Inquirers don't seek, because we know we are awareness; all that is left is to actualize the knowledge. The more you seek the more confused you get and the less confident you become. If there is a problem it is only lack of confidence in the knowledge. The solution is to surrender to the knowledge and apply it until you are completely confident in it. All actions, including the application of knowledge, have results. The result of any worldly action is always limited but the result of the application of self-knowledge is free of limitations. The result is simple: I know that I don't need anything to be happy. I am okay, no matter what.

Self-inquiry

Vedanta is known as self-inquiry. Inquiry means to investigate or to ask. The popular notion, made famous by the recent discovery of the teachings of Ramana Maharshi, is to ask the question "Who am I?" Since Vedanta states clearly that you are awareness, inquiry is not intended to answer that question. What is the proper question? It is "How does the identity I have right now jibe with my identity as awareness?" You can determine the nature of your present identity by asking yourself if you believe that the fears and desires motivating your actions are real. If you believe that getting what you want or avoiding what you don't want will make you whole and complete, you have the wrong idea of who you are.

If you know you have the wrong idea of yourself and you really want to be free of your fears and desires, self-knowledge is for you. What is self-inquiry, then? It is the consistent application of self-knowledge to the Subtle Body, brought about by discriminating the self from the objects appearing in it. Karma yoga takes time but the application of self-knowledge is the fast track; it kills ignorance-inspired vasanas on the spot.

Vedanta is knowledge yoga. It is a strange yoga as yogas go. One of our sages humorously and provocatively called it "the yoga of no-contact," an oxymoron if ever there was one, because *yoga* means contact. The yoga of knowledge is unique among the yogas because it does not speak to the part of you that thinks it is out of contact. It speaks to you as the object of yoga, awareness. In other words, no contact is necessary because you are not apart from yourself.

The Real and the Apparently Real

There is a beautiful and extremely important statement—the essence of Vedanta, in fact—attributed to Shankaracharya, one of the great luminaries of the Vedanta tradition. "*Brahma satyam, jagan mithya. Jivo brahmaiva naparah.*" It is the essence of self-knowledge. I do not mean to trouble you with Sanskrit but please remember Vedanta is an ancient science and Sanskrit is a language that evolved out of the spiritual, not the material, needs of humans.

The first word, *brahma* or *Brahman,* is perhaps the most well known Vedantic term. It is similar to the word *God* and has been used for so long in so many different contexts by people who do not know what it actually means that it has become virtually unusable. It has several meanings, most of which suggest bigness and expansiveness. Over the years a language of nearly pornographic hyperbole has evolved out of the fantasies of experience-oriented mystics around such words, obscuring their simple meaning. *Brahman* does not refer to a vast, mind-blowing, amazing state of consciousness or a place to which you go, "never to return." There is nothing mystical, unknowable, or complicated about it. It is just you, simple ordinary awareness. You can't describe it, because you can't describe you. You can say all sorts of words about what happens or has happened to your body and mind because words do reasonably well where objects are concerned. But there is no word to describe you because you are not an object. This does not mean that you are not knowable.

Limitless Does Not Mean Big

There are many words that mean awareness or consciousness, *chit* and *chaitanya*, for instance. As it is used in Vedic literature the word *brahman* generally implies bigness and greatness. But actually it means limitless, which also tends to imply vastness and bigness.

One word for the self will not do because there is no way to evaluate what it means. You need many words until there is clarity. If you say "you are consciousness" to the self when it thinks it is an individual, it takes the statement to mean that consciousness is limited because that is its experience. So it needs to know that it is limitless.

It Is Ordinary Awareness

Awareness under the spell of ignorance also needs another word or it will continue to suffer. The other word it needs to hear, and hear well, is *ordinary*. This fact about you is difficult to assimilate because the ego wants to think it is special. Awareness cannot be extraordinary because there is only one awareness. This is the meaning of non-duality. It seems as if there are many awarenesses when it is viewed through the body because there are many bodies, but there is only one. Electricity manifests as sound in a radio, heat in a heater and light in a bulb, but all are just one electricity flowing through different instruments.

When the self contemplates its limitlessness and its ordinariness—there are many more words to be unfolded as we go—it is freed of its sense of limitation and uniqueness. In a way you can say that the self is unique because there is only awareness. But this does not really make it unique because something that is not the self is required to make the self unique and there is only consciousness.

What does limitless mean? Does it mean that when you know who you are you will be able to leap tall skyscrapers with a single bound like superman, bi-locate and heal cancer with a wave of your divine hand? Limitless does not mean big or powerful; it means that awareness is not modified—is not limited—by the experiences that present themselves to it. It simply means that experience does not stick to you.

Of course this fact is difficult to accept if you think you are the Subtle Body because experience produces vasanas. As they build up, "you" grow rich in experiences and somehow believe that they all add up to "you." I have had many varied and interesting experiences but I cannot find one experience that is here now. I am exactly the same awareness today that I was the day I was (apparently) born. Where are all those experienced people, places and events? Where are the millions of feelings and thoughts that I have experienced? I cannot find them. They exist as words in "my" autobiography, a life that I did not create, a life cooked up by Isvara that I watched unfold. What happened is not here. But I am. I am like the sky through which clouds pass. I am not contaminated by what happens to me. I am pure, an ordinary experienceless experiencer.

The statement so far reads, ordinary awareness is limitless. But we need another word to make the self clear. The next word, *satyam*, means truth. Truth is what always works. Normally we think of the truth as a statement that corresponds to a particular object appearing in awareness. But since objects change, this kind of truth is not good in every time and place. Once when I was unfolding this teaching someone told me that "THE truth" was okay, but "my truth" was better. There is a truth to the way a limited individual sees reality in terms of negotiating her way through the world but it is not good for everyone at all places and times. Innumerable experiences in life are not resolved based on the knowledge you have gathered through your own experiences. There are as many "my truths" as there are individuals and when life puts you in a situation with someone else's truth, particularly someone whom you need for some reason, and her truth contradicts your truth, your respective truths are often a problem. Or, when you come up against the truth of Isvara, the Creator, your "truth" is often completely unworkable.

The objects in this world are sometimes good and sometimes not, but Truth is always good. You can count on it because it is you. You—the real you—is always loved by you. We know that you are the ultimate good because everything you do, think and feel is for your own sake. Some say they don't love themselves or that they love others more but it is true only because it pleases them to think in this manner. Such statements would be impressive only if "others" actually existed apart from the belief in others. You are the truth. You are all there is. You can count only on yourself.

Satyam also means real or reality. I need to tell you this to negate experience. Anything that changes is not real. This is a challenging statement because it means that all the experiences that I value and pursue amount to nothing more than dream experiences.

You don't necessarily need all these words unless you need all these words. To practice knowledge yoga is to contemplate continually and deeply on the teachings, discriminating the real from the apparent on a moment to moment basis. Grasping the meaning of one word is as good as grasping the meaning of all. We provide many and unfold the meaning of each because ignorance takes many forms and is very clever. I call it the "Yeah, but" monster. It is a cat with nine lives. It does not want to die. You need to be well armed to win the battle.

Another important indicator is the word *purna*. *Purna* means full, complete. It means that you are full. Why do we use this word? Because this is not how we feel. We feel incomplete because we are ignorant of the truth.

The spiritual world is particularly obsessed with the idea of emptiness, legitimized and popularized by centuries of Buddhist thought. It is based on a particular type of spiritual experience that reveals the insubstantiality of objects. Realizing the emptiness of objects can send the poor ego into a funk of cosmic proportions. If you feel disillusioned and disappointed because life has failed to live up to your expectations, Vedanta reveals the fact that the *one who sees emptiness is actually fullness itself*. The sense of incompleteness and emptiness, which is just a feeling and not the truth, drives our karma. If I can see that I am not empty and that the objects actually reflect the fullness of my true nature, I can curtail my mad pursuit of objects, slow down and enjoy myself. This fact obviously inspired the famous Biblical statement, "My cup runneth over."

Purna also means a partless whole. You are a fullness that is not made up of parts. Most of us think that we are an assemblage of parts: body, mind, senses, subconscious mind, self, etc. And, coupled with our knowledge of the impermanence of the world of objects, we are prone to imagine that we are always falling apart. "I have to get myself together," we think. You do not have to get anything "together" except your thinking. You need only look and see that you are already a partless whole.

Another word for you is *kaivalya*. It means perfect. Because the world of objects is never seen to be perfectly in line with what we want, we are always trying to perfect it. Because we feel flawed and sinful we are ever trying to perfect ourselves. It is a vain endeavor because reality is perfect in every way. Even what seems to be imperfect—the ever changing world—is actually perfect, not only because it is the self but because it leads us to the discovery of our innate perfection.

The obvious objection to the idea that the world is perfect is the presence of evil. But evil does not belong to the creation. The creation is perfect in every way. Ignorance of the perfection of the self and the perfection of the creation produces evil. The obvious objection to the idea that I am perfect is due to the very same ignorance.

Another important word is unconcerned, *viragya*. It is important to let us know that worry is no longer an option when our knowledge of who we are is hard and fast. The samsaric life is nothing but an endless procession of petty worries; self-knowledge puts an end to it.

Although there are many others, these words are enough to take care of brahma satyam for now. Brahma satyam covers the subject, the first half of our experience. It refers to the self. I am real. I am whole and complete, non-dual, actionless, ordinary, unconcerned awareness. I witness the experiencer and its experiences.

The second part of the statement, *jagan mithya*, covers the other half of our experience, the objects appearing in me, the objects that present themselves to me: what I see, know, experience. *Jagan* means "what changes." I like to think that it is the root of our word *juggler*, objects in continual motion. Perhaps it is; many Indo-European words have Sanskrit roots. If anyone doubts that experience changes, they are—how can I say this sensitively—intellectually challenged.

The second word, however, is a bit more difficult. *Mithya* means *apparent*. The objects that present themselves to me are apparently real. Remember, our definition of objects is: anything other than the subject, awareness. It means that the objects seem to be real. This word separates the men from the boys spiritually. Modern teachings find themselves firmly in the camp of the boys because they tend to dismisses the world entirely while, oddly enough, addressing nonexistent "people" who are in a nonexistent "world." But the objects appearing in you do exist.

They Exist but They Are Not Real

The impermanence of objects is a problem only if you believe that you need an object for happiness and you expect the happiness to last. Why? Because the sad fact—or perhaps it is not so sad if the absence of something you abhor makes you happy—is that no experience of an object lasts. The beautiful creation lasts a long time, so you could say it is relatively real with reference to the lifespan of individual jivas, but it is not absolutely real because it comes to an end one fine day. In any case, the creation is not a problem. The objects created by ignorance are a problem. These objects are your vasanas. It is easy to understand that they are not real because they change from moment to moment. Objects, subtle and gross, have no intrinsic value. Value is added by your vasanas, your likes and dislikes, which you picked up randomly from the world.

Those who claim that the world doesn't exist make mockery of the very idea of enlightenment and leave us nothing to work with; such "teachings" only arrest the mind for a moment and create a longing to experience something that is apparently unexperienced. They have no meaning because you cannot experience something that does not exist. On the other hand, Vedanta's definition of existence gives us something to work with. Consciousness is existence. It takes the experiencer and what she experiences seriously. It is a bit tricky because it says that the experiencer is actually a "non-experiencing" experiencer, or better yet, a non-experiencing witness and that experienced objects, including the experiencing witness, reflected awareness, are "apparently" real. This is very subtle and useful knowledge that usually takes time to assimilate.

For example, if I want a relationship I should know that it is not real. Knowing life is not real makes it very interesting. It lets me enjoy it without expecting it to fulfill me. If you go to a movie and identify with the hero who gets the girl and makes a million, you are quite happy—in the theater. But when the show is over you do not expect be rich in love and money when you get home. If I want an object I can pursue it happily, or not pursue it at all. If I don't understand that objects aren't real, I pursue them because I think they are real and will fulfill me. Knowing the meaning of "apparent" clarifies my relationship to objects. It is also very useful knowledge because if you know that the person you think you are is not a "real" person, you can stop taking yourself so seriously.

Non-Duality Does Not Mean Sameness

Vedanta offers many illustrations of the relationship of the self and objects, a clay pot for example. The clay and the pot have a peculiar relationship. Even though they are both clay, they are not the same. Non-duality does not mean sameness or equality between you, awareness, and the objects that appear in you, the world of experience.

There is more to non-duality than meets the eye. If it is all one and you are ignorant, then I am also ignorant. But this is not how it is. So we need to understand the word *apparent*. If you look at reality from the perspective of the pot, you are one with the clay, no doubt. But if you switch perspectives and look at reality from the point of view of the clay, you are not one with the pot. There is more to you than there is to the pot. The pot depends on you, the clay, but you do not depend on the pot. You are pot free. Maya can produce a plate or a cup out of you, a production that does not involve any gain or loss as far as you are concerned. Your nature never changes, whereas the nature of the object that depends on you is subject to change. The apparent person that you take to be a real person depends on you, awareness, but you do not depend on that person. When you are illumining deep sleep, that person is nowhere to be found. See the freedom that this understanding implies!

Once the nature of the objects is known, it is very important to know that nothing can be done about the relationship between the subject and the objects appearing in it. It is the unalterable logic of existence. This is why enlightenment is knowledge alone. The freedom lies in the knowledge, not a particular experience, because it frees you of dependence on experience for your happiness. Most believe that moksa is freedom *for* the apparent individual but it is freedom *from* the apparent individual. The apparent individual is never free. It is part and parcel of Isvara's matrix of life.

If you look at reality from the individual's perspective, you will find yourself in a world of constant flux. You will constantly change. You will find it necessary to "reinvent yourself" over and over again. But you can never become free. You will always be dependent on awareness for your existence and on objects for your happiness. Nothing is "wrong" with it, particularly if you understand and accept Isvara, because even though you still take yourself to be a person you will remain more or less stress free. If you take yourself to be an individual and you don't understand and accept Isvara as your boss, you will believe that you need Isvara's impermanent objects to complete yourself and consequently you will suffer. You will suffer because in the absence of the knowledge of Isvara, the doer remains in charge. Being a doer is the problem. Although the desire to be free is necessary to jump-start your inquiry, to not acknowledge and take a stand in your true nature is the greatest suffering.

There is one more sentence after *brahma satyam jagan mithya*. It is: *jivo brahmaiva naparah*. It means "the Jiva and Brahman are non-different." Put simply, it means that the consciousness that I am is not different from the consciousness *in* everything or the consciousness that *is* everything. I can know that I am consciousness and that the world is not real but what about my relationship to other consciousnesses? There are no other consciousnesses. The consciousness appearing as a plant, animal, microbe or any other human being is exactly the same consciousness that I am. Appreciation of this fact basically removes all conflict because it allows me to identify with all life. It is the basis of compassion. If I can identify with you I will not have problems with you. I will treat you as I treat myself—with love. People are fond of criticizing Vedanta as a loveless philosophy, but Vedanta is the essence of love. It reveals the fact that love, which is the nature of the self and manifests as identification with objects, is the only valid response to any object, animate or inanimate.

The Key to Liberation: Understanding Awareness, Jiva and Isvara

Discriminating you, awareness, from Jiva and Isvara is the essence of Vedanta. Understanding the discrimination is moksha. In our literature the words *jiva, Isvara* and *self (atma, brahman, paramatma)* are used in several, often confusing ways so we need to unfold these words a little more carefully.

Here is the key to understanding how you as awareness relate to jiva and Isvara.

Reality, though one, is comprised of three fundamental factors: (1) An apparent person or jiva, the "small self," awareness plus the Subtle Body. It is an experiencing entity. (2) A Causal Body produced by Maya, macrocosmic Ignorance, also known as Isvara. The dharma field is brought into being by Isvara, pure awareness associated with Maya. Isvara is the creator of the experiencing entities and what they experience. Vedanta refers to Isvara as The Unmanifest because it cannot be experienced. It is known by inference. (3) The *knower* of both: pure awareness, the self.

Both the jiva and Isvara enjoy the same identity as awareness. Neither can create because creation is a conscious process and a conscious process obviously requires consciousness. On inquiry, both dissolve into awareness because they are impermanent although, as we have said, Isvara is relatively permanent with reference to the lifespan of an individual jiva. Awareness cannot be dismissed because it is "permanent." *Permanent* and *Impermanent* are not actually good words, because they imply duality and seemingly set the experiencing jivas apart from the objects of experience. But we need these words and others like them to set up the discrimination that brings about moksa, freedom. Awareness is always prior to and free of the jiva and Isvara, the Subtle and the Causal Bodies. Therefore, there is really only one self or awareness, free of all objects, from which everything arises and into which everything dissolves.

If you have problem with the word *impermanent*, you can think in terms of another duality: variable and invariable. Both Isvara and jiva are variable factors and awareness is an invariable factor. Isvara exists only with reference to the creation and the creation appears and disappears. Jiva exists only on the microcosmic level and is subject to transformation insofar as it plays the roles of waker, dreamer and deep sleeper.

Here are four verses that establish these three factors:

Chapter 15, verse 16-19 *Bhagavad Gita*
Two "selves," one perishable and the other imperishable, exist in the world. The conscious beings and matter are perishable, the Unmanifest is imperishable. But other than these is the Self beyond the "selves," the limitless, changeless awareness that has entered the three worlds and sustains them. Therefore I (awareness) am renowned as the supreme being. If you know me in this way you become a knower of everything, the self of all.

It means: The apparent self or jiva is not real because it is not always present (think deep sleep) and is always changing. Although it appears to be conscious, it is not actually conscious; it is modified by Maya/ignorance and is perishable because its lifespan in the apparent reality is very brief. Moksa is freedom from the notion of doership and ownership, notions that are the essence of jivas that are identified with the Subtle Body. Identified jivas are also known as human beings or people. Once ignorance of its true nature is removed, the apparent person continues to exist in the apparent reality, although as the self no longer under the spell of ignorance, it is forever free of the notion that it is limited, inadequate and incomplete. It knows it is nameless, formless, unconditioned awareness.

Isvara associated with Maya is conscious—although it is not a jiva as the words "the supreme being" in the verse seem to imply—and is not modified by ignorance/Maya. But it, too, is dependent on awareness. Isvara is conscious because with the appearance of Maya there is something for awareness to be to be conscious of. Isvara is always present in awareness but it is either manifest or unmanifest with reference to awareness.

Therefore Isvara associated with Maya is not real either. Isvara associated with Maya is eternal or permanent with reference to the jiva and the objects it experiences, but impermanent with reference to awareness. To say that Isvara associated with Maya is eternal with reference to the jiva does not mean that it is limitless because ignorance or Maya applies only to a "tiny fraction" of awareness and because it is resolved back into awareness at the end of the creation cycle. Isvara is just awareness's power to create. This relationship between Isvara free of Maya and Isvara associated with Maya is similar to an individual in the sense that an individual and its powers are not the same. Isvara is the one that wields the powers. An artist, for example, is more than his artistic vasanas and the actions they manifest.

Maya is eternal because it is a power that exists in awareness and awareness is eternal; this is why Maya is said to be beginningless (*anadi*). Personal ignorance (*avidya*) ends when the self is realized, ending its cycle of incarnation and suffering but Maya, or cosmic ignorance, continues unchanged, although it is not always manifest. When ignorance or Maya does manifest, Isvara in its capacity as a creator appears, followed by the apparent creation, the world of sentient beings and insentient elements.

Isvara as Pure Awareness *free of its association with Maya* is called *Paramatma*. If you are a student of Vedanta or familiar with Vedic literature you will perhaps know that the word *Isvara* often refers to *Paramatma*, uncreated non-dual awareness. I have used the word *Paramatma* to avoid this confusion.

Although Paramatma is called eternal and imperishable, it is neither. Eternal and imperishable infer non-eternal and perishable and since Paramatma is non-dual, it is neither. It is isness, being. It is self-knowing and, when objects are present, knows objects. It is prior to and the knower of both the jiva and Isvara. It has no qualities.

As stated, as long as the apparent entity, the jiva, is still embodied in the apparent reality, enlightened or not, it is conditioned by Isvara, the Creator. The liberated person (jivanmukta), who lives in the world of duality, is not affected by it, because he knows that it is a superimposition and that Isvara, the gunas, is the doer. Insofar as this understanding is moksa, the karma yoga sadhana that leads to this understanding no longer obtains, although the karma yoga attitude remains.

Freedom *from* or Freedom *for* Jiva?

We said that moksa is freedom from the jiva and freedom for the jiva. The distinction between jiva, Isvara and Paramatma creates an understanding in the jiva that separates it from its subjectivity and gives it the objective view of Isvara and itself. It makes it clear that the authorship and ownership of everything belongs to Isvara. At the same time it makes it clear that it is not under the control of Isvara because Isvara in its role as creator is not real. How can something that is not real actually create or control anything?

Furthermore, as mentioned, this understanding separates awareness from both Isvara and jiva, the creator and the created. In so doing it makes it clear that its ordinary awareness, which is the essence of its identity, is limitless. The discovery that the self is limitless awareness is moksa, freedom for the jiva. In what way does this understanding come about? Jiva understands that it does not exist unless it is known to exist and the knowledge of its existence is possible only because it is aware. This leads to the conclusion that it is awareness. Try as you might you cannot find two awarenesses.

A jiva that knows that it is limitless awareness is called a jivanmukta, liberated while alive. In reality a jivanmukta is just pure awareness stripped of its identification with Isvara and Jiva. Awareness is neither living (jivan) nor is it free (mukta) since both imply duality.

Limitless Bliss

Because there are two apparently different principles in reality—the self and the objects—it is possible to confuse the self with the objects. Samsaric life is nothing but confusing the real and the apparent. We have a technical term for it: mutual superimposition.

The practice of knowledge is discrimination. Discrimination negates superimposition. Because the self is not known, the gross, subtle and causal bodies are assumed to be real. Taking them to be the self produces suffering because they are only apparently real. You, awareness, are always present and never change.

The three bodies change. They are "not self." They are to be negated until identification with them and attachment to them is dissolved. Negation means that they are understood to be unreal. Knowing they are unreal destroys your identification with them. If you identify with the bodies you will not identify with the self.

When you no longer identify with them, pure non-attachment arises. Non-attachment is not merely the intellectual conviction that the states, bodies, and objects are unreal; it is a sense of limitlessness. You may intellectually appreciate this teaching but until that part of you that does not appreciate it is negated, you need to discriminate until limitlessness, which is always present, is experienced. Moksa means that you know you are free and you experience yourself to be free. It is quite possible to know you are free and still feel limited. The experience of freedom comes gradually as binding vasanas exhaust.

When we say "a sense of limitlessness" and "until limitlessness is experienced" it seems as if we are contradicting the statement that the self cannot be experienced. It cannot be experienced as an object but it is always experienced as myself. Self-actualization is rather like "conscious sleep" in that the jiva experiences bliss continually. It is not the bliss that is opposed to suffering. It is the bliss that observes suffering and enjoying. It is just a sense of satisfaction that arises from the knowledge that while suffering and enjoying *seem* to touch me, they do not actually touch me. If I could not actualize myself and experience my limitlessness as bliss I would not be limitless.

The Five Sheaths

The three bodies are often referred to as sheaths, in the sense that they hide or cover the self. In fact, the self is self-evident and cannot be covered by anything, but attachment to thoughts, feelings and bodily sensations keeps attention on them and not on the self. Although I cannot actually read the words on this page without experiencing the page, my focus on the words keeps me from appreciating the presence of the page. To know the background of my experience, my perceptions, sensations, thoughts and feelings need to be separated from it. Discrimination is not an experiential separation of the subject from the objects. The self cannot be taken out of the bodies because it was never in them in the first place, although often when the self is realized, it may feel like you are out of your body because we are so deeply accustomed to take the physical body as our point of reference. The discriminative shift is purely in terms of understanding and produces a positive result every time the not-self is dismissed. In fact, the bodies are "in" the self, in the sense that they are within the scope of awareness, not outside it, even though they appear as objects.

Discrimination is not "merely intellectual" as some claim; it impacts on jiva's experience of life. But ironically, it only if object experience is negated. To negate experience you have to have experienced enough of life from the samsaric state of mind to have become disillusioned with the *pursuit* of experience. Negated experience is not nonexistent experience. It is knowing that experience is not real unless it is looked at as the self. If you still entertain doubts about the futility of the pursuit of fulfillment in samsara, discrimination doesn't work. But if you are doubt-free on this issue, discrimination works.

The negation implied by discrimination is not intellectual either. To simply assert that an object is not real is only a preliminary step. You have to actually refuse to indulge the vasanas pushing or pulling you into experiences until they are rendered non-binding. You may very well know who you are and who you are not, but your binding vasanas do not. And even if they did, they will not go away on their own. You have to destroy them with inquiry if you want the apparent individual that appears in you to be happy. You can be enlightened and have an unhappy jiva, but what is the point? There is nothing intellectual about it. Discrimination has quantifiable experiential results. There is a certain amount of pain because you are resisting desire but every time you negate the not-self, peace and happiness ensue.

To practice discrimination, you dispassionately observe the incessant stream of thinking (and the emotions it produces) that continually emerges from the Causal Body and determine the impact that identification with it has on your life. As inquiry continues, ignorance cannot support itself, unhealthy patterns of living fall away and the mind becomes increasingly quiet. Consistent observation of the content of the Subtle Body will eventually expose the true observer, awareness. In reality, observation is not an action. It is what one is. However, the jiva needs to mimic the self and discriminate at all times until its attachment with the "not-self" is broken. Remember, the jiva is the self plus the Subtle Body, so when the Subtle Body is negated the ever-free nature of the self is revealed.

We defined objects earlier as anything other than the subject, awareness. The Five Sheaths teaching (*pancha kosa prakriya*) enumerates the objects in a logical way. It says that within the physical sheath is the vital sheath; within the vital sheath is the mental sheath; within the mental sheath is the intellect sheath (or the agent sheath) and within it is the bliss or the enjoyer sheath. This succession of one within another apparently covers the self like the layers of an onion conceal the onion's core.

1. The physical sheath (*anamayakosa*) is produced from the seed and blood of the parents, is made out of food and grows by food alone. It is not the self, for it does not exist either before birth or after death. Since the body did not exist in the previous birth it could not have produced this birth for that would be an effect without a cause. It is impossible to have an effect without a cause. Unless it exists in a future birth it cannot enjoy the results of action accumulated in this birth, which means that one person could suffer and enjoy the karma of someone else, which is not possible. It is in a state of flux and is a known object.

2. The physiological systems, the vital airs sheath (*pranamayakosa*), pervade the body and give power and motion to the perceptive and active senses. It is not the self, because it is not conscious and is in a constant state of flux and is a known object.

3. The emotional sheath (*manomayakosa*) causes the ideas of "I" and "mine" with regard to the body, dwelling and offspring. It is not the self, because it has desires, is moved by pleasure and pain, is subject to delusion, is fickle and is a known object. This sheath is turned outward. It illumines the physical world through the senses. It collects sense data and presents it to the intellect. It doubts and produces emotions.

4. The intellect (*vignanamayakosa*) is the reflection of pure awareness and pervades the whole body up to the tips of the fingers and toes in the waking state but disappears in deep sleep. It is known as the intellect sheath. It is aware of itself, the "subjective" world. It thinks, remembers, believes, imagines, makes determinations and gives orders. It is also not the self, because it is a known object and it changes.

Sheaths 3 and 4 are known as the Subtle Body or the *Antakarana*, the "inner instrument." It is the instrument of action and enjoyment. As such it is called the doer (*karta*) and the enjoyer (*bhokta*).

5. The bliss sheath (*anandamayakosa*). When the Subtle Body gets what it wants, it turns inward, catches the reflection of the bliss of awareness and merges into "conscious sleep." This is known as the sheath of bliss. This sheath cannot be the self, because it is temporal and a known object. The bliss that reflects in the bliss sheath is eternal, immutable awareness.

These five sheaths account for all jiva's experiences. Each is identified by certain signature thoughts. For example, there is not one person in existence who has not thought or said "I walked to the store (or field, hilltop, church, etc.)." Why is this an expression of self-ignorance? Because the "I," awareness—the self—has no feet and it is everywhere so it cannot go anywhere. What would be the correct sentence? "I observed the body walking to the store." If you say "I am hungry and thirsty" you have confused the "I" with the vital air sheath. It is responsible for hunger and thirst. If you say "I am happy or sad" you have owned sensations that do not belong to the self and you are identified with the emotional sheath. The self is free of emotions. If you say "I think" or "I choose" you are identified with the intellect sheath. The self is thought free. Finally, if you say "I feel good" you are identified with the bliss sheath.

In each of these examples the "I," awareness, has confused itself with a particular layer of experience. When you catch yourself identifying with a particular experience—a thought, feeling or action—you should think "This is not me. It is an object known to me. It is not real, because it changes. I am the knower of this object/experience." In this way, you separate the "I" from the object appearing in it at any moment. Then you turn your attention to awareness.

Epiphanies are experiences that usually separate the "I" from the objects and result in a sense of freedom. But because the experience is in the realm of time, the separation is short-lived. When the experience ends, the "I" is reconnected to an object and suffering resumes. It is clear that suffering returns because the desire to repeat the experience arises immediately. In fact, ignorance often appears during the course of the epiphany in the form of a wish to enjoy the experience permanently. Epiphanies do not permanently destroy self-ignorance and identification with objects; they give only temporary relief. Only the persistent application of self-knowledge to ignorance as it manifests in the Subtle Body will eradicate ignorance. It is erroneously believed that enlightenment is some sort of timeless experience, but desirable spiritual experiences are simply experiences of the bliss sheath, which is in time.

The Three States

One of our most sophisticated discriminations involves an analysis of the three states of consciousness and their experiencing entities. The first entity is the waking state ego, the primary identity of everyone. When I say "me" in conversation, I am referring to the waking state entity. The belief that I am a waking state entity comes with the conviction that physical, emotional, and intellectual objects are real.

The Waker

The waking state entity (*viswa*) is consciousness turned outward, shining through the senses, mind and intellect, illumining their respective objects. The waking state entity is a consumer of experience. Vedanta calls it "the one with thirteen mouths." The thirteen mouths refer to the ten senses, the mind, the intellect and the ego. These instruments aggressively eat experience. The physical body consumes matter, the five elements in various combinations. The mind devours emotions; the intellect nibbles ideas; and the ego gobbles any experience it believes will make it feel whole, adequate, and happy.

The Dreamer

The dreamer's consciousness is turned inward, awareness illumining a world similar in some respects to the waking state world and radically different in others. In the dream state, awareness illumines the vasanas playing out as images on the screen of awareness. In the waking state, the vasanas express as the waking state entity's thoughts and feelings. The waking world is not distorted like the dream world, because the senses structure it. Like the waking state entity, the dreamer believes her world is real. The dreamer is equipped with the same instruments for experience as the waking state entity: dream senses to consume dream objects, a dream mind to emote and feel, a dream intellect to think dream thoughts and a dream ego to go about the business of experiencing the dream life. In Sanskrit the dreamer is called *taijasa*, the "shining one," to indicate that it is actually awareness. Dreams appear in light, even though the waking senses are inactive, because awareness shines through the dreamer, just as it shines through the waking state entity.

The Sleeper

Sleep is defined as the state, saturated with happiness, where the self does not desire external objects, does not illumine internal objects and is self-ignorant. The sleeper is called *prajna*, or undifferentiated consciousness. In the other states, consciousness flows outward and inward but in sleep it is formless. The sleeper ego is extremely subtle, its presence indicated by the fact that we experience limitlessness and bliss. In the waking and dream states, bliss is sporadic because it is broken by many divisions of thought and feeling, but in sleep it is continuous. We know of the sleeper's experience because it reports a good sleep after transforming into a waking state entity. Were the waking state entity actually a different ego from the sleeper or the dreamer, it would not recall the experience of sleep or dream. In reality all three are just consciousness.

The deep sleep state is free of both the waking and dream egos and their respective objects, because the vasanas projecting them have become dormant. Hence, it is referred to as the seed state. When the seeds sprout, the sleeper, who is actually the self, seemingly becomes a waking state entity or a dreamer and experiences the appropriate world. Because the gross waking ego is transformed into a very subtle sleep ego when we sleep, we do not think that we are conscious in deep sleep. The subtlety of consciousness in deep sleep (prajna) has erroneously lead metaphysicians to conclude that deep sleep is a void. But it is actually the womb of creation because the waking state entity, the dreamer and their respective worlds, emerge from it. When you wake up in the morning, your whole life is neatly laid out, consistent with the day before, which indicates that the experiencer and its karma had simply entered a dormant state. The macrocosmic sleep state is called the Causal Body and contains the vasanas of every living being.

Because of its association with one of the three states of consciousness, non-dual awareness appears to be three distinct entities. Associated with the waking state, it "becomes" a waking state personality, suffering and enjoying the limitations of its world. The dreamer suffers the limitations of the dream world. And the sleeper suffers self-ignorance and limitless bliss.

These three states and egos are known to everyone and constitute the totality of experience.

Once these facts have been established, the inquiry begins. If I am the waking ego, which I am convinced I am, what happens to me when I become a sleeper? I willingly surrender everything essential to my idea of myself (my body, mind, intellect, and all my physical possessions) and turn into a mass of limitless awareness. Yet in spite of the pleasure of sleep, I am not content, because I sacrifice my sleep identity to suffer and enjoy the worlds created by my vasanas in waking and dream states. My identity as a dreamer is obviously unsatisfactory because I consistently leave it to become a sleeper or a waker. So my status as any ego or ego aspect is limited, and my true identity is open to question. Furthermore, if I identify with experiential happiness, I have a problem, because the happiness experienced in sleep disappears in the waking state. Dream happiness dissolves on waking, and waking happiness does not transfer to the sleep or dream states.

The answer to "Who am I" is: I am not any of these experiencing entities. If I am real I have to exist all the time. I cannot suddenly be one thing one minute and something else the next. I experience life as a simple conscious being. In fact, the three ego entities are non-dual awareness, identified with the particular state they are experiencing. Awareness is the witness of the three states.

It is easiest to understand awareness by considering the dream state because the physical senses are inactive. The dream is playing on the screen of awareness like a movie. Even though physical light is absent and the eyes are closed, the dream ego and the events in which it is participating are clearly illumined. The dream light is awareness functioning as the dreamer, "the shining one." However, ignorance operates in the dream as it does in the waking state. It causes the self to identify with the dream ego and its doings, preventing the realization of the dream light as me, the self.

The self is unknown in the waking state for the same reason. Preoccupied with the happenings in our worlds and minds, we are completely unaware that both the sense objects and our thoughts and feelings are bathed in the light of awareness.

In deep sleep the ego/intellect is dissolved into its source, the dormant seeds of its past actions. It is not aware of the self or anything external. Yet awareness is there, making the experience of bliss possible. And when we wake up we know that we slept, even though we were not there as the waking state entity, because awareness was there.

The three egos are called limiting adjuncts (*upadhis*). A limiting adjunct apparently conceals the nature of something else. If I put clear water in a colored glass, the water, seen through the glass, appears colored. Similarly when I look at myself through my waking, dream and sleep personalities, I seem to be three distinct entities. However, when I remove the adjunct I can see what I really am. The removal or negation of the three experiencing entities is accomplished by simply knowing they are unreal. In the wake of this understanding, I am free to assume my true identity as awareness, because it is the only other option. Awareness cannot be denied or negated.

Over time, the waking state entity becomes fractured into many sub-identities, adjuncts within an adjunct, so that it is possible to be confronted with a confusing array of selves, none of which are real. Remember, real means enduring, unchanging and unlimited. Because something is experienced does not make it real, the blueness of the sky or a mirage on a desert, for example.

With reference to my son, I am a father. With reference to my father, a son. With reference to my wife, I am a husband. To my boss I am an employee. I am a devotee with reference to God and a taxpayer with reference to the government. With reference to myself I am a success, failure, victim, victimizer, sports fan, audiophile or any of the thousands of ready-made identities available today. The many often conflicting roles we play as waking egos are limited by each other, other selves playing similar or different roles, and our ideas about the meaning of these selves. Caught in this thicket of identities, is it any wonder I suffer? In the end, spiritual life, no matter what the path, should always boil down to finding out who I am minus all my roles and experiences.

The Opposite Thought

A binding vasana is one that resists the truth. So we need to turn the truth into a binding vasana. When I hear that I am awareness my whole thought system does not agree. It is a little like being two people. One person says "I am limited, inadequate and incomplete" and the other says "I am limitless awareness. I am capable of dealing with anything life has to offer. Far from being incomplete, I am fullness itself."

If I know that I am awareness and my mind continues to spout ignorance, how enlightened am I? Ignorance and knowledge cannot exist simultaneously. So ignorance has to give way to knowledge, unless I know it is ignorance. If I know it is ignorance I will not identify with it and it will have no power to create suffering. That I take ignorance to be knowledge is the problem, not ignorance per se. If I expose my mind to Vedanta in a dedicated way I will learn the difference between ignorance and knowledge, making it unlikely that I will identify with ignorance.

Ignorance has many forms. For example, the idea that "I am unique or special" is ignorance because you are just the five elements, mind, intellect, ego, tendencies and awareness like everyone else. The belief that someone other than myself can make me happy is ignorance because there is not anyone else. The notion that something is right or wrong with the world is ignorance because the world is only in your mind and your mind is not real. If it is real, where is your mind and the world in deep sleep? Why does the world not bother you when you sleep? The thought that I may get sick and die is ignorance because what is born dies and what is never born never dies. Since I am awareness, I am never born. Therefore, death has nothing to do with me.

To catalogue all ignorance-inspired ideas would take centuries. To make it easy, self-inquiry has reduced ignorance to a list of one—I am the body-mind-intellect-ego entity—because this is where they all come from. The war with ignorance is not a fair fight at first. Is it reasonable to expect weak little David to knock out great Goliath with a small stone? But it is reasonable for him to take steroids and go to the gym every day and bulk up, giving him a fighting chance. You win the war by consciously substituting the "I am complete" thought for the "I am incomplete" thought when it arises—which it does with every illegitimate fear and desire. Fears and desires are just proxies for the idea that I am incomplete and inadequate. If you feel depressed because you are not getting what you think you want at work or in your relationships, ask yourself who is depressed and who wants the depression to go. Then, with the help of the knowledge "I am the one in whom this depressing feeling is occurring," notice the natural separation between you and the feeling. Identify with the one who knows, not the feeling. The feeling dissolves and the vasana that gave rise to it is weakened.

Knowledge is very powerful. Nothing more than the conscious thought of awareness is required to "reach" awareness because you *are* awareness—even when you think you are someone or something else. Substituting truth for untruth builds a truth vasana, which neutralizes the likes and dislikes that keep us tied to the wheel of action. It will eventually neutralize the ego-doer completely. Nothing can be done to make you complete and whole except to cancel the thinker-feeler-ego-doer. You were complete and whole before your body was born. You are complete when you think you aren't.

The voice of ignorance is like an entity within. It seems real and conscious. It will find many reasons to sabotage your practice. It will say that it cannot assert the truth because it does not "feel right" to do so. It will tell you that it is dishonest to say that you are free. Aside from the fact that the truth does not feel like anything, except perhaps the absence of suffering, it should be encouraged to take its steroids and pump iron. In other words, it is precisely when you do not feel good that you need to remind—bring the knowledge back to your mind—yourself who you are. Who you are is not a feel-good experience, but practicing knowledge feels good.

It is necessary to stand up to the lie, over and over. Substituting the true for the false is not brain washing. It is a continual conversation with your ego. You cannot fail to win the argument if you explain the logic of the teachings to it. Although there is resistance, at some secret place within itself the ego knows that it stands to gain from accepting the knowledge. Patiently win it over.

Self-inquiry works only for mature people who desire freedom strongly, have created a lifestyle that allows them to monitor the mind on a moment-to-moment basis and who know the difference between knowledge and ignorance. It does not work for extroverted people with a weak or middling desire for liberation. Neutralizing the doer does not mean that actions are meant to be given up, only that the true source of action is known. The true source of action is not the doer; it is a complex web of impersonal forces illumined by awareness that animate the body mind like a battery animates a toy.

If attention is not properly introverted and the lifestyle is too active, applying the opposite thought will not work. In this case, the mind can be purified with the karma yoga attitude until it becomes prepared for the direct application of self-knowledge.

Those who take enlightenment to be a thought-free state dismiss this practice. They say that the presence of any thought, including the thought "I am awareness," shows that the goal has not been reached. Aside from the fact that enlightenment is not a state of consciousness that can be reached, no thought, including the thought "I am a limited ignorant suffering person," stands in the way of the self, because the self is present before, during and after every thought. It is a different order of reality. If you step on a person's shadow, the person is not injured. Many discover the self precisely when they are completely identified with the suffering ego. Identification with the idea that the self suffers or enjoys is all that stands in the way of enlightenment. The knowledge) ignorance that brings on the identification.

The Three Gunas

In the last chapter we discussed how the three gunas affect the assimilation of experience, their relationship to spiritual experience and how knowledge of them can be a powerful purifier. But this teaching has another purpose: to directly discriminate the self from experience. If you are really interested only in liberation, you are not interested in gaining a particular experience or the effect of experience on the experiencer. As we know, awareness is experience-free and we also know that experience appears in the form of the three energies. In this discrimination the inquirer simply pays attention to the guna operating in the mind and identifies with the awareness of the guna. Ignorance, of course, would like you to think that "you" are dull and sleepy (tamasic), busy, passionate and agitated (rajasic) or clear, still and happy (sattvic). But you know better so you use self-knowledge to separate from the experiencing entity, the Subtle Body, that ignorance insists is you. As always, the guna in play cannot be me, because it is known by me. Like all the other discriminations it is simply a way to distinguish my self from the objects—in this case the gunas—appearing in me.

CHAPTER TWELVE

VALUE OF VALUES

Hearing and reflecting on the teachings of Vedanta are the primary means of self-knowledge, but you cannot hear or reflect properly if the mind is not prepared. Therefore, a secondary means of knowledge—the knowledge of values—is required.

Sadly, the modern spiritual world is averse to teaching values, much to its detriment, preferring instead to focus exclusively on the self, the ultimate value. But you cannot ignore the moral dimension of reality in your quest for freedom, because values or lack thereof impact directly on the ability to understand and assimilate knowledge.

This important chapter is based on Swami Dayananda's discussion of the values required for self-inquiry presented in the *Bhagavad Gita* and other texts. I cannot claim authorship of it, although I think the discussion is enhanced by my edits.

Knowledge Requires Three Factors

For knowledge of any kind to take place, three factors are required: the knower, the object of knowledge and a means of knowledge. To know a sound, I—the knower—must be present. Second, the sound must happen, and thirdly, I need ears.

The first two factors are obvious but the third is not always obvious. If I am within the range of a sound and did not hear it, I have to see if my ears are working. If I have my ears checked and they are functioning properly, the problem lies elsewhere. The only other possibility is my attention. If it was engaged elsewhere when the sound occurred, I will fail to hear the sound. For basic perceptual knowledge the sense organs are not enough. They need to be backed by attention.

Mind Must Be Prepared

When all factors, including an attentive mind, are present, sometimes knowledge does not take place. For instance, if I really want to know the meaning of the theory of relativity and I attend a university class and attentively listen as a famous scientist explains formula E=MC2, yet fail to understand, it is because my mathematics background is insufficient. To solve the problem I need to bone up on my calculus because my mind is not prepared to understand.

Words as a Means of Knowledge

For Vedanta to work, the teacher needs to communicate the vision of non-duality and the inquirer's mind must be prepared. Vedanta is a means of self-knowledge whose words and sentences reveal the self. They can give indirect self-knowledge if the self is beyond my field of perception and direct knowledge if it is within my field of experience. Since the subject matter of Vedanta is me and I am always and only experiencing me, words can give me direct self-knowledge.

For the words to work, the inquirer needs to understand them as the teacher understands them. Imprecise definitions don't work, because they are open to interpretation. Vedanta does not work if it is interpreted. The words of Vedanta carry precise meanings. To appreciate the intended meaning, unintended meanings must be eliminated. So the teaching establishes a context in which unintended meanings are removed. Without the proper context, self-knowledge will not happen in the teaching situation. If words like unlimited, eternal, transcendental and samadhi are used but are not contextualized, they will only create confusion.

However, even if you have a teacher skilled in the methodology of teaching, one who can unfold the exact meaning of the words, and a dedicated inquirer who is seeking self-knowledge, it will not happen unless the inquirer's mind is prepared. Without a prepared mind Vedanta is like calculus for a person still working on the multiplication tables.

This does not mean that Vedanta cannot be understood, only that a prepared mind is required. Knowledge takes place only in the Subtle Body. If the conditions are favorable and knowledge does not take place, there is an obstruction.

Values a Secondary Means for Self-knowledge

Spiritual practices are useful for quieting the mind but they do not prepare the mind for Self-knowledge. One does not need to be a mature or morally sound person to breathe a certain way or twist one's body into a yoga pose. A prepared mind reflects non-dual values and ethical attitudes. Values are the primary means to prepare the mind for inquiry. Specific practices are secondary. The knowledge of values is not self-knowledge. It is a means and self-knowledge is the end.

Self-knowledge does not necessarily happen when the appropriate values are present, but it may happen. Without the right value structure, self-knowledge will probably not happen and if it does, it will be basically useless.

Universal Values – Samanya Dharma

Because reality is non-dual there is only one person, awareness with three bodies. The implication of this statement in terms of values is obvious: you and I are one. If we are one spiritually, appearances created by Maya to the contrary notwithstanding, I should value you as I value myself. And since my actions reflect my values I should treat you like I treat myself. I treat myself well because I love myself and you deserve the same.

A behavioral norm based on the non-dual nature of reality is called a *dharma*, or right action. How I do not want to be treated is called *adharma*, wrong action. I don't lie to you because I don't want you to lie to me. I don't injure you because I don't want you to injure me. Dharma and adharma are universal and stem from a common sense regard for one's own interests. They vary slightly from culture to culture.

Situational Ethics – Visesa Dharma

Although dharmas and adharmas are more or less universal, they are not absolute. The context that calls for a response plays an important role in determining how I behave. If I have a ruptured appendix I will surrender my value for non-injury and go under the knife without surrendering my general value for non-injury to others. Although my standards for behavior and attitude may not be subjective, my interpretation of these values is very likely to be. For example, I may strictly apply my value for truthfulness to the words of others but not so rigorously to my own.

Values cannot be dismissed, nor can they be contravened with impunity. A thief locks up his stolen property because he cannot escape the value for non-stealing. If he was not disturbed he would not hide his loot. Universal values are built in to the very fabric of creation and my mind is an integral part of it. Failure to live up to a value puts me in conflict with the world and with myself. It creates guilt and guilt is not an aid to self-knowledge.

To assimilate the teachings of non-duality, I must follow dharma. If I understand that both good and bad actions are apparently real, then values are no longer a problem for me. However, this does not mean that my actions transcend dharma and adharma. It means that my actions in the apparent reality will be dharmic because I have nothing to gain or lose by violating dharma. Only when I imagine that the apparent reality does not exist is it possible for me to violate dharma, disturb my mind and the minds of others. A conflicted mind is not helpful. It produces counterproductive emotions: anger, sadness, regret, low self-esteem and a sense of failure.

When my values are the same as those of others operating in my environment they cause no conflict, but if I am not willing to behave according to the expectations of others I cannot expect others to behave according to mine. For example, if I have a value for non-injury, the number one universal value, and I do not like to be criticized, if I criticize others I will be conflicted. If the world expects me to be truthful, which it does, and I expect the world to be truthful, which I do, yet being truthful conflicts with a personal value for money, for example, I may lie to get or keep my money. I am quite happy to follow my personal values, but when they conflict with universal values there is scope for suffering because universal values do not go away when I override them to gain some passing comfort; they are built into the very fabric of my being.

In fact, my personal values are often the source of significant agitation irrespective of the correctness of my behavior. My value for clean air or healthy food puts me at odds with the whole world because virtually everything these days is polluted. If I am particularly concerned with justice, which is based on the non-dual nature of reality, I will become agitated when someone treats me unfairly or even if I believe they might treat me unfairly. Spiritual values for truth, beauty and justice can cause as much mischief as petty worldly values.

The Knower-Doer Split

If I value truth but tell a lie, I feel guilty because I have created a split between the knower and the doer. For example, the knower goes on a diet but the doer has a second helping; the knower decides to get up early and go for a walk but the doer turns off the alarm. This angers the knower, who starts to condemn me, making me feel useless and uncomfortable.

At the same time the disturbance hides the deeper reason for my actions. I never want what I want for the reason I think. An unconscious force is always at work. The situational things that I value are not valued for their own sake, only for how they make me feel—for a sense of security or pleasure or virtue. A vegetarian does not value vegetables for the vegetables' sake but for the feeling that she is doing animals a favor. So what I really value is feeling comfortable with myself. If I understand this and appreciate the fact that there is an upside and a downside to every action, I am in a position to inquire directly into the self because the joy that comes from fulfilling any value, personal or universal, comes from it. Nonetheless, this analysis of values is intended to heal the knower-doer split and make inquiry workable.

Swami Dayananda says:

> The source of a situational value is that I expect to feel good through exercising choice based on it. When I clearly see that a particular choice will make me suffer, I do not make that choice. Thus, when I become thoroughly convinced that acting contrary to a general value will result in suffering for me, my compliance with that value becomes choiceless, like the answer to the question, 'Do you want happiness or unhappiness?' If speaking truth is a value for me, and I am completely convinced that non-truth brings suffering, there is no choice but to speak the truth. Speaking truth becomes natural and spontaneous and my partial value for a universal value has now become a well-assimilated personal value.

When I want certain unassimilated universal values to become part of my value structure, I must exercise deliberation in following them until I am convinced of their value in terms of knowledge. When I am convinced, observing them becomes spontaneous. For the person with assimilated ethical values, life becomes very simple. No conflicts cloud the mind. For that one, the teaching of Vedanta is like the meeting of gas and fire. Knowledge ignites in a flash.

For values to be valuable for me their upside and downside must be understood and not simply imposed from without in the form of religious or social dogma. Therefore Vedanta calls these values knowledge. The following values are interrelated and define a harmonious frame of mind in which knowledge can occur. Each term highlights a certain attitude, the value for which must be discovered personally, so that the attitude becomes a natural aspect of the inquirer's frame of mind.

A "Better Person?"

Vedanta is not self-improvement. An inquirer is not trying to become a perfect or better person, because both good and not so good people suffer a sense of limitation and crave freedom. He is trying to realize his primary identity, the ever-free self, the non-experiencing witness of the person. Most approaches to enlightenment involve denial of the person, punishment of the person, transcendence of the person, or thoughtless transformation of the person, probably because making a person acceptable to himself is very difficult. But it is the person who wants freedom and it is the person that needs to seek it, so we have to take the person into account.

Our discussion of values is challenging because it clearly states that we may be saddled with values that prevent us from inquiry, which is to say that we are not up to the mark spiritually, which in turn may make us think that we are not good people. The investigation of values is intended only to get our minds settled enough to discriminate, not improve us. However, insofar as a person is little more than her priorities and values, any change in one's value structure amounts to a change in the (apparent) person. In general a good person is one who thinks and acts conforming to universal values and a bad person is one who doesn't. So if you have a feeling of inadequacy and low self-esteem and want to be a better person, the following analysis of the moral dimension of reality will be useful, whether or not you are a seeker of freedom.

Understanding Values

1) Inquiry into Pride, Vanity, Conceit, Self-Glorification

A simple, factual self-respectfulness is a good quality. However, most of us have doubts about our adequacy. We secretly fear that we are not good enough and are unable to provide ourselves with the confidence we need to be happy with our lives. So we look to others to validate us. In order to gain validation we are often tempted to exaggerate our qualifications and accomplishments so that others will think we are special and glorify us. If I am completely certain about my talents and abilities I take them for granted and have no need for validation or support.

Demanding respect from others invites many disturbances because the one who asks for respect is not in control of the result. People give it for reasons known only to them. When their minds change, the validation is withdrawn and hurt arises. Any form of hurt is due to pride, an inflated ego, one that is excessively attached to what it thinks it knows, believes, or possesses or how it looks. For example, body-conscious individuals who spend an inordinate amount of time grooming or calling attention to their bodies with expensive clothing, outlandish hairdos, tattoos and piercings often do so to attract attention they are incapable of giving themselves. Such egos, inflated by pride and vanity, invariably end up deflated. Often they waste time and energy trying to save face or plotting revenge. Additionally, it is not always easy to determine another person's true feelings. A person who lives by the opinions of others squanders his valuable mental resources and is not qualified for inquiry.

THE SOLUTION – INQUIRY INTO ISVARA

If I take time to analyze the factors involved, I will clearly see that demanding respect from others cannot bring comfort or satisfaction, even if I am a highly accomplished person. First, I should investigate the basis of the factors that motivate me to demand respect from the world. The answer is that I believe that I am the author of my actions, the producer and owner of my gifts and skills. But is this true? What did I actually create? It is clear that I did not create my body. I appeared here one fine day encased in a fleshy meat tube by no effort of my own.

I did not create my sense of individuality either: it came along with the body and the world in which the body exists, a world that I definitely did not create. Certain tendencies—skills and abilities—sprouted from within me by no will of my own. I can utilize them but I cannot claim authorship of them. Whatever achievements I claim depended on opportunities that were provided by life itself. I did not cook them up. I just happened to be in the right place at the right time. How I got there is a mystery.

If I am a reasonable person I should conclude that whatever talents, skills and gifts I enjoy are given by Isvara. I should appreciate them as such and make use of them, or not, without fanfare. They should speak for themselves. Whether or not they are noticed and appreciated by others should not concern me. A flower in a vacant lot in a slum blooms unnoticed for no other reason than it is its nature to bloom. Pride ceases to be important when I see that it is a false value that does not work.

Once I understand the psychology of pride I should remain alert, and when it raises its ugly head I should examine my thinking dispassionately without a sense of guilt or self-condemnation. Why do I care what people think? Because I feel inadequate. Is it true that I am inadequate? Will the attention of others remove my sense of inadequacy? Even when I am acknowledged by people, the sense of satisfaction it engenders does not last and I am forced to seek approval once more. When does it end? Is it reasonable to claim these things when it is clear that I did not create them? Is this whole samskara real? Who is this for? It is for my ego. Is my ego real? It is not even apparently real, because it disappears when I look into it. Why do I invest so much energy in something that is not even real?

I cannot just drop my prideful ego but by meeting it head on, I see how pointless my expectations are and after some time, this samskara loses its power to disturb my mind. The habit of seeking approval eventually winds down and I become an uncomplicated person.

2) Pretension, Affectation

Pride is based on real accomplishments or abilities but pretension is self-glorification without a cause. I want to give the impression that I am something I am not. If I dress like a prince and my bank account is overdrawn and I am dodging bill collectors, I am pretentious. If I claim to have a country estate in the south of France when I live in a rent-controlled apartment in the ghetto, I am preten-tious. If I can't answer the doorbell without first tidying the living room for fear that someone might think I am a messy person, or I cannot appear in public in a mis-matched outfit without my lipstick and every hair in place, I am a poseur. If I have done no meaningful spiritual work but wear orange robes, shave my head, carry a staff and wander around spiritual centers with a beatific smile pasted on my face to convince others of my mystic attainments, I am not a *mahatma*. I am a phony.

All unhealthy samskaras stem from the same basic reason, the understand-ing of which should never be far from my mind. It is: I do not feel good about myself. I cannot accept myself. I want to be different. I am so extroverted that I cannot see my own psychology and take responsibility for it so I rely on others to do what I should be doing for myself, i.e., make me feel good. I need to impress people so they will validate me.

This is a particularly difficult problem because I don't even have the satisfac-tion of knowing that what I am saying about myself is true. I am therefore com-mitted to falsehood and find myself in direct conflict with truth. This attitude is particularly vexatious because there is no way to compel others to respond favorably to my lies. Because I badly need others to respond and because at any time my lie may be exposed, I am subjected to a surfeit of stress. To make it work I need to be very alert, keep all my friends apart and have a very long memory. There is a belief that karma yoga—leaving the result to Isvara—works in this sit-uation, but it doesn't, because karma yoga assumes that one's values are in order. It does not get your values in order. It is not to be used to mask a psychological problem or manage an adharmic situation.

Obviously, a mind practicing untruth is too agitated to dispassionately in-quire. It is telling me that I am unacceptable and Vedanta is telling me that I am acceptable both as a jiva and as awareness. So there is a glaring disconnect between what I am pursuing—validation for a part of myself that is not even real—and what I say I want: freedom from the suffering produced by my iden-tification with that unhealthy part.

The solution is to admit the problem, accept scripture's idea of who I am, and be willing to consider other's views because they see what I don't see about myself. Or I should have the confidence to discount their views because I know that they are projecting a false image on me owing to their own lack of clarity.

There is no learning and no growth for poseurs. I cannot solve even the basic problems of desire and anger if I am a proud, pretentious person. Without it I become a simple individual capable of honest self-examination.

3) Non-Injury

I have a value for non-injury because I do not want to be hurt. It is the same for all living beings. Non-injury is a nuanced value difficult to apply, owing to the apparent nature of the world in which we live. Three categories of injury prevail: actions, words and thoughts. The most obvious expression of an injurious action is physical violence.

A common expression of non-injury favored by spiritual types is vegetarianism. The argument is: Although life eats life, human beings are not in the same choiceless category as animals, whose food is dictated by instinct. We are self-conscious and endowed with free will, and since there are many means of survival we are free to choose a non-ambulatory food source. Although plants are living beings they are not conscious as animals are, so eating grains, fruits and vegetables is morally superior to killing conscious beings. Swami Dayananda, a great champion of vegetarianism, says, "To bring meat eating in line with dharma I would have to kill my prey bare-handed, without the assistance of weapons, thus exposing myself to the possibility of becoming some animal's dinner." If I am not willing to do this I am little more than an unethical, cowardly hypocrite "owing to an incompletely assimilated value for non-injury revealed by my failure to risk the possibility of suffering the same result."

For many, vegetarianism is sufficient as far as the value for non-injury is concerned, but the definition of non-injury includes two other types of karma: thoughts and words. Words should be truthful and pleasing. White lies are okay in certain situations because compassion trumps honesty. Our sensitivity to physical violence needs to extend to include a careful consideration of the effects of our words on others and the effects of harmful thoughts on our own minds. You may think that your bad feelings are justified by the adharmic behavior of others but they do not punish the offender or make the situation right; they serve only to hurt your own mind.

It is a shame that since the sixties, when hedonistic individualism became acceptable—if it feels good, do it!—society became increasingly disturbed and the traditions of civility, manners particularly, gradually declined. The solution to negative thoughts and actions is to develop an appreciation of the feelings of others because, considering the non-dual nature of reality, there are no others. "Others" is only an idea in an ignorant mind. To develop such an appreciation I need to look beyond my own needs. Such an attitude is conducive to self-inquiry insofar as both inner and outer conflict is not conducive to self-inquiry.

The Psychology: When I feel small, inadequate and incapable of getting what I want I may resort to violence to achieve my ends.

The Solution: Develop an appreciation for the feelings of others.

4) Accommodation, Commodiousness

To cheerfully and calmly accept any type of person or a given situation—not resigned indifference—is to be accommodating. It is based on a clear understanding that, owing to the law of karma, things cannot be different from the way they are. A person's behavior is a consequence of his conditioning and is not subject to will power. People are incarnated to work out karma, not to please me. Situations are the result of all the factors in the dharma field and are beyond the control of individuals. It is foolish to like or dislike them. All successful relationships depend on one's ability to accommodate to others. Similarly, I cannot be different from what I am and my situation is the result of my karma, so I should cheerfully accommodate my apparent self, not desire it to be different or struggle to change its circumstances. Those who refuse to adjust to reality are constantly disturbed and unfit for inquiry.

To develop this important quality I should learn to appreciate variety, cultivate an attitude of diversity, and constantly monitor my mind for a sense of dissatisfaction. When I find myself dissatisfied, I should reduce my expectations. It is helpful to see myself and everyone else as helpless fools or inert objects. I have good relationships with inert objects because I expect nothing of such things. I suffer fools gladly because I know they cannot be otherwise.

The key to accommodation is to respond to and identify with the person, not to their actions. Understand that the person is the self, temporarily bewitched by Maya. Try to remember that Isvara is behind an angry outburst, a fit of jealousy or a domineering action, and appreciate the fact that if they have no control, I have even less. With this kind of understanding it is easy to become accommodative.

Mechanical reactions stifle accommodation. To be free to respond
son I must act consciously, not react like a robot according to my vasana
miji again:

> A reaction is a mechanical, non-deliberate behavior, a conditioned re-
> sponse borrowed from previous experiences, one not given prior sanction
> by my will. That is to say, it is a response which I do not measure against
> the value structure which I am trying to assimilate, but which I just allow
> to happen.
>
> Reactions can go against all my wisdom and experience; these factors
> get relegated into the background and the reaction comes. I may have
> read all the scriptures of the world; I may be a great student of ethical
> systems; I may be a professional degree-holding giver of counsel to others,
> but when it comes to a reaction, my reaction will be just as mechanical as
> that of anyone else.
>
> Therefore, until universal values become thoroughly assimilated pro-
> viding a ground out of which right attitudes and actions spontaneously
> arise, I must consciously avoid reacting and deliberately choose my atti-
> tudes and actions.

WANT TO BE A SAINT?

If you are aiming for sainthood, non-injury and accommodation are the minimum requirements. Wisdom and scriptural knowledge are not necessary, only
these values. Saints do not consciously hurt others with their words, thoughts
or action. They accept people – good or bad – as they are and have an endless
capacity for forgiveness and mercy. They respond to the person, not their actions,
because they know that Isvara is the doer. This attitude expands the heart.

5) *Straightforwardness, Truthfulness*

Alignment of thought, word and deed is straightforwardness. Saying one thing
and doing another or doing something and saying something else is not conducive to peace of mind and inquiry. Straightforwardness includes not only truthful
speech, but thought and actions. Non-alignment fragments the person, subjecting him to a restless mind disturbed by many conflicts.

Service to the Teacher

uires a lot of discrimination, particularly for West-
ood reason, are not used to the idea of surrender
a frame of mind that constitutes surrender of will,
slikes, a willingness to give without asking anything
le of respect. Service should not be given lightly and
given only to a teacher of great integrity who does not ask for it, because she has
no need for it. If a teacher demands surrender, she is not a true teacher and the
student who surrenders to such a person is asking for suffering. Only the student
should benefit from the surrender.

Service is a state of mind that does not require physical action, only the willingness to act. In the ideal student-teacher relationship there is no give and take
as in other relationships. There is only giving on the part of the student. The
teacher is a stand-in for the self and serves by providing an object of meditation for the student. If the teacher is established in the self as the self and has
worked out all his personal issues, the opportunity to serve a teacher is the greatest blessing.

I was fortunate to have had a true teacher; the benefits were enormous. It was
the highpoint of my life. My desire for freedom grew leaps and bounds because I
could observe first hand a free being living free in samsara. I was asked to do very
little except to be present and alert at all times and when I needed something,
which was exceedingly rare, my teacher was there for me.

7) Cleanliness

The value of external cleanliness and orderliness is obvious, as it makes life pleasant and brings about attentiveness of mind. Dayananda again:

> Even as every day while I go about my business, a little dust settles on my
> skin, some dirt smudges my clothes, my desk becomes littered, my mind
> gathers dust in my transactions with people. Smudges of envy settle, a
> spot of exasperation lands, streaks of possessiveness appear and overall a
> fine dust of self-criticism, guilt and self-condemnation spreads. Each day,
> until my false identification with the mind dissolves and self-knowledge
> arises, the mind must be cleaned. What is the detergent for the mind? It
> is applying the opposite thought. It should be applied even though my
> negative attitude seems justified by circumstances.

A resentment settles in my mind even though I was legitimately wronged. Allowed to remain, it can build up to hatred. So I deliberately look for reasons to like the person that harmed me. He is liked by others, loved by his wife, takes care of his children properly, gives to charity, goes to church on Sunday. When I look into any other person I will find love. I am capable of loving and everybody is capable of love. Even a rank criminal has within him the elements of love and sympathy. It may be that his capacity for love is so obscured that it manifests only in the sympathy he shows himself—when he accidentally bangs his thumb with a hammer, for example. But it is there to be discovered. Apparent or not, everyone has saintly qualities—compassion, mercy, love, harmlessness. Therefore, to clean the mind of resentment and various dislikes, which will solidify into hatred and other negative feelings, I should deliberately search for those things which indicate humaneness and saintliness. When you do so, attribute the bad things to wrong thinking, bad upbringing or a bad environment. Take it as a blessing that you are not in his shoes. With a similar background you would do the same things. Saintly qualities belong to the self and constitute human nature. Negative qualities are incidental; they come and go.

So when resentment, dislike and hatred towards someone arise, see the person behind the adharmic action from an opposite viewpoint and you will discover some sympathy or understanding. Your attitude should be accommodating. In this manner, any resentment, any hatred, is cleansed daily.

Selfishness is perhaps the most common impurity. When I discover that I am caught in non-consideration of the wants, needs and happiness of others, I should deliberately do an unselfish action. When a resolution to clean up unselfishness is backed by an action, it is hard for selfish vasana to perpetuate itself. There are many opportunities every day to put down what you are doing and give a helping hand.

Self-condemnation, like selfishness, is just an impure thought. When something does not go according to plan or I find myself in conflict with a universal value and a feeling of guilt, inadequacy and self-judgment arises, I can counteract it by deliberately bringing self-knowledge to mind—"I am whole and complete, ever-pure awareness."

Here is a statement that should be spoken out loud every day that will help to root out negative thoughts about oneself:

> The body-mind sense complex, the doer, which I think is me, cannot be condemned because all its parts are inert. They do their jobs automatically or at the behest of the mind. It is innocent. The mind is also innocent. It is only an ever-changing aggregate of thoughts in motion, programmed by vasanas which are born unconsciously out of unconscious actions and attitudes. It is only an insentient instrument. I cannot condemn it. I cannot condemn an impure thought because it belongs to ignorance, not to me.

Purifying guilt and regret alerts the mind to further transgressions of dharma. If I think I am the doer, regret will arise. If a particular thought is responsible, I am off the hook. Without the emotional disturbance I can address the ignorance that produced the thought.

Here is a mantra that should be chanted every day:

> Desire does it. Desire is the Doer. I am not the Doer. Desire causes action. I do not cause action. Salutations to you, Desire. Anger does it. I don't do it. My prostrations to you, Anger. Ignorance caused it. I am not ignorant. Obeisances to you, O Ignorance.

It places the blame where it belongs, and at the same time, acknowledging the transgression frees the mind to contemplate on the self. If you are fear oriented, substitute the word *fear* for *desire*.

Another value that falls under this heading is chastity, which amounts to a respectful attitude toward the opposite sex, not lack of physical intimacy.

8) *Jealousy and Envy*

One of the most common and unreasonable impurities is jealousy, a pernicious form of duality. It exists because the world is vast, filled with millions of entities that provide myriad opportunities, real or imagined, for self-demeaning comparative judgments. Jealousy and envy are transformed anger and usually lead to depression. They are produced by a sense of lack brought on by comparison to someone I think is superior in some way to me. It is unreal for this reason: I am never jealous of the whole person, only some aspect. He is more intelligent, beautiful, wealthy or popular than me. The fact that I would like to be like this person shows that there is some sympathy for him. The qualities that invoke jealousy cannot be separated from the complete person. Because the complete person, who is actually the self, can never be completely an object of envy, there is no real place for my bad feelings to attach themselves. Finally, it is also clear that there are certain things in that person that I do not want. Additionally, if I am honest, I will find that I too am not perfect and am the possessor of certain unenviable qualities, knowing which makes it difficult to judge others. If the shoe fits, wear it.

Jealousy is actually an unwarranted reaction to the apparent nature of reality. It is completely without merit. In other words, jealousy is a projection that masks an insufficient appreciation of my own nature and the abundance of good qualities that spring from it. A self-realized person is never jealous, because she is mindful of her fullness.

Although the Bible's statement that God is "a jealous God" means that when you know God you cannot love anything else, many people believe that God is a superbeing sitting somewhere else, who is endowed with certain human qualities, one of which is jealousy. But God is not a person subject to any form of limitation. It is the creator and possessor of everything and, like an enlightened person, knows it is fullness itself. So jealousy and other emotions, positive and negative, do not apply to God.

When I feel jealousy I should apply the opposite thought and nip it in the bud, lest it devolve into schadenfreude, delight in the misery of others, a truly despicable emotion. I should think "I am happy for the good fortune of this person. I admire his good qualities. I am happy that he is happy."

Any negative feeling that is opposed to peace can be neutralized by applying the opposite thought. At first it may seem untruthful to think this way—after all I really don't *feel* it!—but a deliberate daily practice will cleanse the mind and prepare it for self-knowledge.

9) *Steadiness, Constancy, Perseverance*

A consistent effort to achieve a stated goal is required for self-knowledge because self-knowledge is not partial knowledge, like worldly disciplines. It is absolute, the essence of all knowledge. Certain actions flow from my commitment to my goal and I should steadily perform them. Most of us are totally resolved at the beginning of any endeavor but we quickly lose interest when we are confronted with the enormity of the task and seize some pretext to opt out of the required dharmas. Steadiness, sometimes called devotion, implies an acute appreciation of the power of rajas and tamas, to distract and cause laziness. To give in to them is to generate a sense of guilt that will eventually paralyze the mind and lead to failure.

10) Mastery of Mind

To value a controlled mind is to understand the way the mind thinks and to bring it in line with the way the self would think if it was a person living in the apparent reality. It means that although the mind is capricious I need not fulfill its fantasies and yield to its caprices. It means that I am the boss, not the mind.

There are four basic ways of thinking, three of which are necessary to understand and master if I want to prepare my mind for self-knowledge:

1. *Impulsive.* Unexamined thoughts born of instincts dominate the mind. I do what I feel without thinking about it.
2. *Mechanical.* Thoughts of which I am conscious but have no power to control because they are produced by binding vasanas.
3. *Deliberate.* Thoughts subjected to discrimination that are accepted or dismissed with reference to my value structure.
4. *Spontaneous.* Without evaluation my thinking automatically conforms to universal values and my actions are always appropriate and timely. This kind of thinking applies only to those for whom self-knowledge has destroyed binding vasanas and negated doership.

Spontaneous thought is not included in this value because it applies only to self-actualized individuals. If my thinking is impulsive, conditioned or deliberate I am not a master, but by deliberate thinking the mind can be controlled. Relative mastery is simply alertness (sattva) and involves deliberately submitting all thoughts and feelings to rational scrutiny and substituting the appropriate logic whenever ignorance-born mechanical thinking dominates the mind. If I am conscious of my mind I can learn from my mistakes and exercise choice over the way I think, allowing me to fulfill my commitments to my goal in the face of various distractions and to change my behavior so that it conforms with universal values.

In chapter 4, control of mind, control of senses, and single-pointedness were listed as qualifications for inquiry. In this chapter we present them as values. Here, mind control is discipline over one's thinking at the level where the thoughts arise, sense control indicates discretion at the level of the senses and single-pointedness is the consistent capacity to stick with the teachings in the face of unhelpful thought patterns—applying the opposite thought, for example. The first two make the mind capable of single-pointedness.

11) Dispassion Toward Sense Objects

An extremely important value that amounts to existential maturity, dispassion was defined in chapter 1 as a clear appreciation of two hard-to-assimilate facts: (1) the joy I seek is not to be found in objects and (2) life is a zero-sum game. It strips false emotion created by my vasanas and presents the world as an objective fact to my mind. In chapter 4 it was presented as indifference to the results of my actions. If you are not clear about *viragya* please review these sources. Inquiry is second nature to a dispassionate mind.

12) Renunciation, Austerity

It would be difficult to find a more spiritually useful value than renunciation. Postwar World War II prosperity has created societies chock to the brim with needy, wanting creatures. I want what I want the way I want it and I want it NOW! This attitude, inspired by the wholesale spiritual emptiness of huge populations has produced an intensity and volume of disturbing thoughts that is unprecedented in human history. The solution: cultivate a value for renunciation. The holy mantra of the renunciate is "Less is more." The fewer gross and subtle objects I crave and possess, the more peace I enjoy.

13) Absence of Egoism

Because we are discussing the topic of values, absence of egoism is not the complete freedom from the sense of localized "I-ness" afforded by self-knowledge. It is simply recognition of the difference between the ego and the self.

Pride is little more than ignorance of the relationship between the individual and the world. The individual is *an* ego, a conscious being, brought here to fulfill its destiny. Egoism is an idea of self, purely a notion of separateness. It is born of ignorance and is the capital with which I-ego begins life and which it spends liberally throughout. It amounts to little more than the groundless claim to ownership of various objects, talents and abilities that belong to Isvara, not to the apparent individual. For an understanding of this value, refer to the analysis of pride above because pride and egoism are more or less synonymous.

Swami Dayananda presents an interesting inquiry, contemplation on which will make the absurdity of egoism clear. He says:

> Although I am graced by free will and have the power to choose my actions, I have no power over the result, which is no more than a possibility among probabilities. The result of any act is the outcome of many circumstances, past and present, known and unknown, which operate in concert. If my strong, skillful arm throws the winning pass in the final seconds of a football game there are too many material and circumstantial factors coming together for the win to be considered a matter of personal pride. I am creator neither of the football nor of my athletic body. Many experiences contributed to the development of the skill in the arm that threw the football. I am not responsible for the clearing of the pregame rainstorm so the event could take place or for the sharp earth tremor that occurred two seconds before I threw. Nor can I claim credit for the skill of my teammate who caught the winning pass. When pride and ego are examined they become so silly that humility really cannot be considered a virtue. Humility is simply understanding the world—including myself because I am part of the world—just as it is. Absence of egoism allows me to appreciate all the wonderful opportunities that the world affords, opportunities that provide a source of learning and a chance to shed my ignorance.

14) Appreciation of Time

The objects on which I depend for my happiness are obviously subject to time. To make samsara work for me I need to be willfully ignorant of this obvious fact. Ignorance of it prevents inquiry because it keeps me tied to objects. This value is little more than looking at the downside of the very process of life itself. Birth is wonderful perhaps, but it ceases to be so wonderful when you consider death. And the space between birth and death is no bed of roses either; we are all treated to various physical and psychological pains daily. Today you may be happy, but tomorrow you may suffer. Time is a ravenous mouth, consuming everything, including pain. Nothing can be done about it, so keep your goal in mind. Don't fritter it away. Make conscious use of it to do what can be done. Become a master of time and hasten slowly.

15) *Absence of Ownership*

This value is similar to absence of pride and absence of ego. Here is another clever analysis by Swami Dayananda:

> A few years ago a young friend told me that he had brought a new place in Bombay, which he invited me to see. When we arrived at his house, I found myself looking at a seven-story structure. Since this young man has a relatively modest position, I was surprised.
>
> "You bought this!" I said.
>
> "Not all of it," he laughed, "I own a flat on the third floor."
>
> So we went to the third floor and he ushered me in, saying, "This is mine. That is the flat I own."
>
> This was the first time I had heard of such an arrangement, so I was still puzzled.
>
> "Do you own the land? I asked.
>
> "No," he said, and explained that a co-operative management society owned the land. All he owned was one rather small flat—two rooms and a kitchen.
>
> So I asked, "Do you own the floor?"
>
> "No. My floor is the ceiling of the fellow downstairs."
>
> "Do you own the ceiling?"
>
> "No, the ceiling is the floor for the family upstairs."
>
> "How about the walls?"
>
> "Well, the inner walls are shared with other flats. The outer wall, of course, belongs to the whole building as part of its structural support.
>
> "So what do you own?"
>
> "Well, Swamiji, I own the space."

Is the body mine? My mother can claim it, in that it is made out of her flesh. The father can claim it, in that it cannot come into being without his seed. It cannot survive without parents to take care of it. The family has a claim, the society too, the bank that keeps your money safe, for instance. Myriad creatures, including bacteria of all ilk, air, fire, water and earth, the sun and moon, and so on, all have a claim. At best I am a trustee, a caretaker or a tourist taking up temporary residence as the karma for this incarnation plays out. Without the idea of ownership my relationship with objects becomes purely factual and in the absence of attachment my mind becomes settled and capable of inquiry. Isvara "owns" it all.

Two positive values that correspond with absence of ownership are charity and generosity. Spiritual life is about giving not getting. The heart that gives, gathers.

16) Absence of Excessive Attachment to Loved Ones

I am here to add value to the creation; the beings I love are meant to be loved by me. For the same reason that I own nothing and have created nothing, sticky attachment to loved ones is not justified. However, I should look after them in a caring and dispassionate manner.

17) Sameness of Mind in All Circumstances

Based on an understanding of Isvara, this value is a variant of dispassion. It is a state of mind that does not swing between elation (rajas) and depression (tamas). To achieve this state of mind I need to strip my projections from the objects, usually people, including myself, and view them factually. Once subjective feelings are reduced to fact, the mind assumes a stance that makes it easier to appreciate the vision of Vedanta. It is true that Vedanta reveals "facts" to be mithya, apparent realities, but to understand what mithya means and free myself of it, it is necessary to remove subjectivity.

18) Unswerving Non-Dual Devotion to God

We refer to awareness as Isvara, God, not pure consciousness, in the discussion of values because values are only an issue for someone who does not know who they are, so the devotion mentioned here is not hard and fast self-knowledge. It is an understanding that a jiva seeking freedom would do well to assume, as it produces the steadiness of mind mentioned in the last value.

It is karma yoga, an attitude of grateful acceptance brought about by seeing Isvara as the giver of the results of actions. Like inquiry, it frees the mind of projections and brings it in line with objective reality, making the assimilation of the teachings possible.

19) *Love of Solitude*

Love of solitude is an obviously valuable value, as one cannot inquire when the mind is connected to and surrounded by other busy minds. Love of solitude is not escapism, because the need to escape indicates an inability to face oneself. An activity that leaves you feeling incomplete when you cannot do it has become an escape. Love of solitude is a mind that enjoys being with itself and is the perfect environment for self-inquiry.

20) *Absence of Craving for Company*

This is a companion value to love of solitude. A quiet place in and of itself is not intrinsically good, nor is the company of others bad. Fear of people and craving company are not healthy values. The value touted here is a value for a happy, non-escaping mind that enjoys its own company.

21) *Constant Practice of Self-knowledge*

In every waking moment, keeping in mind that all I really want in life is freedom and knowing that ignorance of reality obstructs my experience of freedom is the value indicated here. Furthermore, it includes knowing beyond a doubt that self-knowledge—knowledge of myself as awareness—is the only solution. This conviction should be so firm that samsaric goals—security, pleasure and virtue, as discussed in chapter 1—do not turn my head. This value was discussed in the chapter on qualifications as a burning desire for liberation. When this value is assimilated, the next and final value is easy to understand.

22) *Resolution, Completion*

Excessive rajas is the bane of spiritual life. While individuals with tamasic minds find it difficult to initiate projects, individuals with predominately scattered (rajasic) minds find it difficult *not* to start projects and to complete them. Unless you follow through on a resolution, your mind will become more and more disturbed as unfulfilled vasanas build up. So it is necessary to have a strong value for completing actions. To master this value do one thing at a time—no multitasking! Only when a given project is completed do I take up the next. In addition to karma yoga, it is necessary to investigate the source of my many needs and plethora of activities, identify it for what it is—a false idea of who I am—and neutralize it with the knowledge "I am whole and complete. Nothing that I do will change who I am. And once I am committed to liberation and understand the value of inquiry I must stick to my practice until I am free."

23) Precaution, Deliberation and Restraint

To correct the inclination to impulsively initiate projects, it is important to value caution. I should deliberately think things through, carefully considering the upside and the downside before jumping in with both feet. Once committed, I should work patiently. In the name of speed and the feeling "I am doing," rajasic individuals waste inordinate time and effort on unnecessary actions.

CHAPTER THIRTEEN

LOVE

How Is Consciousness Love?

Those who do not understand that self-knowledge and love are one often criticize Vedanta as a "merely intellectual" path, implying that the path of love is superior because it produces states of ecstatic love. We need to mention that because love motivates all conscious endeavors and because all rituals are actually karmas, there is no "path" of love. Furthermore, we also need to mention that Vedanta is the knowledge behind all paths, so it could not be said to be a path at all. However, leaving these arguments aside, Vedanta might reasonably be called a "pathless path," as it encourages action and action always leads somewhere. Insofar as it is a path, we contend that it is a path of love that leads to the realization that the self is love. This misunderstanding is due to an inability of seekers to connect the idea of the self as consciousness/awareness and the self as love. There is a logical connection: if reality is non-dual consciousness as Vedanta contends and if love exists—which it does—then there can be no difference between love and consciousness.

There is also a simple practical connection. The bridge between them is attention. In terms of the apparent reality, love is willing attention. To say that I love my cat means that I pay attention to it. I feed it, cuddle it and think about it. If I do not pay attention to my husband or wife, he or she will inform me that I do not love him or her. Attention is consciousness directed through the Subtle

Body toward an object. Because I am always paying attention to something, I always love something. Love is not a special state or a special feeling. It is the nature of consciousness, my self. It does not come from objects, though certain objects invoke it.

You may argue that there are many things that you do not love, but this is true only because it pleases you not to love a particular object. It pleases you not to love an object because you love your dislikes. Not loving an object because you dislike the object does not mean that your nature is not love. It means that for the sake of yourself, which you love above all objects, you indulge a dislike. Your likes and dislikes, fears and desires do not come from outside. They bubble up from within you. They are born of consciousness, your awareness, as it is filtered by ignorance. Likes are "positive" love and dislikes are "negative" love. They are you, but you—love—are free of them.

If you say that you do not like your job but remain in it because you need the money, it means only that you love money more than you dislike the job. And you love money because you love yourself. Everything we do, everything we think and feel, is for the sake of the self. We do everything for the self because the self is loved beyond all else.

It is difficult to accept the fact that you do not love an object for the sake of the object because we want to believe that we love unselfishly. But all love is self-ish because there is only one self. The object that you love or don't love is just you, appearing as the idea of an "other" in your consciousness.

Relationship Love Is Based on Duality

The belief that reality is a duality is responsible for the idea of relationship love. It accounts for the sad fact that this form of love is fraught with anxiety. When you are caught in duality, even though the love that you are is fullness itself, you believe that you lack love. Ignorance of this fact causes you to project love on objects. It makes you think that if you possessed a particular object—let's say a person—you would feel complete. The feeling of completeness is the experience of love, your self. The knowledge of your completeness is liberation. It results in an acute appreciation of the fact that I am love.

Passion for an object, particularly a person, is not love even though desire is a form of love. But if you look into it you will discover that when you love someone or something it is your self—the love—in the object that you love. You do not know that when you contact the object you are only contacting yourself. The object invokes the love that you are. Remember, the joy is not in the object— ever! Because of ignorance of this fact, you become attached to the idea that you need the object, usually a jiva of some sort, to complete you. This kind of "love" is thought to be love but it is ignorance masquerading as love.

Some texts say that the desire to love an object and be loved by an object is the primary cause of suffering because it generates an incessant stream of bind-ing emotions, both positive and negative. Nonetheless, it is not a desire that can be immediately renounced, as it is hard-wired from birth. So it needs to be sublimated, not by demanding and expecting love but by giving it. Giving love is the essence of devotion. It is the simple recognition that by your very pres-ence as consciousness you are offering yourself to the world in the form of your thoughts, words and deeds. It is awareness of the presence of "others" and their need for love. You do not lose love by loving. On the contrary, your experience of yourself as love grows the more you give. Devotional yoga is also loving the "you" you think you are—the one that wants love—because from the point of view of the self, the actual lover, you are an object too. It redeems the loveless past.

Because every transaction with an object is actually love, owing to the fact that the self is love, how do we account for fear and pain? If the doer, the cogni-tive person, is ignorant of her nature as love, the love will be hijacked by the likes and dislikes and express in negative, often perverted, ways. Inquiry aids devotion because it makes the cognitive person, the Subtle Body, aware of her prejudices and biases, likes and dislikes. When you are aware of your projections, they sub-side and the energy invested in them is converted into devotion; you love yourself more because you have freed yourself of painful emotions.

Who Is the Devotee?

The devotee is the jiva, the reflected self, the basic person. Just as the moon de-pends on the sun for its light, the basic person depends on consciousness for its claim to be a conscious living being. An ordinary worldly jiva becomes a devotee when it recognizes its inviolable relationship with Isvara, pure awareness in the role of the Creator. Devotion is the recognition by the jiva of its total depen-dence on Isvara. This simple basic person finds itself in a complex ever-changing environment that it did not create and over which its influence is very limited. To succeed, it needs to come to terms with its life by resolving its identity into Isvara. Isvara is the script and the devotee is the actor in the play of life. Because Isvara appearing as the apparent reality is complex, the devotee is required to play many roles. With reference to my mother I am a son. With reference to my children I am a father. With reference to my wife I am a husband. With reference to the man next door I am a neighbor. With reference to the bank I am a customer. The list goes on.

Responding to the demands of Isvara in an appropriate and timely fashion is the duty of a devotee and requires considerable skill. The devotee must be intellectually and emotionally agile, changing roles at the drop of a hat as Isvara presents new situations. A common reaction to the stress of role playing is to withdraw from the world because one does not have confidence to respond in different ways. Owing to the demands of Isvara, a devotee may retreat into a few simple roles—or even a single role that does not require alertness, like a hermit. But dropping out is not always possible in this day and age, nor is it necessarily advisable to avoid relationships. Recognizing one's connection with Isvara cushions the devotee from the stress of role playing because she understands that the roles belong to Isvara, not to the devotee. Playing the appropriate role to the best of one's ability is devotion. You love yourself when you discharge your duty to your self.

Conversion of Emotion into Devotion

Keeping in mind that devotion is not a special path, it is fair to think of devotional yoga as converting emotion born of love for impermanent objects into devotion for the eternal subject, the self. Transforming emotion into devotion requires sustained and persistent commitment to the practice of non-attachment, without which serious devotional progress is impossible. It requires the devotee to abandon craving for the fruits of action and the belief that objects— people and experiences like romantic love, particularly—are a legitimate source of lasting love.

Renunciation confers power, understanding and love. For example, people willingly sacrifice less attractive objects for more attractive ones. When someone addicted to sensuous pleasure discovers the subtler pleasures of the mind, physical objects lose their luster. And when a devotee finds the state of love that is the innermost self, the small personal loves that captivate the heart pale. As the practice of letting go grows, love grows.

Strip away the shallow cravings for romance and excitement that are the hallmark of the unenlightened and discover that your deepest need is the desire to love and be loved. Nothing is more attractive than love, realizing oneness with one's self. When the real object of our desire is unknown, we chase object love, but when we wake up to the self, we understand that we only ever loved the self. We see that our small daily loves are merely faint reflections of the love that is our nature, the love that pervades every atom of the universe. Devotional practice directs our attention to the true object of our affections.

You cannot properly practice devotional yoga without the knowledge that reality is non-dual consciousness/love. With this understanding it is easy to worship yourself. If reality is non-dual love appearing as gross and subtle objects—inanimate and animate things—each and every transaction with an object provides an opportunity to worship. Since life is nothing but endless transactions with objects, your life can easily become a temple, an offering, a prayer, an appreciation of yourself. It is easy to worship the objects that present themselves to you when you know that they are actually you because you love yourself beyond all else. If this idea makes you feel uneasy—as if it were a form of arrogance—you have the wrong idea of who you are.

If the non-dual understanding escapes you, however, all is not lost: you can worship dualistically. It may or may not lead to freedom. Religion is dualistic worship: the object of worship and the worshipper are believed to be different. It is worship according to your predominant guna or the guna that is predominant at the time. Unlike the modern spiritual world, which does not appreciate the value of the religious impulse, Vedanta encourages a religious attitude because it is this attitude—exemplified in the karma yoga practice—that instills awareness of Isvara, which makes the jiva objective and harmonizes it and its environment. Your environment, your life, is nothing but Isvara.

Devotion with Qualities

If your Subtle Body, the instrument of worship, is predominantly tamasic, you will believe that the self is a special God or perhaps a spirit being, something other than you. And, because your mentality is primitive you will worship as if you were a child or a slave. You will open yourself to all manner of extraordinary magical beliefs and find yourself thrilled and fascinated by the dark feelings invoked when you visualize demons, devils and ghosts. Fear will be your predominant emotion and you may not be above using satanic practices, casting spells for instance, to bring harm to others. You may love miracles and bizarre rituals. In India, some sects drink the sacrificial blood of animals to display their devotion. You will probably believe in heaven and hell, interpret scripture literally, and be obsessed with sin. You may have an unholy affinity for cults and be easily manipulated by corrupt priests or take delight in surrendering yourself to powerful "spiritual" personalities, allowing yourself to suffer abuse at their hands. You may hate anyone who dares to question your guru or religion. Religious history is replete with examples of the many excesses caused by this narrow state of mind, the Inquisition and fundamentalist Islam come to mind.

On the other hand, this type of faith tends to be rock solid and allows the devotee to withstand not only the small pinpricks of life but her major crises as well. The conviction that an external God exists is steady, deep and heartfelt.

If your Subtle Body is predominantly rajasic, you will also project some sort of God or spirit figure as an object of worship. Rajas, the projecting power, a restless dissatisfied energy, keeps the mind and emotions perpetually disturbed. It acts like an opaque moving screen, effectively concealing the love that is your nature. This type of devotion is narcissistic and the devotee is not above bargaining with God for power, position and wealth. The idea that material "abundance" is evidence of spiritual virtue appeals to rajasic people. Rajasic devotion tends to be status and image conscious and such a devotee is not above using it to impress others. Scratch the surface of this mentality and you will find a person more interested in presenting a devotional front to the world than a pure heart to God. Unlike the steady dependability of the dark type, the restless devotee will change religions, beliefs, teachers and practices at the drop of a hat.

Rajasic devotion, unlike the sleepy innocence of tamasic mother-father God worship, is passionate. For rajasic devotion to evolve into sattvic devotion, the devotee must be convinced that knowledge of God, not accumulation of God's goods, is the true goal of life. Once committed to self-knowledge through worship, this devotee becomes a spiritual dynamo and makes rapid progress.

Devotees with predominantly tamasic and rajasic Subtle Bodies do not understand that reality is impersonal; for them everything that happens is personal. Consequently, their view of Isvara is personal, to their detriment insofar as they often find themselves at odds with Isvara, their environment.

Sattva, the third strand in the psychic rope and the highest of the three lower stages of devotion, is rooted in awareness, *sat*. It is the most secure foundation for a devotional life because the sattvic heart is a clean mirror, capable of accurately reflecting God's image; to see the self reflected in a pure heart is to love the self. Sattvic devotees are blessed with curiosity, intelligence, discrimination and powerful epiphanies. Sattvic devotion is characterized by a strong value for renunciation, dispassion, dedication of action and its results to Isvara, deep attachment to non-dual scripture, love of spiritual culture, unhappiness when the current of love is broken by a worldly vasana, humility, ability to recognize and serve great souls, and rigorous conformity with dharma.

The downside of sattva: because the veil separating the devotee from the self is so thin, the devotee may become spiritually conceited and suffer attachment to purity, goodness, beauty and knowledge—golden chains difficult to break if devotion is to flower into primary devotion, the fourth and final stage. Primary devotion is free of all positive and negative qualities. It is impersonal, non-dual love.

Thinking of yourself as a particular type of devotee is not helpful, because it fails to take into account the fact that the ultimate purpose of devotion is to dissolve our limited identity into our limitless identity. Devotion destroys the fear that sets up the apparent boundaries between the devotee and his true nature. Rather than develop an identity based on the predominant quality, it is better to use the guna model to assess and transform rajasic and tamasic devotional tendencies into sattva, setting yourself up for liberation.

If you beg Isvara for something other than Isvara, it means your vasanas are rajasic. It is fine to ask Isvara for the things you are too incompetent or lazy to acquire on your own, but you need to know that Isvara may refuse your request because it is not in the best interests of the dharma field, or even in your best interest. And even if it is in your interest, Isvara has to work through the law of karma to deliver the results you want because the law of karma is Isvara. Because the availability of objects that you might want is limited, or you would not be praying for them, and the desires of others vying for the same result, who in Isvara's eyes are just as important as you, are virtually limitless, you will have to wait your turn. This will not be a happy situation, because rajas is the mother of frustration.

Nobody asks Isvara for air because air is not in short supply. If your heart is pure, you will have the good sense to ask Isvara for something that is readily available. Because Isvara is readily available as the self of the devotee and self-realization is the fulfillment of all desires, a sattvic prayer would be: "Reveal yourself to me."

Prayer Is Not Worship

Prayer is an intelligent use of free will because it takes Isvara into account, but it is not worship. It is not worship because it belies an imperfect understanding of both one's nature and the nature of Isvara, the Creator and giver of the results of action. Prayer is a supplication based on the belief that who one is and what one has are insufficient. But worship is based on the knowledge that Isvara created the devotee in its own image and that everything she has is Isvara and is more than enough. Worship is an offering, a settling of accounts with Isvara. But prayer is necessary; for a seeker of liberation, there is only one prayer: remove my ignorance and reveal yourself to me.

Secondary devotion leads to primary devotion. Sattva is the springboard for non-dual devotion. Primary devotion will not develop when the heart is tamasic. Rajas is the way out of tamas. Tamasic devotees believe in Isvara but are too lazy to actually seek Isvara. If the tamasic devotee becomes devotionally proactive and takes up a purification regimen, it will generate epiphanies and insights. Eventually, as the devotee experiences the self reflected in a full heart, more and more sattva develops and the desire for self-knowledge arises. The desire for self-knowledge is the highest form of devotion because self-realization is the purpose of human life. You love yourself totally when you do the noblest thing for yourself. The more the self is experienced, the firmer self-knowledge becomes. Knowledge "of" the self is indirect, but inquiry will convert it to direct knowledge, the hard and fast understanding that my nature and the nature of everything is non-dual love.

Devotion Is Knowledge and Action

Devotion is knowledge, clear seeing. Devotion is a childlike and intense love of Isvara. It is the recognition of my total dependence on Isvara. Why should I love Isvara? Because everything I value is given to me by Isvara. Devotion is karma yoga, because when I see that my likes and dislikes stand in the way of the vision that everything is Isvara and Isvara is me, I patiently eradicate them. Devotion is a sense of reverence. As my likes and dislikes are effaced, a sense of reverence ensues. It is the wonder that appears when I see the vastness and complexity of Isvara. It is a sense of irony that arises when I see the non-dual whole that I am sitting side by side with the incompleteness that I am not. How can Isvara create an ocean of mercy and beauty and an ocean of ugliness and suffering at the same time? How can Isvara be both day and night, knowledge and ignorance, freedom and bondage? How can there be free will when everything is programmed by Isvara?

Devotion is worship of Isvara. Worship means that you understand that you are who you are by no fault of your own and the world is the way it is by no fault of its own. It is an understanding of the helplessness of everyone, which gives rise to compassionate appreciation of everything. You understand that we are all like children who can't help themselves, so the heart goes out to everyone. When the judgments about how life should be cease, love flows and lifts you up. A devotee stops trying to change herself or control her life and the lives of others. The devotee does not see the self "in" the creation or beyond the creation but knows that the creation is nothing but Isvara, the self. If some aspect of life is seen to be defective, the devotee understands that Isvara is not defective; only her vision is defective. Isvara is not responsible for the evil. The devotee knows that the cruelties that arise from the sense of difference belong to ignorance of Isvara, not to Isvara.

Devotion Is Free Will

Devotion is choosing Isvara as the goal. Isvara is not a big individual who decides everything that happens. If Isvara decides everything, then there is no choice whatsoever. All conflicts arise out of choice. If there is no choice, there are no conflicts. But we have conflicts every day. This means that there is free will. A sattvic devotee is free to see himself as an instrument of Isvara's will. There is very little free will for someone under the spell of rajas and tamas. But dispassion is a characteristic of sattva, which separates the devotee from his likes and dislikes and makes clear the value of substituting dharma for likes and dislikes. Since dharma is Isvara, the devotee becomes an instrument for Isvara and his life blends into Isvara.

Devotion for Isvara is a means for liberation. Karma Yoga is devotion because to practice it you need to have devotion for liberation, Isvara's nature. It is adding value to the world by doing what you do with an attitude of gratitude, which neutralizes your likes and dislikes and prepares the mind for inquiry. But devotion will not set you free unless it is devotion for Isvara, not for security, pleasure and virtue. Devotion is a burning desire for liberation.

Devotion to Isvara is difficult because the devotee needs to live in the world, which implies a certain need for Isvara's stuff. If the mind is occupied with security, etc., it will not contemplate on Isvara, so the security issue needs to be turned over to Isvara, which requires trust. Pure devotion is the firm knowledge "I am protected by Isvara." If we leave the direction of our lives to Isvara, it means we trust and love Isvara. The *Bhagavad Gita* says if you turn your life over to Isvara, It will "take care of your getting and keeping." We see the same idea in the Bible: "Seek to know the Lord and all else will be added unto you." It is absolutely true.

Devotion is contemplating Isvara's qualities. Contemplation is a constant flow of similar thoughts unobstructed by dissimilar thoughts. Wherever you see brilliance and dullness, compassion and indifference, dispassion and passion, discrimination and attachment, forbearance and frustration, restraint and indulgence, devotion and carelessness, fearlessness and fear, understanding and ignorance, accommodation and selfishness, satisfaction and dissatisfaction, charity and miserliness, beauty and ugliness in yourself or others, you are seeing Isvara. Isvara is everything that is. Understanding the qualities of Isvara allows the devotee to eschew the negative qualities and cultivate the qualities that lead to pure devotion.

Worship of Symbols

When you take the apparent reality to be real, you do not know that you are what you are devoted to. You know there is something more than what you experience and you have a certain degree of love and respect for it, even though it is not clear what it is. So you become devoted to selective objects that remind you of it. Symbols can take us to the self because the self is always present. It is not apart from you. When we worship a symbol, Isvara works through the symbol to provide the experiences and insights necessary to draw us ever closer to it in love and understanding. So even though you think that Isvara is someone or something other than the symbol, the symbol is actually Isvara too. Any object that invokes the self in the form of love can be used to get love flowing.

Strip every object of its secular meaning and instill it with a divine aura. See your body as Isvara's temple, your home as the house of Isvara, your family as Isvara's family. Consider every spoken word the name of Isvara and every activity, spiritual or otherwise, service to Isvara. Bending, lying or kneeling should be seen as prostration to Isvara and all lights as symbols of self. One should see sleep as meditation and eating as Isvara eating Isvara. In this manner, every object and activity gradually loses its worldly associations and becomes a living symbol of the divine.

When you see a mountain, see it as a symbol of your self. Mountains are good self symbols, because they are relatively eternal. They rise above everything and provide an unsurpassed view. The self is the highest part of our being, jutting above the plains and valleys of our body-mind territory, affording us unlimited vision. They are unmoving, like the self. The self cannot move because it is non-dual. They are silent like the self, "the unstruck sound." When you see a river, see it as your self. Like the self, rivers give life, nourishing everything with which they come in contact. See the sky as the limitless self.

If you favor religious icons, see that the deity you worship is compassionate, conscious, peaceful and beautiful. Choosing a deity with these qualities is an indirect way of invoking and recognizing them in your self.

A human being is an excellent symbol of the self. Humans, like everything else, are "cast in the image of God," i.e., they reflected awareness. The love light that is awareness shines with particular brilliance in human beings because they are endowed with intellect and are capable of knowing who they are. The worship of humans with discrimination, particularly great souls, is an essential step on the devotional path, because the worshipper is a human being brought into this world and looked after by human beings. Worship of humans purifies childhood hurts and resentments. By loving others, you learn to love yourself.

The worship of others does not mean that you value them more than you value yourself but that you see no difference between them and you.

To the materialist part of the mind, projecting divinity into objects seems to be irrational, but the practice is good psychology. Just as an actress becomes the person she portrays by totally identifying with every aspect of the character's life, the devotee discovers identity with the self through intense identification with the symbol. The more you love your symbol, the more likely it is to produce a vision of the self. Having experienced the beauty of the self, it is impossible not to fall deeper in love and become passionately attached. Because worldly beauties pale in the presence of the self, attachments to objects dry up.

Worship is not a grand gesture like going to church once a week. It is being there for yourself and others when you are needed. It is attending to small needs. See the request as the self asking for worship. Refusal to give is refusal to love yourself because there are no others. Loving others is a valuable practice because conflicts with others are a major source of agitation. Eventually this practice destroys duality and results in self-realization, the understanding that there are no others.

Worship of the Formless Self

How can you worship something that has no qualities? By subjecting your mind to the teachings of Vedanta. Anyone can worship objects, but to worship the formless self, i.e., to gain liberation, the mind must be prepared. Worship of the self in its manifold forms prepares the mind for Vedanta.

Vedanta is the highest form of worship because it is the truth. Isvara is truth. How does Vedanta work? It works by removing the barriers between the worshipper and the object of worship, the self. What are those obstacles except ignorance-inspired beliefs and opinions that maintain duality and cause suffering? The devotee offers his ignorance up to the teaching and gladly accepts the result. When the last shred of ignorance is gone, it is clear that the self is love and that the devotee is non-separate from it.

CHAPTER FOURTEEN

THE ENLIGHTENED PERSON

If you want to know what you will be when you are enlightened, this chapter is for you. If you have a lot of energy invested in the idea that you are enlightened, you should read this chapter—or maybe you shouldn't, as it may call your enlightenment into question.

What is an "enlightened" person? Obviously, if reality is non-dual consciousness there are no enlightened persons. Enlightened people, like ordinary people, are nothing more than limitless awareness appearing as human beings. Or, if you prefer a slightly less radical notion, can't accept that "people' is only an idea in awareness and want to think of it differently, you could say that everyone is enlightened, meaning each of us is illumined by awareness, "in the light," so to speak. In fact every living organism is enlightened according to this definition because without awareness nothing exists. You might even successfully argue that insentient objects are enlightened according to this definition because insentient objects have meaning only if they are known to exist and they can be known to exist only if consciousness illumines the knowing faculty, the Subtle Body.

Though true, these definitions of enlightenment are understood by very few indeed. In addition, they are certainly unpopular with those in the spiritual world who would use their idea of enlightenment as a special status or those who need a more liberal definition, one that allows them to impress, manipulate, intimidate, exploit and hoodwink unsuspecting seekers. You may believe that all spiritual people are somehow…well…spiritual, but you would be wrong.

Spiritual people are just worldly people dressed up in special clothing. While they have a vasana for otherworldly intangibles, they are not necessarily immune to the assortment of everyday attractions favored by their worldly brothers and sisters: the pull of security, pleasure, power, and fame.

The first definition denies the existence of the individual and the second voids the idea of enlightenment altogether. Enlightenment as the non-existence of an individual is not a workable idea. In addition to our nature as limitless awareness, we all enjoy a limited existence as ordinary human beings. As a normal person seeking freedom I need to know what enlightenment is and why I should seek it. So the question "What is an enlightened person?" is relevant. How will my life look when I know who I really am? Remember, Vedanta is not concerned with the details of your personhood. These you know full well. You have lived with yourself for a long time and are quite familiar with your narrative. We do not denigrate, dismiss or diminish that person at all. We only say that that you have a much more spacious identity and that knowledge of that identity will make your life wonderful indeed.

Enlightenment is the loss of ignorance of that spacious, ever-free identity. Our teaching strips away the beliefs and opinions we have about ourselves, leaving us naked and free as we really are. In our tradition we shy away from the word *en-lightenment*, even though I have used it shamelessly in this chapter and in the title to make my book appealing because it is a popular word. *Enlightenment* is similar to the word *God* in that it can mean what you want it to mean. But generally, we don't endorse it, because it gives the impression that it is a special event that confers a special status, whereas it is much more simple and profound than that.

So far we have explained Vedanta's view of reality and unfolded the tools needed to qualify for it and to understand it. If you have been seeking for some time, and nearly everyone who is reading this book probably has, you will understand that, compared to the meager fare dished up in the modern spiritual soup kitchen, Vedanta is a classy joint that serves red meat: a time tested, complete, seriously nutritious means of self-knowledge you can sink your spiritual teeth into.

Now we need to explain what freedom looks like to make your way easier as you wend your way through the spiritual marketplace, and to guide you once you have realized who you are. You may think you have a choice but you have no choice about seeking; you are driven by a self whose powerful need for freedom will not be denied. We need to explain what it means to be free so you can avoid enlightenment sickness, bad teachings and bad teachers. Bad teachings are vague and incomplete teachings based on the personal experience of the teacher and/or cobbled together from books that have no methodology and no epistemology. Bad teachings tend to heartily endorse duality or deny the apparent reality and ignore any one or all of the obviously essential topics: the need for qualifications; dharma; values; the relationship between the apparent and the real; the relationship between experience and knowledge; the need for spiritual practice; the downside of action; the lack of a complete and dispassionate analysis of consciousness, the psyche, and the material world; and finally, Isvara and the necessity of devotion to Isvara.

Enlightenment Sickness

Bad teachers are those who have not worked on themselves, because they have been seduced by the idea that an epiphany or a series of epiphanies means that they are enlightened and are therefore qualified to teach. It so happens that epiphanies happen to individuals at every stage of evolution. They do not happen exclusively to saints. In fact, many saints have never had an epiphany. Bad teachers are rarely bad people. They are often charismatic and well meaning but unpurified individuals who have prematurely hung out a shingle advertising themselves as world saviors or they are ambitious people who would like to accomplish in enlightenment what they failed to accomplish in the world. Rarely do they realize that spirituality is a samsara like none other, that enlightenment does not make them special, nor does it lend gravitas to their words. It is quite amazing how utterly banal are the vices that have brought so many modern gurus down.

A Fallen Yogi

Recently I received an email with a link to a web blog by a reasonably famous "enlightened" teacher in the Neo-Advaita world. He said he was renouncing gurudom to work on himself and become a "better person." It was a surprising event because arrogant people invariably live in an ironclad state of denial, the better to project their emotional problems on others. Evidently the chorus of angry voices that followed him for twenty-seven years swelled to such a din that it became too loud to ignore. His statement will undoubtedly be seen by some as a courageous act of contrition, the uplifting resolve of a newly minted reprobate taking the first halting steps on the road to redemption and by others as a disingenuous attempt to make the public believe that he was not forced to step down by his organization, leaving the door open for a triumphant return once he had atoned for his sins.

The real lesson, however, is not his personal story but what it says about his view of enlightenment, since it was behind this view that he perpetrated so much misery. Had he been taught by a proper teacher in a proper tradition he might have known what enlightenment is and hundreds, perhaps thousands would have been spared much heartache.

He was obviously not enlightened by even the most liberal definition. What he called enlightenment was merely an epiphany that had a profound effect on his ego and convinced him that there was something more than his way of seeing at the time. It convinced him wrongly that he was "enlightened." In fact enlightenment, as it is popularly conceived, is not something that happens, because there is only one eternal you—nothing ever happens from your point of view—and you are, have always been, and ever will be the light of awareness and the light alone. As such you are unborn and never die. Experiences are born and die. They do not change you and make you into something other than what you are. If you take yourself to be an experiencing entity, an ego, you will be apparently, but never actually, modified by what happens, spiritual or otherwise.

If I am awareness there is no way to conclude that I am special or unique. Or perhaps there is: since there is only one of me, I am unique. However, this fact is not helpful if you are looking for a way to distinguish yourself, since there are no others to appreciate it. The understanding of my nature illumines the ego, because the ego is just a notion of specialness and uniqueness. If I see my ego it cannot be me. Vedanta does not want it to disappear or expect it to transcend the world. It simply views it as an object, an idea of separateness. It should be noted once more that most of the mischief in the spiritual world over the centuries can be laid squarely at the feet of the idea of ego death and transcendence, two signature features of the experiential view of enlightenment.

What actually happened to our yogi? He imagined he had transcended himself, came to believe that he now inhabited a special experiential niche reserved only for the few, and convinced himself that his epiphany empowered him to enlighten others. Along with it came the companion belief that the end justifies the means, opening the door to a remarkably abusive "teaching." The craving for power, born of his sense of smallness and inadequacy, present from childhood, survived the epiphany—as such things do—and immediately manifested in his environment with predictable results, blinding him to life's number one moral value, non-injury.

Although he spoke non-duality, his version of enlightenment was pure duality. It amounts to splitting the ego into a transcendental self and a self to be transcended. To make this idea work, the ego needs to be in a state of complete denial. It must imagine that the non-transcendent part of itself doesn't exist. It didn't exist for him, at least not officially, although it must have troubled him all along, but sadly it existed for his devotees—some say fools—until they put a stop to it, after twenty-seven years! To keep the myth of transcendence alive and transfer his emotional problems elsewhere, the enlightened one is forced to lay them at the feet of the devotees, usually immature sycophants who, for reasons related to their own self-esteem issues, believe in the myth of transcendence. Nobody is transcendent because reality is non-dual. There is only one self. Ironically, the myth of ego death, aided by the guru's attacks on the ego, is counterproductive insofar as it reinforces the belief that the seeker is the ego.

You are awareness and awareness is apparently other than what it perceives, meaning that what it perceives is itself. During "awakening" moments you are actually experiencing yourself as you are, but ignorance survives these moments and projects the experience on the ego. Vedanta calls this phenomenon *super-imposition*. I call it *enlightenment sickness*. It is a state of delusion. You think that what belongs to you, awareness, belongs to the ego. When the transcendent experience wears off you go back to the ego level but now somehow believe you are something other than your ego. You declare yourself enlightened and imagine that you are qualified to teach others.

The Blades of a Fan

Although karma is one, it is described in three ways with reference to a jiva. The karma that will take place in the future as a result of actions you are doing now is called *agami* karma. The total store of karma that is standing in your account waiting to fructify is called *sanchita* karma and the karma that is manifesting now is called *prarabdha* karma. It is a hot day and the fan in my room is on. It suddenly cools down and I switch off the fan two seconds before you enter the room. Seeing the still whirling blades of the fan, you remark that the fan is on, but I say it is off. Who is right?

The fan is on but it is off. An epiphany is just karma, an experience. It arises in the long cue of your experiences and subsides back into the cue to become a part of your story and perhaps a vasana that may or may not fructify again. This vasana does not obliterate the *sanchita* karma you have accumulated. The *sanchita*, all the tendencies that make up your apparent person from birth onwards—let's leave reincarnation out of it—and manifest as the apparent person's behavior in the world, has to work out. There is no logic to the idea that an epiphany, which is just a peculiar kind of short lived karma, suddenly erases all the other karmas stored in your account, leaving you as a karma-less "enlightened" person. You are karma-less and beyond the world already, but not as a person.

The person stays. He chops wood and carries water just as before. If he suddenly jettisons jeans and t-shirts and a day job, dons flowing robes, puts up a website informing the world of his new status, refers to his former self in the third person, speaks unintelligible mumbo jumbo slowly in low tones and generally puts on airs, you will know that you have a poseur on your hands, not an enlightened person.

But when firm self-knowledge removes the last vestiges of ignorance, there is a subtle shift from the point of view of the jiva to the point of view of awareness. You can't say it is an experience and you can't say it isn't. It bears repeating that this shift does not change the jiva and its karma, at least not immediately. The knowledge destroys the notion that you are a jiva and changes the way you regard the jiva. When this happens the fan is off, meaning that while the body and mind continue to function as they did before the shift, awareness does not identify with them. It seems they belong to another person. It is like watching yourself in a dream.

Once this shift is no longer shiftable you become very happy and there is a natural tendency to want to share your happiness with others. However, *how* you share it reveals whether you are enlightened or enlightenment sick. Happiness attracts people. You needn't say or do anything extraordinary to share it. It is a very subtle energy that shares itself. If you put a lit candle close to an unlit candle the flame jumps from one to the other as if by magic. The idea that you need to "teach" enlightenment needs to be considered in light of this fact. The bliss of self-realization is different from the happiness that comes from happenings. Happenings unhappen. The bliss of self-realization doesn't unhappen. It is constant and steady and "deepens" as the Subtle Body is purified by the knowledge.

This bliss is Isvara teaching through you. If you take credit for it and make people dependent on you without acknowledging the source, you are violating dharma. If you open your mouth and speak about enlightenment and your experience of it, you need to be very careful to speak the truth, not your idea of it, or you will mislead people, regardless of how happy they feel in your presence. Enlightenment without knowledge of Isvara is no enlightenment because knowledge of Isvara makes you humble. Truth spoken by a humble teacher invariably clarifies, uplifts and upholds dharma. Truth coming from an unpurified mind serves only to confuse and leads to adharma.

Self-Realization/Self-Actualization

We make a distinction between realization and actualization because dharma trumps enlightenment. Or to express the issue differently, enlightenment is as enlightenment does. The idea that enlightenment somehow justifies adharmic behavior—popularly known as "crazy wisdom"—is one of the most pernicious and long-standing beliefs in the spiritual world. Fortunately, as the Western spiritual world matures, crazy wisdom does not seem to enjoy as much traction as it once did. However, there are still many vasana-laden individuals on both ends of the guru disciple relationship with low self-esteem who are susceptible to it. It probably happens because jivas, continually bedeviled by desires and fears too numerous to mention, find inhibiting rules inconvenient at best and threatening at worst. Therefore they are inclined to cut corners. Depending on how you view it, the dharma field is a stifling matrix of laws designed to thwart the need to be free, a necessary evil insofar as it keeps life from sliding into the abyss at the hands of the wicked, or a benign structure that makes success possible. The alternative is chaos, which does not bode well for purposeful work and happiness.

To many, enlightenment seems to promise relief from Isvara's myriad tyrannies. Without putting too fine a point on it, the jiva is often prone to feel that once it is enlightened, it is free to do what it wants and reap no untoward consequences. It soon learns otherwise, although many transgressors are slow learners, like the teacher mentioned above, the power of the vasanas being what they are. However, until it learns its lesson, it inflicts misery on itself and others. If you come by your enlightenment through an experiential teaching that ignores the qualifications, dharma, and Isvara and does not encourage a purification sadhana, you will be susceptible to the crazy wisdom disease or some variation thereof.

Essentially all problems centered around enlightenment are a result of superimposition, confusing the self with the jiva. Since we are looking at enlightenment from the jiva's perspective it is important to know that in all matters transformational, tamas rules! Enlightenment—the hard and fast knowledge "I am limitless, non-dual, ordinary awareness'—leaves the eternal jiva alone but it does change the apparent jiva, the specific individual. If it doesn't, the knowledge is only intellectual. It changes the jiva because it renders binding vasanas non-binding and destroys the doer's sense of doership. How does it change the individual and how soon do the changes manifest?

Recently, in the first case of its kind in our lineage that I know of, a self-realized teacher lost his ashrams, money, power and—most significantly his reputation—for sexually abusing his students. He got away with it for years but eventually Isvara brought him down. I met him years ago, was impressed by his teaching, and more or less endorsed him in spite of one small inconsistency in his appearance. In our tradition teachers usually let their hair grow naturally and when it gets too unwieldy they shave it off and let it grow again. They are not unkempt but they do not make an attempt to draw attention to their bodies. But this teacher was different. He put a little too much attention into his hair. He had a hairdo. Hair is fine, but a "do" is a little fishy in the context of the tradition of Vedanta. In any case I did not think much about him over the intervening years but whenever I did, I was always amused by this peculiarity. When I heard about his self-imposed misfortune, it all made sense. He was insecure and vain and wanted to make himself attractive to women. He may have been self-realized but he was not self-actualized, because he was not attractive to himself. When you really know who you are, you are so attracted to yourself that you don't care what people think.

Self-actualization means that your life reflects the teaching. You cannot wall off a particular vasana, refuse to apply the knowledge to it and claim to be self-actualized. The two most obvious vasanas that self-realized people are loath to examine in light of the knowledge are money and sex, or to quote a long-deceased teacher, "women and gold." Individuals, worldly or spiritual, who chase money are insecure. Money makes them feel secure. People who chase sex don't feel good about themselves. Sex is the ultimate worldly pleasure and obsession with it is an attempt to compensate for low self-esteem. A self-actualized person is in a state of perpetual pleasure because the self's nature is bliss. Small blips of sexual bliss do not enthrall, coming as they do with an obvious downside: they end.

Other tendencies often bedevil self-realized people, three of which deserve mention: power, love and respect. The first guru mentioned above was addicted to power, hence the psychological and physical abuse. Power-hungry gurus have low self-esteem born of a feeling of impotency and inadequacy. To compensate they seek power. Gurudom is an easy route to power, as the guru is dealing with a gullible public with its own self-esteem issues. A person who does not feel his own spiritual power will be attracted to and surrender to a powerful person, hoping one day to exercise such power. The sense of power that accompanies self-knowledge has nothing to do with power over people. It springs from the sense of mastery over the vasanas that comes with the firm knowledge that you are whole and complete. Knowing beyond a doubt that you are whole destroys the network of desires that render jivas powerless and dependent.

Gurudom is also an easy route to respect. In most societies people respect intelligence and knowledge. A jiva that does not respect itself will seek the approval and respect of others. Although it is a more benign impurity, teachers who are otherwise disinterested in money or sex may expect constant acts of devotion, which indicates low self-esteem. When you go to a guru you are already primed with the idea that he knows more than you do, so you respect him or her. Of course, you should respect your teacher but not because he demands it.

The least intuitive and perhaps most benign impurity that bedevils the self-realized is the desire for love. If the desire to be loved motivated your search and you have figured out ways to get people to love you, you will feel you hit the jackpot when you realize who you are. Combined with your previous skill you may use your new-found attractiveness to get many people to love you. Before you know it, a cult of personality will be centered on you. It is very hard to tell if the attraction is coming from the purity of the teacher's mind or a skillful manipulation of love-starved devotees by a cunning, needy guru. This kind of love is very needy. One sign is a total lack of appreciation of the need for boundaries. If you have this vasana, you will have people hanging on you day and night sucking the love out of you. You will find yourself completely exhausted because you will be unable to say no. And you will not understand that you asked for it. Seeking or giving anything creates a vasana for more seeking and more giving because the doer has not been neutralized. All that is required to help the world understand is a pure mind, one that effortlessly reflects the great wisdom of Isvara.

The idea behind the self-actualization teaching is the understanding that life is very conservative. There are no radical changes, although it may seem so at times. Things do change, but they change incrementally. The body that was there when you realized who you are is the same body that you inhabit after you realize who you are. The basic structure of your personality, your svadharma, remains the same. Although in the euphoria of the *rediscovery* of your limitless nature, it seems like everything has changed, nothing has actually happened. One small doubt, the last uncertainty about your nature, dies, and life goes on. So self-actualization is a commitment to continue to apply the knowledge to your mind after you have realized who you are. If you worked out all your binding vasanas before you realized, you are self-actualized when you become self-realized and nothing needs to be done. The sattvic lifestyle and habits of mind that purified you will continue to serve once you know who you are. If self-realization destroyed the remaining binding vasanas, you are self-actualized when you realize. If you realize and still have binding vasanas—it is the norm in Western societies where seekers tend to have rajasic/tamasic lifestyles—you are only self-actualized when the last binding vasana bites the dust as a result of continued inquiry.

The Self-Actualized Person

So what do these enlightened people look like? The first thing to know is that you cannot tell by looking at them. They don't walk funny or float a few inches off the ground. They don't wear special clothing, sport halos, and speak slowly with their eyes closed. They can be found in every country and in all manner of occupations. They speak normally. So what distinguishes them?

The most comprehensive definition of a self-actualized person is found in one of Vedanta's most important scriptures, the *Bhagavad Gita*. In it the perennial seeker asks his enlightened teacher to describe a person of "steady wisdom, one whose mind is not disturbed by anything and abides in the Self."

The teacher replies, "*When a person gives up desires as they appear in the mind and remains happy with only her Self, she is a discriminating person.*"

The question itself removes the experiential idea and defines enlightenment as "steady wisdom." We have harped on this point sufficiently—hopefully not ad nauseam—but the word *wisdom* needs a comment. Why the word *wisdom* and not the word *knowledge?* The question does not use it because knowledge is just knowledge. It is useful only when it has an impact on the mind. Wisdom is applied Self-knowledge. It transforms the mind from a reactive instrument to a clear reflector of awareness.

What kind of mind does this person enjoy? A mind that is not disturbed by anything. Why is it not disturbed? It knows that nothing in this world is worthy of agitation because nothing here is real. Earlier in the conversation, in response to the seeker's existential grief brought on by his contemplation of death, the teacher said, "The wise grieve neither for the dead nor for the living." If you go to a movie and a character loses all his money, you do not suffer grief, because his grief is only movie grief. A self-actualized person always feels that what he experiences, including the experiencer, is just a play of consciousness cooked up by Maya.

What makes the mind free of suffering? It "abides in the self." The mind is an interesting object. Its nature is that it has no nature of its own. It becomes whatever it is paying attention to. If it is paying attention to an emotion, for instance, it becomes emotional and moves here and there. If it pays attention to the self it becomes an abiding mind. An abiding mind stays put. Why does it remain with the self? Because the self is beautiful. It is love. It is peace.

In other verses on this topic the person of steady wisdom is referred to as a "discriminating" person. This person's mind abides in the self because the person—who is actually the self—knows the difference between the self and the objects appearing in the mind. He knows that objects disturb and the self fills the mind with bliss, so he keeps the mind on the self and it abides in bliss. It abides because the bliss of the self is always present, unlike objects, which come and go.

This person "*doesn't yearn for pleasure and is free from longing, fear, and anger.*"

Fools yearn for pleasure because they do not know that the self is *paramasukka*, limitless wellbeing. Because they feel incomplete, jivas don't feel good about themselves, but when a jiva realizes the self, she experiences the completeness and wholeness of the self. The self-actualized are free from fear and anger.

Why are they free? For the same reason they don't long for things: they don't need anything to make themselves feel complete so their desires dry up. Desire is painful and anger is painful. If your desires are neutralized, your angers are also neutralized by self-knowledge because fear and anger are just thwarted desire.

This person is *"unattached to the outcome of all situations, does not rejoice in pleasant circumstances, nor is he uncomfortable in unpleasant situations."*

The statement does not say that a self-actualized person experiences only pleasant circumstances. Uninformed seekers imagine that once they get enlightened their lives will become a bed of roses. These individuals do not understand Isvara. The self-actualized person's understanding takes Isvara into account. There is no escape from pleasant and unpleasant circumstances because the enlightened person lives in the dharma field. But circumstances have no effect because they belong to the field, not to the self. If a soldier realizes who he is in a war zone, his life is unaffected, only his relationship to it changes.

"And if a person is able to withdraw her sense organs from the sense objects like a turtle withdraws its limbs, her knowledge is steady."

Because we live in the world, our senses are always active. But because sense contact with objects produces pleasure and pleasure creates vasanas for more pleasure, jivas can easily become prisoners of their senses. A self-actualized person is not averse to pleasure. The verse implies that her sense organs will be connected to objects. But self-knowledge saves the day because a self-realized person knows that the pleasure that comes from objects is actually a faint, reflected, transient blip of the eternal bliss of awareness. Experiencing herself as the source of that bliss neutralizes the bliss vasanas, but not the bliss. Therefore a self-actualized person can enjoy any experience and step back from any experience to protect her apparent self.

"For one who does not feed the senses, the senses come back to the Self, leaving the longing behind. When the Self is known to be one's self even the longing goes away. When the mind no longer tries to connect the sense organs with their respective objects it becomes permanently fulfilled. Pleasure arising from the contact of the organs and their objects is a source of pain because it begins and ends. The wise do not celebrate it."

A self-actualized person knows that the senses are driven by the insatiable need for wholeness. If they are denied objects they turn inward and center on the reflection of the bliss of awareness.

"*Even for a person who practices yoga and whose goal is clear the senses can pull the mind away from the Self. Keep your senses under control and contemplate on Me (awareness) with a discriminating mind. Self-knowledge becomes established in a discriminating controlled mind.*"

You can take the word *yoga* in this statement to mean jnana yoga, self-inquiry. Although the verse is addressed to someone striving for liberation, the statement applies to self-realized individuals in that discrimination is also the means for self-actualization. Once you have realized who you are, it is still possible to lose your discrimination when binding vasanas arise, so you need to continue to apply the knowledge if you want the knowledge—and therefore the bliss—to be steady.

Recently a well respected "enlightened" teacher declared himself unenlightened shortly after his wife left him for another man. His enlightenment, it seems, occurred in the context of a marriage, the basis of which had never been subjected to inquiry. He must have assumed that his wife would always love him. When he realized his assumption was untrue, his self-knowledge deserted him and he became emotional. Had he been a self-actualized person he would never have assumed that a worldly situation was not subject to change. Furthermore, a self-actualized person knows that the love for the object is actually love for the self in the object and he would have been happy to see her pursue happiness according to her nature. Finally, non-duality means that the wife is none other than the self, as he is, and therefore that the wife could never be apart from him. A self-actualized person knows that "my wife" is only ignorance, claiming for jiva what actually belongs to Isvara.

Liberation is more than the knowledge "I am awareness." It includes clear knowledge of the apparent reality, which modifies the jiva's life in the world. Here is an example of the well assimilated self-actualized knowledge that is freedom:

> When you dwell on objects attachment arises. Attachment causes desire and when desire is obstructed anger arises. An angry mind is easily deluded and delusion leads to the loss of memory. When memory goes the mind is incapacitated. And when the mind no longer functions properly one's life is destroyed. Even when you move in the world of objects it is possible to attain tranquility if the sense organs are controlled and you stand apart from your likes and dislikes. Self-knowledge, easily established

in a tranquil mind, destroys existential sorrow. But for the agitated mind there is no self-knowledge. Contemplation does not take place and without contemplation on the self there is no peace. Without peace how can there be happiness? Self-knowledge will not stick in a mind distracted by changing sensations. They carry it away just as a strong wind carries a small boat across the water. Therefore, the self-knowledge of one whose senses are free of their respective objects is steady. In that dark daylight world in which all beings sleep, the wise person who has mastered the senses is awake. Just as water flows into an ocean leaving the ocean unchanged, objects arising in the mind of a self realized person leave it unchanged. But the desirer of objects is never peaceful. The one who abandons the belief in "I" and "mine" and moves through life without longing is peaceful. This is steadiness in the self. The self-realized are not deluded appearances.

Self-realization takes place in the Subtle Body, but unless the knowledge impacts positively the emotions and one's actions in the world as outlined in these verses it is not actualized. The proof of the pudding is in the eating.

"The one who sees actionlessness in action and action in actionlessness is wise and has done everything that is to be done."

A self-actualized person knows that when something is happening in the apparent reality, nothing is happening to the self. A person sitting in a stationary train that has been travelling in one direction will feel as if the train is moving when a train on an adjacent track moves in the opposite direction. Self-actualization is identifying with the unchanging station, not with the trains coming and going. From the station's point of view, nothing is happening. The feeling "I am doing" is caused by ignorance. The "I" is always free of action.

"Actionlessness in action." For example, a boat on the horizon rapidly moving out to sea will seem to be unmoving to a person standing on the sea shore. Although apparently there is nothing happening, something is happening. A lot of people think that the knowledge "I am not the doer," which is tantamount to self-realization, means that an enlightened doer does nothing. In India many people believe that a person who sits in one spot for years on end is enlightened because he is free of action. But sitting is an action, just like walking. It may give the appearance of inactivity but it is an action nonetheless. The doer cannot help but act. It is always acting. Self-actualization is the understanding that freedom from action cannot be attained by doing nothing. Understanding this, the self-actualized person is apparently engaged in the world like everyone else. "I am not the doer" means "I am limitless, non-dual, actionless awareness." It is not a statement about the jiva.

"*The sages say that a person is wise if his actions have been burned in the fire of self-knowledge. Such people act without desire for the results of their actions. Consequently they are content because they do not depend on results to make them happy. They are free of doership even when they act. Those who are free of expectations, whose bodies, minds and senses are well disciplined, who are free of attachment to possessions and act only to sustain the body, are happy with what comes by chance, unaffected by the opposites, without envy, even-minded in success and failure and free of the need to act, while acting, are free. The karma of those who are free from attachment, whose minds have been liberated by self-knowledge and who perform action as an offering is completely cleared.*"

A self-actualized person is a karma yogi who does not need to practice karma yoga to purify the mind. The attitude is natural, effortless. *Karma yoga* is just a description of how the actionless self, appearing as a jiva empowered to act by the power of Isvara/Maya, relates to action and its results.

This apparent person is actually the self. This person lives differently in the body from the rest of us. While it seems as if this person is a he or a she, there is no feeling of gender for it. It doesn't think that it owns anything. It acts only to maintain the body because it doesn't need anything from the world. It is here only to enjoy. It waits for what it needs to come to it. It has complete faith in Isvara to take care of it. It doesn't want to be like anyone else—"free of envy." It can act, but it need not act when subjective or objective situations demand a response. It sees its actions as contributing to, not extracting value from, its environment.

"*Those who see no difference between a humble Brahmin endowed with knowledge and a cow, an elephant, a dog or a dog eater are wise.*"

Of course these people would not confuse a cow with an elephant, nor a dog and a dog eater. They know that cow, elephant, dog and dog eater are only thoughts in the mind, the essence of which is consciousness. A verse from the Yoga scriptures says "A yogi in *Samadhi* sees no difference between a lump of gold and the excreta of a crow." This does not mean that such a person will try to deposit crow poop in the bank. It means that the essence of everything is consciousness. *Samadhi* is a compound word. *Sama* means equal and *dhi* is a contracted form of *buddhi*, which means knowledge. So the word means someone who values everything equally. If she sees other selves, she values them as much as she values herself. The utility of this vision in terms of happiness is obvious, as people who see differences are continually conflicted.

"If you are awake to the self, revel in the self and are satisfied with the self alone you are free."

The self-actualized person is completely free of dependence on objects for happiness. Insofar as the absence of an object causes a sense of loss or the presence of an object is required to make you feel good, you are not self-actualized.

"You have attained liberation when you are no longer attached to the sense objects or to action and you have removed the cause of desire."

Non-attachment to sense objects and action is not enough. You need to be free of ignorance of the wholeness of the self, as it is the cause of desire. This is not to say that enlightened people do not have desires. It means that they don't take them to be commands, or as the verse says, they "(can) *give up desires as they appear in the mind."* It does not mean that they cannot act on the basis of desire. If reality is non-dual and desire exists it has to be the self—although the self is not desire. It is the desire that is not opposed to dharma. In other words a self-actualized person performs only actions that are in harmony with dharma, the cosmic order. In the seeking phase and in the self-realization phase, desires that spring from incompleteness and inadequacy are to be renounced. A self-actualized person has no desires that spring from a sense of inadequacy. His desires are Isvara's desires. Since Isvara is the source of dharma, there is no danger that such a person will act selfishly, as all of Isvara's desires relate to the maintenance of the cosmic order. You will be attached only to you own vasanas, not the vasanas of others.

A self-actualized person is not, however, required to act out Isvara's desires. To restrict him in this way would limit his freedom because the self is beyond dharma and adharma. Sometimes the interests of dharma are sustained by adharmic acts, so you may observe a self-actualized person *occasionally* breaking the rules. The question concerning action, which takes place in the dharmic order, is always about knowledge. What does a person know when he is acting? A self-realized person knows that Isvara is the doer but still has ego-centered vasanas left over from his stay in ignorance. He will not develop new vasanas because the ignorance is gone but he still has to put up with the effects of ignorance. So discrimination is necessary for the self-realized until the effects of ignorance are reduced to ashes in the fire of self-knowledge. The self-actualized person knows that Isvara is the doer but does not need to discriminate because his actions are automatically aligned with Isvara's desires and because the effects of ignorance have been burned by self-knowledge. So selfish desire and action are no longer an issue. This is why scripture says that the self-actualized person is Isvara. He does not have the capacity to create, sustain, or destroy the Macrocosmic Gross, Subtle and Causal Bodies but he is one up on Isvara and one up on Jiva because he is actually the self and the self is unaffected by jiva and Isvara.

"The one from whom the world does not shrink, nor who shrinks from the world, who is self-reliant and stable, not inclined to initiate self-centered actions, who is not carried away by joy, anger or fear…"

How self-realized people deal with the doer can be a problem because it is clear to them that action and its results cannot complete them. Yet they often feel disillusioned and adrift and seem to think that life is meaningless when they discover that it is a dream; *emptiness* is the most common word used to describe it. Most believed the doer would disappear and the problem of action would be solved. But the doer remains, as it Isvara's creation and is a necessary factor in the karmic stimulus-response mechanism. The doer is active as long as you are embodied. Because you are identified with the doer, you feel you have to cook up something new. One of the most obvious knee-jerk reactions to this problem is to hang out a shingle and "teach." But this verse says that a self-actualized person does not "initiate self-centered actions" because he is satisfied with the bliss of the self alone. The solution: continue inquiry until you understand the difference between the doer and doership. Doership is the notion that you are the doer. When you truly understand the nature of the gunas the problem disappears because the gunas generate action without the doer's permission.

More often than not, in the euphoria of realization, the seeker sees that there is nothing to do and gives up inquiry. Inquiry is not something the doer gives up. It stops when the knowledge has been completely assimilated and the effects of ignorance removed. But the scripture's statement that there is nothing to do for the self-realized does not mean that action is no longer required for successful living, only that actions centered around solving the identity issue are no longer necessary. So during this stage, you keep contemplating the teachings on action until the doubt is cleared. Self-inquiry is noble work. Once you know who you are, your vision expands to include the whole world. So the endless needs of others for freedom become your needs and you contribute in whatever way you can to helping them.

"The one who treats enemies and friends alike, sees success and failure in the same light, remains unchanged when honored or disgraced, views pleasure and pain, heat and cold equally, stands free of objects, is disciplined in speech, has no place to call his own" is self-explanatory. And finally, *"Such people are not averse to any state of mind—even tamas—when it predominates. Nor do they long for any state of mind when it is gone."*

Finally, our definition of enlightenment includes how the self-actualized relate to their states of mind. They are not bothered by bad feelings—tamas and rajas. So they don't expect the mind to feel good, because they know that their moods are controlled by the gunas.

❧

The modern spiritual world, dominated by Neo-Advaita in the last twenty years, is not unlike the culture in which it has taken root. No blame. It took the Vedanta teaching, which is truly a science of consciousness, a couple of thousand years to develop into a refined, comprehensive and proven means of knowledge, so we cannot compare the two. Modern spirituality is a lazy fast food culture. It seeks the easy way, a quick fix. "There is nothing to do, no qualifications required; you can just get it," the hucksters claim. Because people are eager to distinguish themselves, they are susceptible to this message. They can't wait to be respected and loved, to gain an identity with real meaning, unlike the vast but insubstantial offerings to be plucked from the endless shelves of the supermarket of identities that is modern life. So a third rate epiphany will suffice as a flimsy structure on which to construct a spiritual identity. "Eureka! I found gold. I'm enlightened!"

Vedanta's daunting list of the signs of enlightenment unfolded in this chapter separates the enlightened men from the boys. If you are tempted to think you are enlightened, particularly if your enlightenment involves informing others, you should carefully contemplate this chapter. It is a checklist. It will tell you where you stand. Has your self-knowledge transformed you into a truly cultivated human being or is your enlightenment simply a baseless claim? If you appreciate the comment of the thirteenth Zen master Dogen, the founder of Soto Zen, "Next to good manners enlightenment is the most important thing in the world," you are a great soul. If not, not.

ABOUT THE AUTHOR

JAMES SWARTZ grew up in Montana and attended Lawrence University in Appleton, Wisconsin and the University of California at Berkeley before finding his niche in the world of business. He saw great success as a businessman, but in 1967 he experienced a major epiphany that turned him away from that path. Instead, he traveled to India on a spiritual journey, searching for the path to enlightenment. It was here that he learned of the famous Indian sage Swami Chinmayananda, whose knowledge and teachings proved to be the means to set James free.

Now a disciple of the sage, James travels extensively to cities in America, Europe, and India to hold seminars on Vedanta, the science of self-inquiry. He provides resources for understanding non-duality through his website, www.shiningworld.com.

James has previously self-published three non-fiction books: *Meditation: An Inquiry into the Self* (1998), *The Mystery Beyond the Trinity* (1998), and *How to Attain Enlightenment: The Vision of Non-Duality* (2009).

Sentient Publications, LLC publishes nonfiction books on cultural creativity, experimental education, transformative spirituality, holistic health, new science, ecology, and other topics, approached from an integral viewpoint. We also publish fiction that aims to intrigue, stimulate, and entertain. Our authors are intensely interested in exploring the nature of life from fresh perspectives, addressing life's great questions, and fostering the full expression of the human potential. Sentient Publications' books arise from the spirit of inquiry and the richness of the inherent dialogue between writer and reader.

Our Culture Tools series is designed to give social catalyzers and cultural entrepreneurs the essential information, technology, and inspiration to forge a sustainable, creative, and compassionate world.

We are very interested in hearing from our readers. To direct suggestions or comments to us, or to be added to our mailing list, please contact:

SENTIENT PUBLICATIONS, LLC
1113 Spruce Street
Boulder, CO 80302
303-443-2188
contact@sentientpublications.com
www.sentientpublications.com